Bovine Tuberculosis and the Culling of Badgers

David Hill

Callisto Reference

www.callistoreference.com

Callisto Reference,
118-35 Queens Blvd., Suite 400,
Forest Hills, NY 11375, USA

Visit us on the World Wide Web at:
www.callistoreference.com

ISBN: 978-1-64116-778-9 (Hardback)

Cataloging-in-Publication Data

Bovine tuberculosis and the culling of badgers / David Hill.
p. cm.
Includes bibliographical references and index.
ISBN 978-1-64116-778-9
1. Tuberculosis in cattle. 2. Cattle--Diseases. 3. Badgers--Diseases.
4. Old World badgers as carriers of disease. I. Hill, David.
SF967.T8 B68 2023
636.208 945 420 941--dc23

The *"How-To-Win"* Appeal Manual

WINNING APPELLATE ADVOCACY IN A NUTSHELL

by

Ralph Adam Fine
JUDGE, WISCONSIN COURT OF APPEALS

Juris Publishing

Library of Congress Cataloging-in -Publication Data

Fine, Ralph Adam, 1941-
The "how-to-win" appeal manual : winning advocacy in a nutshell / by Ralph Adam Fine.
p. cm.
Includes index.
ISBN 1-57823-077-2
1. Appellate procedure--United States. 2. Trial practice --United States.
I. Title

KF9050 .F56 2000
347.73' 75--dc21 99-057854
CIP

Manufactured in the United States of America.

For Kay and Matt

ABOUT THE AUTHOR

Ralph Adam Fine has been a judge on the Wisconsin Court of Appeals since 1988. He served as a judge on the Wisconsin circuit court from 1979 to 1988, and presided over in excess of 350 jury trials. He was the presiding judge in the PBS ***Frontline*** production *Inside the Jury Room*, which was the first time jury deliberations in a criminal trial were filmed and broadcast.

Ralph Adam Fine has taught trial-advocacy, evidence, and appellate-advocacy at more than one-hundred continuing-legal-education programs around the country, in-house trial-advocacy programs to law-firm litigation departments, and as Professorial Lecturer in Law at the George Washington University National Law Center in Washington, D.C. In January of 1995, the University of Virginia School of Law honored Ralph Adam Fine with the Honorable William J. Brennan, Jr., Award for his contributions to the teaching of trial advocacy.

In addition to ***The "How-To-Win" Appeal Manual***, Ralph Adam Fine is the author of ***The "How-To-Win Trial" Manual*** (Juris 1998) as well as the annually supplemented ***Fine's Wisconsin Evidence*** (Juris). Judge Jack B. Weinstein, original co-author of *Weinstein's Federal Evidence*, called ***Fine's Wisconsin Evidence*** "probably the best single-volume state treatise on the subject that I have seen."

Ralph Adam Fine has also written: ***Escape of the Guilty*** (Dodd, Mead & Co. 1986), which was called "must reading" by *The Wall Street Journal*; ***The Great Drug Deception*** (Stein & Day 1972); and ***Mary Jane versus Pennsylvania*** (McCall 1970). He is a senior contributing editor and reporter for the four-volume treatise ***Evidence in America*** (Lexis); a contributor to the ABA publications ***Emerging Problems Under The Federal Rules of Evidence 2d Ed.*** (West 1991) and ***Emerging Problems Under The Federal Rules of Evidence 3d Ed.*** (Lexis 1998). He also has written two chapters for ***Criminal Justice?***, edited by Robert James Bidinotto and published in 1994–1995 by the Foundation for Economic Education; a chapter on the Eighth Amendment in ***A Time for Choices*** published in 1991 by the First Amendment Congress; and more than thirty professional-journal articles.

Ralph Adam Fine has analyzed legal issues on CBS' **60 Minutes**, ABC's **Nightline** and **Reader's Digest: On Television**, PBS' **MacNeil/Lehrer NewsHour**, CNN's **Both Sides with Jesse Jackson**, as well as a periodic guest on CNN's **Crossfire** and **Larry King Live**. From May, 1974, through

December, 1975, he was a reporter for WITI-TV, the Milwaukee CBS television affiliate. Two of his reports won awards from the Milwaukee Press Club for journalistic excellence. From 1975 to 1978, he was host of *A Fine Point*, which featured such guests as Nobel laureates Elie Wiesel and Milton Friedman.

A 1962 graduate of Tufts University, and a 1965 graduate of the Columbia Law School, Ralph Adam Fine is an elected member of the American Law Institute.

ACKNOWLEDGMENTS

Many thanks to De Vonna Joy, Beth Kushner, William H. Levit, Jr., superb lawyers all, and to the Honorable Neal P. Nettesheim, one of my colleagues on the Wisconsin Court of Appeals, who also teaches appellate advocacy, for their thoughtful review of the typescript and their many helpful suggestions.

I would also like to thank Gayle Dubensky for her superb editing and formatting; Candice Dubensky and Bob Frasca for making everything smooth and easy; and of course, to Chuck and Mike Kitzen, the publishers, who took the chance of thinking outside the box in our efforts to help lawyers be better trial and appellate advocates.

I would also like to acknowledge all the caring men and women with whom I have enjoyed working on the Wisconsin Court of Appeals during my last twelve years: Daniel P. Anderson, Richard S. Brown, R. Thomas Cane, Patricia S. Curley, David G. Deininger, Charles P. Dykman, William F. Eich, Paul C. Gartzke, Michael W. Hoover, Daniel L. LaRocque, Gordon Myse, Neal P. Nettesheim, Gregory A. Peterson, Patience D. Roggensack, Charles B. Schudson, Burton A. Scott, Harry G. Snyder, Michael T. Sullivan, Robert D. Sundby, Margaret J. Vergeront, and, especially, Ted E. Wedemeyer, Jr.

TABLE OF CONTENTS

I.
HOW JUDGES DECIDE CASES
(*And Why That Is Important To You*)

Sol Wachtler, the former Chief Judge of the New York Court Appeals, New York's highest court, is reported to have proudly told his wife after his first day as chief judge that he was "sitting behind Cardozo's desk." Her reply? "And it will be called 'Cardozo's desk' long after you're gone." And so it will be, irrespective of how history resolves the complexities surrounding Wachtler's plunge from his lofty perch behind Cardozo's desk to a prison cell for stalking a former lover.

Benjamin Nathan Cardozo is and will forever remain an icon in American jurisprudence because, if for no other reason, he is the Robert Frost of American law. His decisions, like Frost's poetry, are ubiquitous in all the student anthologies and first-year courses. Thus, it is fitting that we look to Cardozo for an insight into what is often viewed as the mystery of the appellate process. Louis Nizer, one of this country's most skilled trial lawyers, tells us that Justice Cardozo "defined judicial process as the instinctive reaching of a conclusion and with subsequent research and reasoning to justify it."[1] What this means, of course, is that judges, especially appellate judges, will do what they damn well please. And, given the plethora of reported decisions (West and Lexis each pump out more than one-hundred thousand every year), a judge can find a precedent to support almost *any* proposition. To paraphrase Judge Harold Leventhal, late of the United States Court of Appeals for the District of Columbia Circuit, judges parse precedent like a person entering a crowded cocktail party: he or she looks over the heads of strangers to find friends.[2]

---

1 Louis Nizer, *My Life in Court* 444 (1961).

2 Thus, for example, several years ago, the Wisconsin Supreme Court considered a negligent-supervision tort claim brought by a woman against the Roman Catholic Diocese of Madison alleging that a priest assigned by the Diocese as a hospital chaplain abused that position by having a sexual relationship with her. In holding that the First Amendment barred the claim, the Court relied extensively on an article published by the St. Thomas Law Review, whose lead author was a former elected member of the Ohio Bishops Advisory Council and former chairman of the Pastoral Council of the Archdiocese of Cincinnati, JAMES T. O'REILLY, JOANN M. STRASSER, CLERGY SEXUAL MISCONDUCT: CONFRONTING THE DIFFICULT CONSTITUTIONAL AND INSTITUTIONAL LIABILITY ISSUES 7 ST. THOMAS L. REV. 31, 73 (1994). *L.L.N. v. Clauder*, 209 Wis.2d 674, 563 N.W.2d 434 (1997).

Although law schools and continuing-legal-education seminars put on by state bar associations love to perpetuate the myth that the judicial decisional process is a careful, neutral-principled winnowing of precedent until the governing law emerges from painstaking research, the reality is quite different. True, there are judges who approach their responsibilities that way; but the simple fact is that many, if not most, judges get their jobs because they are either politicians or the friends of politicians. Judge Richard S. Arnold of the United State Court of Appeals for the Eighth Circuit noted that his "merit" was that he was "a friend of a senator."[3]

All judges, whether politicians with agendas or not, bring to their decision-making responsibilities a whole host of ideas, ideologies, biases, predilections, philosophies and the like—all of which color their view of "the law." If this were not true, most appellate-court decisions would be unanimous. That they are not, tells us that judges see the same facts and the same legal principles through different filters. Some of these filters are created in college and law school; it may make a difference as to how a judge analyzes policy decisions if that judge went to Berkeley rather than to the University of Chicago, or grew up in a barrio rather than Long Island's Gold Coast.

Judges also get lobbied at continuing-judicial-education courses by those with axes to grind. These courses give those with special-interest agendas an incredibly valuable forum at which to inoculate judges with concepts that will tilt judicial analysis their way. Some, like the "Economic Institutes for State Judges" sponsored mostly by Koch Industries and run by the University of Kansas, put the judges and their families up at luxury resorts. But it is not only the private sponsors of judicial education who indoctrinate. I recall that when I was a trial judge attending the "sentencing institutes" sponsored by the Wisconsin office of continuing judicial education, the "mentors" and outside lecturers (some of whom were either defense lawyers or persons involved with Wisconsin's very liberal probation and parole system) tried to persuade us that judges should impose the least restrictive sentence—whether that was probation or a minimal prison term. I do not recall ever hearing a different suggestion—except by some judges in the audience, who were clearly disgusted by the attempt to brain-wash them. More recently, a plaintiffs' personal-injury lawyer gave a continuing-judicial-education "lecture" on why he believed that the then just-enacted legislative restrictions on insurance coverage should not be applied "retroactively."

---

[3] Richard S. Arnold, 9 *Litigation* No.4 at 5 (Summer 1983).

Sometimes, judges' predispositions go beyond selective legal analysis. Richard A. Posner, Chief Judge of the United States Court of Appeals for the Seventh Circuit, researched Justice Cardozo's most famous case, ***Palsgraff v. Long Island RR Co.***, 248 N.Y. 339, 162 N.E. 99 (1928), where Cardozo, writing for a bare four-to-three majority of the New York Court of Appeals, held that a plaintiff injured by a defendant's negligence could not recover damages from that defendant unless the plaintiff's harm was a foreseeable consequence of that negligence. Posner tells us that Cardozo fiddled with the facts in the ***Palsgraff*** case to make it come out the way he wanted. Worse, Cardozo *advocated* fudging the facts in order to reach a desired result:

> "Cardozo defended the right of a judge to deliberately misstate facts: 'I often say that one [a judge writing a judicial opinion] must permit oneself, and that quite advisedly and deliberately, a certain margin of misstatement' (Selected Writings 339, 341)."[4]

And Cardozo's view was no roaring-20s quirk; Judge Posner tells us that judges do this today: "It is not the invariable practice of appellate judges to slant the facts in favor of the outcome, although goodness knows it is common."[5]

All of us know of decisions that have traversed a tortuous path to reach a desired result. The most famous example is ***Mapp v. Ohio***, 347 U.S. 634 (1961). That watershed Fourth-Amendment decision, which imposed the exclusionary rule on the states, started out as a case raising only First-Amendment issues.

Dollree Mapp lived alone with her teenage daughter on the second story of a two-family house in Cleveland. Three police officers came to her house early one afternoon. They were looking for a person they wanted to talk to about a recent bombing; they thought that he was hiding in Mapp's home.

Mapp called a lawyer who was representing her at the time on a civil matter. He told her that she did not have to let the officers in unless they had a warrant. For the next two and one-half hours, the police—in the words of Justice William O. Douglas—"laid siege to the house." More police arrived, and when Mapp's lawyer showed up, they told him that they had a warrant, but they refused to show it to him.

---

4 Richard A. Posner, *Cardozo* 43 (1990). (Bracketing by Posner.)

5 Richard A. Posner, *Cardozo* 55 (1990). (Emphasis in original.)

Finally, a police officer broke into Mapp's home through the back door. When confronted by Mapp, the officer waved a piece of paper, which he described as a warrant. She grabbed the paper and stuffed it down the front of her blouse. After a brief scuffle, the officer retrieved it and had her handcuffed. She was taken upstairs and made to sit on a bed while the police rummaged through her house. Although they did not find the man for whom they were looking, they did come across a comic book regaling the sexual exploits of Popeye, some racy photographs, and a drawing, all of which the officers believed were pornographic. Mapp was arrested, tried, and convicted for the possession of obscene material.

Mapp's case came to the Supreme Court on the obscenity issue: namely, whether under the First Amendment, as phrased by her lawyer's brief before the Court, Ohio law could "dictate to the mature adult what books he may have in his own private library." The only place an exclusionary rule was mentioned was in a perfunctory comment in an *amicus* brief submitted by the American Civil Liberties Union on Mapp's behalf. The ACLU asked, without argument, that the Court reconsider ***Wolf v. Colorado***, 338 U.S. 25 (1949), an eleven-year old ruling permitting the states to devise their own methods to protect Fourth-Amendment rights: "It is our purpose by this paragraph to respectfully request that this Court re-examine this issue and conclude that the ordered liberty concept guaranteed to persons by the due process clause of the Fourteenth Amendment necessarily requires that evidence illegally obtained in violation thereof, not be admissible in state criminal proceedings."[6]

As Bernard Schwartz tells us in his biography of Earl Warren, *Super Chief*, when the justices met in conference to discuss Mapp's case, it was their general consensus that her conviction should be vacated on First-Amendment grounds—they believed that Ohio's anti-obscenity statute was unconstitutional. Justice William O. Douglas, however, thought that Mapp's appeal was a good case with which to extend the search-and-seizure exclusionary rule to the states. Chief Justice Earl Warren and Justice William J. Brennan, Jr. quickly agreed, but the plan was dropped because none of the others would go along.

Justice Tom C. Clark was assigned to write the decision reversing Mapp's obscenity conviction on First Amendment grounds. Then, a little later, as some of the justices were riding on the elevator, Clark, who had been thinking about the issue in the meantime, turned to Justices Hugo Black and Brennan and

---

6 ***Mapp v. Ohio***, 347 U.S. 634, 673 n.5 (1961) (Harlan J., dissenting).

asked: "Wouldn't this be a good case to apply the exclusionary rule and do what *Wolf* didn't do?" They agreed, and Clark circulated a decision that did precisely that.

The justices outside of the liberal coterie were not privy to the change. In a 1983 article in the *Columbia Law Review*, Justice Potter Stewart says that he was "shocked when Justice Clark's proposed court opinion reached my desk," and he wrote Clark a note telling him so, Stewart warned against such a precipitous ruling: "In all honesty, I seriously question the wisdom of using this case as a vehicle to overrule an important doctrine so recently established and so consistently adhered to."[7] Justice Stewart complained that the question of imposing the exclusionary rule on the states "was not even discussed at the Conference, where we all agreed, as I recollect it, that the judgment would be reversed on First Amendment grounds." Not only was the exclusionary rule not discussed at the justices' conference, but, indeed, it had not been discussed during oral argument, except when Mapp's lawyer was asked by one of the justices whether he believed that *Wolf* should be overturned. His response? In the words of Justice Harlan, Mapp's lawyer "expressly disavowed any such purpose.[8]

Mapp is, perhaps, the poster-child example of judges doing what they want. The United States Supreme Court and the highest courts of every state are in the enviable position of not being answerable to any court higher than they (except when federal constitutional rights are concerned, the decisions of state high courts are final). As Robert H. Jackson, who served as a justice on the United States Supreme Court in the late 1940s and early 1950s wrote, the Supreme Court is not "final" because it is "infallible"; it is "infallible" because it is "final."

Sometimes, judges bent on changing the law will reach out in order to do that. A good example of this happened in Virginia several years ago.

Lowell Stanley, a lawyer in Virginia Beach, Virginia, won an appeal that he and his client did not want to take. The client claimed that she was fired from her job with a private employer in Virginia because she was black. For some reason, Stanley could not bring the client's case in federal court. Virginia

---

7 Potter Stewart, THE ROAD TO *MAPP V. OHIO* AND BEYOND: THE ORIGINS, DEVELOPMENT AND FUTURE OF THE EXCLUSIONARY RULE IN SEARCH AND SEIZURE CASES, 83 COL. L. REV. 1365 (1983).

8 ***Mapp v. Ohio***, 347 U.S. 634, 673 n.6 (1961) (Harlan, J., dissenting).

had a very strict employee-at-will doctrine, which permitted employers to fire for any reason those of its workers without employment contracts. The only exception was an amorphous "public policy" exception that, essentially, protected whistle-blowers who were fired because they alerted the authorities to something their employers either did or wanted to do that jeopardized the public health or safety. Under Virginia's employee-at-will doctrine, therefore, an employer could fire with impunity an employee—even if the reason was that employee's race or sex. Stanley recognized this and attempted to frame his client's case to fit within the whistle-blower exception. His theory was that she was fired not because she was black but because she complained about how blacks were being treated. The state trial court did not buy the distinction, and dismissed the case. Stanley filed a protective notice of appeal to give him time to discuss with his client whether she wanted to appeal. She did not.

In Virginia, appeals cannot be taken unless an appeal bond is filed or the court grants a waiver. Inasmuch as Stanley's client did not want to appeal, Stanley never filed an appeal bond. Before expiration of the time within which the appeal bond had to be filed, Stanley got a letter from the Virginia Supreme Court asking him if there were some problem with the bond and whether he needed an extension of time within which to file it. Having decided not to appeal, Stanley ignored the letter. Next, the clerk of the Supreme Court called to ask whether Stanley's client needed an indigency waiver for the bond. Finally, Stanley got the point, and filed the bond. Guess what? He won the appeal. The Virginia Supreme Court used his case and a companion case alleging sex-based employment discrimination to carve out two new exceptions to Virginia's employee-at-will doctrine—race and sex discrimination. ***Lockhart v. Commonwealth Education Systems Corp.***, 439 S.E.2d 328 (Va. 1994).

I tell you all this not to heighten your skepticism or paranoia, or even to make you more cynical than your years of practice may have already done, but to level with you so that you may best represent your clients in what may very well be an imperfect world. They deserve no less; *you* deserve no less. You must know this, and use it to help you win your appeal. Recognize the "hot buttons" of the judges before whom you appear. Know how to frame your issues, marshall your facts, and make your arguments, to hit those "hot buttons" dead center. With this in mind, we turn to the fundamentals of winning on appeal.

II.
Too Many Cases

Mastering fundamentals of appellate advocacy is even more critical than it used to be, given the crush of cases that appellate courts decide and the growing trend by many courts, including some of the United States courts of appeals to issue one-word "decisions." Thus, Rule 36(b) of the Federal Rules of Appellate Procedure instructs the clerk to "mail to all parties a copy of the opinion—or the judgment, if no opinion was written—and a notice of the date when the judgment was entered." Often, the judges don't even read the briefs that are submitted, but, rather follow the recommendations made by staff counsel. In a 1999 article, Patricia M. Wald, a long-serving judge on the United States Court of Appeals for the District of Columbia Circuit, pointed out that in her circuit more that forty percent of the appeals filed in circuit are handled in that summary way.[9] It used to be that conscientious judges would go the extra mile to help a litigant whose cause is retarded by poor lawyering. No more—there just isn't time.

Your submissions to your appellate court must make the court see that your appeal is serious and make the court *want* to give it the serious attention to which you and your clients believe it is entitled. Of course, your submissions must also make the judges and staff attorneys want you to win, and must give them the tools to decide in your favor. This book shows you how to do that—how to make your argument forceful, compelling, and persuasive. This book also will let you to practice the winning techniques with two real appeals. The first is a copyright fight over a popular computer game. The second is a criminal case that was ultimately decided by the United States Supreme Court. Before we get to those cases and use them to sharpen our analytical and advocacy skills, we must erect our framework of winning appellate advocacy.

III.
The Brief

The brief is the backbone of appellate advocacy. Often, it will be your only shot, as intermediate appellate courts are increasingly eliminating many or most oral arguments. Even in cases where appellate courts hear oral arguments, the briefs are pivotal. Thus, the PRACTITIONER'S HANDBOOK FOR

---

[9] PATRICIA M. WALD, 19 TIPS FROM 19 YEARS ON THE APPELLATE BENCH, 1 *The Journal of Appellate Practice and Process* 8 (1999).

APPEALS published by the United States Court of Appeals for the Seventh Circuit says that "[m]ost appeals are decided largely on the basis of the briefs." PRACTITIONER'S HANDBOOK FOR APPEALS 82 (1999 ed.) Moreover, the Handbook advises:

> "In writing the brief, one must bear in mind that the Seventh Circuit judges read the briefs in advance of oral argument. Thus, it is the first step in persuasion, as well as being the far more important step. After oral argument, it is usually reexamined by the judges and will be used in the writing of the opinion."

Ibid.

Given the critical role of briefs in appellate advocacy, it is somewhat surprising to learn that they are a relatively recent innovation. The United States Supreme Court did not even require briefs from the parties until 1821. But those early written submissions were a far cry from what we see today. The "brief" was to set out "the substance of all material pleadings, facts, documents, on which the parties rely, and the points of law and fact intended to be presented at the argument."[10] And this was before carbon paper and photocopies! Indeed, the first American patent for the typewriter wasn't even issued until 1829, and they weren't in general use until the 1870s. The first Xerox machine was not sold until 1959. To paraphrase the ubiquitous advertisement for Virginia Slims cigarettes in an era when cigarette advertising on television was permitted, legal briefs have come "a long way."

1. *You Must Show Why Your Client Deserves to Win.*

Irrespective of their philosophies, appellate judges—like jurors—want to do what they believe to be right. But what is "right"? That, as we used to say, is the "$64 question."

In some cases the answer is easy; in other cases it is difficult because there are competing equities on both sides. A good test is one that was devised by the great pre-Conquest English king, Ælfred, who decreed, in an inversion of the "golden rule": "What ye will that other men should not do to you, that do ye not to other men." According to Ælfred, this was the essence of law: "By bearing this precept in mind," he reflected, "a judge can do justice to all men. He needs no other law books."

---

[10] SUP. CT. R. XXX, 6 Wheat. b (1821).

Let Ælfred's paradigm guide you as you distill the jumble of facts that ricochet in your case into coherent lines of argument—the essence of which *must be* that "right" is on your side.

Thus, to be a winning appellate lawyer you *must*:

- Persuade the appellate judge (and law clerk) that "right" and "justice" is on *your* side for both:
  - Your *specific* case
  - The *general* proposition, of which your case is an *example*

Those reading your appellate brief, be it the judge or a law clerk or staff attorney must be *made to see* that your client *deserves* to win. This is essentially a fact-specific and fact-driven analysis. In most appeals of civil cases, the law is generally sufficiently ambiguous that the case can go *either* way—if the law were 100% clear, an appeal would be frivolous. Moreover, bringing an appeal that a lawyer did not believe was winnable would violate his or her duty to the client. It would also violate Rule 3.1 of the American Bar Association's Model Rules of Professional Conduct:

> "A lawyer shall not bring or defend a proceeding, or assert or controvert an issue therein, unless there is a basis for doing so that is not frivolous, which includes a good faith argument for an extension, modification or reversal of existing law. A lawyer for the defendant in a criminal proceeding, or the respondent in a proceeding that could result in incarceration, may nevertheless so defend the proceeding as to require that every element of the case be established."

How do you show an appellate court that your client deserves to win? As Judge Wald has observed, you must formulate the legal issue in your appeal so that an answer that is favorable to you "is inevitable after you read the upcoming 'Fact' section."[11]

Justice between the parties, however, is not the only issue with which you must be concerned. Appellate courts write for posterity; they shape legal principles that govern our society so that it is orderly and

---

11 PATRICIA M. WALD, 19 TIPS FROM 19 YEARS ON THE APPELLATE BENCH, 1 *The Journal of Appellate Practice and Process* 12 (1999).

predictable—unpleasant surprises are as much a death-knell for community well-being and safety as they are to orderly commerce. Thus, interplay between the importance of justice between the parties on the one hand, and the importance of the general issue on the other hand, varies with the tribunal before which you are appearing. The United States Supreme Court, for example, is—in theory at least—not concerned with justice between the parties; rather, it will take a case solely because the issues at stake are important to the nation. Thus, Rule 10 of the Rules of the United States Supreme Court provides:

> "Review on a writ of certiorari is not a matter of right, but of judicial discretion. A petition for a writ of certiorari will be granted only for compelling reasons. The following, although neither controlling nor fully measuring the Court's discretion, indicate the character of the reasons the Court considers:
>
> "(a) a United States court of appeals has entered a decision in conflict with the decision of another United States court of appeals on the same important matter; has decided an important federal question in a way that conflicts with a decision by a state court of last resort; or has so far departed from the accepted and usual course of judicial proceedings, or sanctioned such a departure by a lower court, as to call for an exercise of this Court's supervisory power;
>
> "(b) a state court of last resort has decided an important federal question in a way that conflicts with the decision of another state court of last resort or of a United States court of appeals;
>
> "(c) a state court or a United States court of appeals has decided an important question of federal law that has not been, but should be, settled by this Court, or has decided an important federal question in a way that conflicts with relevant decisions of this Court.
>
> "A petition for a writ of certiorari is rarely granted when the asserted error consists of erroneous factual findings or the misapplication of a properly stated rule of law."

Except in those states where the highest court does not have discretionary jurisdiction, similar limitations apply—a state's highest court will generally only take those appeals that concern issues beyond the parochial interests of the parties. What does all this mean for you as an advocate? It means that you have to shape your issue to meet these criteria; a petition for writ of certiorari filed with the United States Supreme Court that asks for review of a judgment that is claimed to be not supported by the evidence adduced at trial will get nowhere—except as an example of shoddy lawyering that will be passed from clerk to clerk for their mutual amusement.

Intermediate appellate courts, on the other hand, consider both the impact of the case on the parties as well as the general issue. They are both error-correcting courts and courts that clarify and make law. Thus, they will consider whether the evidence is sufficient to support a jury verdict, whether the trial judge made a legal error during the trial, and whether the law applied by the trial judge needs to be modified. You must understand all of this in framing your issues and in shaping your statement of facts.

Strategy:

> ☞ Know the criteria that the appellate court uses: 1) to accept appeals; 2) to decide appeals

2. *Give the appellate judge the tools to decide in your favor.*

As I already mentioned, both West and Lexis put a torrent of written decisions into the system every year. Indeed, West publishes, in its hard-bound volumes some 60,000 opinions *a year*, plus approximately 90,000 *more* opinions in various forms online in its ***WestLaw®*** service. I am certain that Lexis keeps pace. Rarely will a case be on "all fours" and, thus, dispositive. If there were such a binding case in your jurisdiction, you probably would not be bringing the appeal, except to argue that the case should be overruled. By the time you get to your brief's legal-analysis section—the reasons why you believe you should win your appeal—you *must* have already made the appellate court *want* to decide in your favor. Your legal analysis must give the judges and law clerks and staff attorneys the *tools* to decide your way. As Judge Wald has put it, you will, in essence, be showing the appellate court that "the law *allows*" the result you want.[12]

---

[12] PATRICIA M. WALD, 19 TIPS FROM 19 YEARS ON THE APPELLATE BENCH, 1 *The Journal of Appellate Practice and Process* 12 (1999) (emphasis by Judge Wald).

3. *Why Briefs Must Look a Certain Way.*

An appellate brief is a highly-structured presentation. The winning appellate lawyer must be able to use that structure to forcefully argue his or her case.

- The rules *require* that briefs look a certain way.
- Appellate judges *expect* to see briefs structured as the rules require.
- Appellate judges, like the rest of us, do not like surprises.

Every profession or calling has rules that govern what the way things look—articles written for *The English Journal*, for example, will look different than articles written for *The Harvard Law Review*. Authors for the former will follow the Modern Language Association style manual; persons writing for latter will follow the *Blue Book*. Even movie scripts must have a certain look about them:

> "Like every other industry on the planet, Hollywood has its standards. This is especially true when it comes to the screenplay. Either a screenwriter conforms her work to industry standards or she doesn't. If she doesn't, she tips off the reader that she is unfamiliar with screenwriting in general and that her work will probably have significant problems with character, story, and structure."[13]

Courts have their standards as well, and those are set out in the rules. A lawyer who submits a brief that does not comply with the rules risks having it not accepted. Even if a non-conforming brief is accepted, however, the judges will think, and rightfully so, that the lawyer was either too ignorant or too lazy to look up the rules. Why should the judge then believe that the lawyer has done any better a job with the record or the law?

4. *Content.*

Briefs generally must have the following:

- The questions presented for review.

---

[13] JENNIFER LERCH, 500 WAYS TO BEAT THE HOLLYWOOD SCRIPT READER 19 (1999).

- The procedural history of the case.
- The statement of the facts.
- The argument.
- The conclusion.

Some courts also require:

- A statement on jurisdiction.
- A statement on the applicable standards of review.
- A summary of argument.
- Statutes Involved.

Appellate-court rules vary from jurisdiction to jurisdiction. There are the rules of the highest court in your state system, and for the intermediate appellate courts (if your state has one). There are also rules for the United States Supreme Court and for the intermediate federal appellate courts—the United States Courts of Appeals for the various circuits. The rules governing appeals in the various United States Courts of Appeals are the Federal Rules of Appellate Procedure, which may, however, be modified by "local" rules of a particular circuit. Let's look at these rules, bearing in mind that other rules of appellate procedure are similar. They will give us a backdrop against which we can see how to make our briefs easier to read, more efficient, and, therefore more persuasive.

Rule 32(a) of the Federal Rules of Appellate Procedure provides (my comments are in **bold univers type**):

Form of a Brief.

(1) *Reproduction.*

(A) A brief may be reproduced by any process that yields a clear black image on light paper. The paper must be opaque and unglazed. Only one side of the paper may be used.

[This is merely common sense. Even if your appellate court does not have such a rule, why would any lawyer want to submit a brief was did not have "a clear black image on light paper." Yet, my court has received briefs from lawyers with barely legible dot-matrix printing! Additionally, briefs with the writing on one side of the paper help you in two ways: First, they give the judge the feeling that he or she is making some progress through the brief. Don't forget, appellate judges read a lot of briefs, and they want them short and to the point. Judge Wald makes the point with a frankness that may surprise you:

> **"Many judges look first to see how long a document is before reading a word. If it is long, they automatically read fast; if short, they read slower."[14]**

The Handbook published by the United States Court of Appeals for the Seventh Circuit gives similar advice:

> **"The brief writer should never forget that the judges are reading the briefs in six cases in preparation for each day of oral argument. The writer must select what is important and deal only with that; all that is not necessary should be ruthless discarded."[15]**

Judge Wald tells lawyers: "The more paper you throw at us, the meaner we get."[16] A brief with the words on one side of each page, even when a court does not require it (the Wisconsin Court of Appeals does not), gives the judge the heady feeling that the brief is shorter than it first appeared. Additionally, a brief with the words on one side of the page permits the judge (or law clerk or staff attorney) to annotate it easily. You are making the judge's job easier; subconsciously at least, he or she appreciates it.]

---

14 PATRICIA M. WALD, 19 TIPS FROM 19 YEARS ON THE APPELLATE BENCH, 1 *The Journal of Appellate Practice and Process* 10 (1999) (emphasis by Judge Wald).

15 PRACTITIONER'S HANDBOOK FOR APPEALS 86

16 PATRICIA M. WALD, 19 TIPS FROM 19 YEARS ON THE APPELLATE BENCH, 1 *The Journal of Appellate Practice and Process* 09 (1999) (emphasis by Judge Wald).

(B) Text must be reproduced with a clarity that equals or exceeds the output of a laser printer.

[Only a fool would submit a brief that was hard to read. Follow this rule even if your own court does not require it!]

(C) Photographs, illustrations, and tables may be reproduced by any method that results in a good copy of the original; a glossy finish is acceptable if the original is glossy.

[Again only a fool would submit graphics that were not good copies of the original.]

(2) *Cover.* Except for filings by unrepresented parties, the cover of the appellant's brief must be blue; the appellee's, red; an intervenor's or amicus curiae's, green; and any reply brief, gray. The front cover of a brief must contain:

(A) the number of the case centered at the top;

(B) the name of the court;

(C) the title of the case (see Rule 12(a));

(D) the nature of the proceeding (e.g., Appeal, Petition for Review) and the name of the court, agency, or board below;

(E) the title of the brief, identifying the party or parties for whom the brief is filed; and

(F) the name, office address, and telephone number of counsel representing the party for whom the brief is filed.

[This is the way judges expect the briefs to look. The covers are color-coded so the judge can pick out easily a brief and know whose it is without having to read the legend. Additionally, this standardized form lets the judge determine immediately the pertinent procedural information.

Sometimes the clerks who accept briefs for filing get a bit too picky. Once, a frantic lawyer called me on a late-Friday afternoon. He told me that the clerk in Madison would not accept his

appellee's brief because it was the "wrong" shade of red. I told him to do two things. First, to tell the clerk that I had authorized her to take the briefs nevertheless (and to call me if she still had a problem). Second, to send me a small slice of the cover. The clerk never called me, the briefs were filed, and the color was the shade of fresh salmon—certainly "red" enough to distinguish it from a blue brief-in-chief, a grey reply brief, a white appendix, or a green amicus curia brief.

And it is not only in state court where the clerks are picky. Indeed, the United States Court of Appeals for the Seventh Circuit is especially hard on lawyers for fairly *de minimis* transgressions of Rule 32 of the Federal Rules of Appellate Procedure. We'll see later how the court almost imposed sanctions because a brief contained too many words—through no fault of the lawyer. The clerks reflect the judges' super-sensitive, low threshold of irritation. Thus, a friend of mine recently received the following letter together with a box load of briefs that the clerk's office would not accept for filing:

"Dear Counsel: BRIEF/PETITION DEFICIENCY NOTICE

> "Documents that are determined by the Clerk's Office to be procedurally deficient must be corrected and returned for filing within seven days from the date of this notice. Previously set deadlines will not be automatically extended by this deficiency notice. Copies of the corrected document must be served upon all other parties. The substance of the document must not be changed; only the procedural deficiency is to be corrected. If the initial filing was untimely or if the corrected document is not returned to the Clerk's Office for filing within the seven days, a motion for leave to file instanter must accompany it, and must also be served upon all other parties.
>
> "Today this office Received' your brief/petition, which has been deemed deficient for filing due to the following procedural concern(s)
>
> > The brief should be clearly readable and the page size, margin and spacing requirements must be adhered to. See FRAP 32. FRAP Rule 32(a) (5) allows either proportionally spaced or monospaced type. Proportional type must include serifs for text and footnotes but sans-serif type may be used for headings and captions. Proportional type (text and

footnotes) must be 12 points or larger. Monospaced type may not contain more than 10.5 characters per inch. The typed matter must be set in clam roman style. This type size rule applies to briefs, petitions, answers, motions and responses. See FRAP Rule 32.

"A copy of this notice should accompany the corrected filing when resubmitted. The resubmission will be deemed timely if the mailing is accomplished within seven days of this notice, except that Petitions for Rehearing must be physically received in this office within that time."

What was the problem? The letter, a form letter, does not say. The lawyer had to *call* the clerk's office to ask. It seems that the font in the footnotes was too small. The briefs had to be redone, re-served, and re-filed! The irony is that the case was an *appointed* criminal case, which the lawyer and his firm took on, essentially, a *pro bono* basis.]

(3) *Binding.* The brief must be bound in any manner that is secure, does not obscure the text, and permits the brief to lie reasonably flat when open.

[You must make your brief easy to read and handle. Beware of using staples to bind briefs, even if the brief is short. I've been stuck by many a staple that has drawn blood—not the most pleasant experience. No judge would decide against a lawyer because the judge was stuck by an errant staple prong, but it doesn't make you happy. The best binding is, of course, one that will let the briefs lie flat—by themselves. Again, the whole idea is to make it easy for the person reading your brief.]

(4) *Paper Size, Line Spacing, and Margins.* The brief must be on 8 1/2 by 11 inch paper. The text must be double-spaced, but quotations more than two lines long may be indented and single-spaced. Headings and footnotes may be single-spaced. Margins must be at least one inch on all four sides. Page numbers may be placed in the margins, but no text may appear there.

[This rule ensures that the briefs will be the same size (so a brief does not stand out like a cumbersome sore thumb in the judge's brief case), and will be easy to read—plenty of white space and

typographical diversity to highlight and, thereby, easily identify, quotations. Even if your appellate court's rules are not this detailed, set your pages up so they will be easy to read, and so that the highpoints will stand out.]

(5) *Typeface*. Either a proportionally spaced or a monospaced face may be used.

> (A) A proportionally spaced face must include serifs, but sans-serif type may be used in headings and captions. A proportionally spaced face must be 14-point or larger.
>
> (B) A monospaced face may not contain more than 10 1/2 characters per inch.

Large type is a must. Judges read many, many briefs. Large type is easy to read—no, let me rephrase that: Large type is a joy to read! When I get a brief with large margins, large type, and plenty of white-space, I savor it as one might a fine wine or a vintage port. Other judges feel the same way. So, even if your appellate court's rules do not require "14-point type or larger" (emphasis added), do not try to squeeze words in, by either shrinking the type size, by decreasing the margins, or by narrowing the space between the lines. Lawyers who believe that they are helping their clients by jamming in more words are making a big mistake.]

(6) *Type Styles*. A brief must be set in a plain, roman style, although italics or boldface may be used for emphasis. Case names must be italicized or underlined.

[This rule is designed to make the page easy to read. Follow it, even if your appellate court does not have a similar rule. You should not use courier, the typeface that looks like typewriter type; it is harder to read than plain roman or the other normal proportionally spaced fonts. Of course, if your appellate court requires a different typeface, use it.]

(7) *Length.*

(A) Page limitation. A principal brief may not exceed 30 pages, or a reply brief 15 pages, unless it complies with Rule 32(a)(7)(B) and (C).

(B) Type-volume limitation.

(i) A principal brief is acceptable if:

- it contains no more than 14,000 words; or
- it uses a monospaced face and contains no more than 1,300 lines of text.

(ii) A reply brief is acceptable if it contains no more than half of the type volume specified in Rule 32(a)(7)(B)(i).

(iii) Headings, footnotes, and quotations count toward the word and line limitations. The corporate disclosure statement, table of contents, table of citations, statement with respect to oral argument, any addendum containing statutes, rules or regulations, and any certificates of counsel do not count toward the limitation.

(C) *Certificate of Compliance.* A brief submitted under Rule 32(a)(7)(B) must include a certificate by the attorney, or an unrepresented party, that the brief complies with the type-volume limitation. The person preparing the certificate may rely on the word or line count of the word-processing system used to prepare the brief. The certificate must state either:

(i) the number of words in the brief; or

(ii) the number of lines of monospaced type in the brief.

[Here it is! The page or word limitation. All appellate courts have it. Why? Because judges are busy and are inundated with words—words that obscure rather than clarify. Judges are immersed in a fog of words. Judge Wald is equally blunt:

"It's my view we can, should and will do more to stem the paper tidal wave. Repetition, extraneous facts, over-long arguments (by the 20th page, we are muttering to ourselves, "I get it, I get it. No more for God's sake") still occur more often than capable counsel should tolerate. In our court [the United States Court of Appeals for the District of Columbia Circuit] counsel get extra points for briefs they bring in under the 50-page limit."[17]

Remember, Judge Wald's court is one of the preeminent courts of the land. Its judges come from all over the nation, and the appointment process is further removed from crass political considerations than almost any other court in the country (there are no local United States Senators to please!). Remember how she described the reaction of her colleagues to briefs that were not "brief":

> "The more paper you throw at us, the meaner we get, the more irritated and hostile we feel about verbosity, peripheral arguments and long footnotes."[18]

As noted earlier, the United States Court of Appeals for the Seventh Circuit recently toyed with imposing sanctions on a lawyer because the lawyer's word-processing program *undercounted* the number of words. Here is the decision in full:

> "*Per Curiam.* Our opinion in this case directed appellants' counsel to show cause why they should not be sanctioned for filing a brief that exceeded the type-volume limit. Counsel's attempt to incorporate some other document by reference led us to check whether this had been done in order to dodge the limit. Here's what we found: "The certificate under Fed. R. App. P. 32(a)(7)(C) represents that the brief contains 13,824 words, only 176 short of the maximum. Our check reveals that the certificate is false. The brief actually includes 15,056 words, substantially over the maximum. Appellants counted only the words in the text of the brief, although Rule 32 provides that '[h]eadings, footnotes, and quotations count toward the word and line limitations.' Fed. R. App. P. 32(a)(7)(B)(iii). Appellants' brief has 20 footnotes with a total of 1,232 words." Appellants' brief was

---

[17] PATRICIA M. WALD, 19 TIPS FROM 19 YEARS ON THE APPELLATE BENCH, 1 *The Journal of Appellate Practice and Process* 9–10 (1999).

[18] PATRICIA M. WALD, 19 TIPS FROM 19 YEARS ON THE APPELLATE BENCH, 1 *The Journal of Appellate Practice and Process* 9 (1999).

prepared with Microsoft Word 97, and an unfortunate interaction occurred between that software and the terms of Rule 32. All recent versions of Microsoft Word (Word 97 for Windows, Word 98 for Macintosh, and Word 2000 for Windows), and some older versions that we have tested, count words and characters in both text and footnotes when the cursor is placed anywhere in the document and no text is selected. In recent versions on both Windows and Macintosh platforms, choosing the Word Count function brings up a window listing the number of characters and words in the document. A checkbox at the bottom of the window reading "Include footnotes and endnotes," when selected, yields a word count for all text and notes. But if the user selects any text in the document this checkbox is dimmed, and the program counts only the characters and words in the selected text. Microsoft Word does not offer a way to count words in those footnotes attached to the selected text.

"This complicates implementation of Fed. R. App. 32(a)(7), which limits the allowable length of a brief to 14,000 words, and of a reply brief to 7,000 words. Under Rule 32(a)(7) (B)(iii), footnotes count toward this limit, but the "corporate disclosure statement, table of contents, table of citations, statement with respect to oral argument, any addendum containing statutes, rules or regulations, and any certificates of counsel do not count toward the limitation." To determine the number of words that are included in the limit, counsel selects the "countable" body portions of the brief—which causes Microsoft Word to ignore countable footnotes. Counsel who do not notice that the count-footnotes box has been dimmed out may unintentionally file a false certificate and a brief that exceeds the word limits. That's what happened to appellants' lawyers. Older versions of Word have separate columns for text and footnote counts (plus a summation column), giving a visible cue that footnotes were not being counted when text had been selected, but current versions give only a consolidated count. When the count-footnotes checkbox is dimmed, even counsel who are aware that the brief contains footnotes may suppose that the software included these automatically.

"Current versions of Corel WordPerfect (for both Windows and Macintosh platforms) do not have this problem. WordPerfect does what lawyers may suppose that Word does (or should do): it automatically includes footnotes in its word and character counts. If no text is selected, the word count feature includes all words anywhere in the document; if text is selected, then WordPerfect includes words in footnotes that are attached to the selected text. We have not tested other programs, because the vast majority of briefs filed with the court are prepared using either Word or WordPerfect, but law firms that use other programs must find out how their software treats footnotes attached to selected text.

"Lawyers who produce their documents with WordPerfect software have an easy job of things under Rule 32. They select the "countable" portions of the brief, and the program tells them how many words are in both text and footnotes. Lawyers who use Word, by contrast, must infer from the dimmed checkbox that footnotes have been omitted from the count. They must open a separate footnote window, select the footnotes attached to "countable" body text, and have the program count the words in these notes. Then they must add the text and footnote counts manually in order to determine compliance with Rule 32(a)(7).

"Long-run solutions to this problem must come either from Microsoft Corporation—which ought to make it possible to obtain a count of words in footnotes attached to selected text—or from the national rulemaking process. We will send copies of this opinion to those responsible for such design decisions. In the meantime, we will flag this issue in the court's Practitioner's Guide and in materials distributed to counsel when an appeal is docketed. Law firms should alert their staffs to the issue pending a resolution at the software level. *Our clerk's office will spot-check briefs that have been prepared on Microsoft Word, are close to the word limit, and contain footnotes. Noncomplying briefs will be returned, and if the problem persists after there has been ample time for news to reach the bar we will consider what else needs to be done.* (Counsel who use Word are not entitled to a litigating advantage over those who use WordPerfect.) For now, however, sanctions are inappropriate, and the order to show cause is discharged."

DeSilva v. DiLeonardi, Nos. 99-1754 & 99-1769 (7th Cir. July 21, 1999) (Coffey, Easterbrook, & Rovner). (Emphasis added.)

If a body of serious, scholarly jurists react as Judge Wald describes, and if a panel of the Seventh Circuit has the words in a brief *counted*, and considers imposing sanctions because the brief had an extra 1,056 words (through no fault of counsel), you can imagine how the less scholarly, more street-wise judges of

other appellate courts will respond to the type of briefs Judge Wald describes.]

5. *The Keys to Writing an Effective Brief—A Part-By-Part Analysis.*

Later, we will examine briefs submitted in real cases, and analyze their good and bad parts—as well as the courts' ultimate verdict on their advocacy: the decisions. First, let us look at the brief part by part and see how to make it an effective tool to help you win.

A. *Be Honest and Forthright*

When you write your brief or present your oral argument, avoid the temptation to put an unfair, overly clever spin on either the facts or the law. Winston S. Churchill was a master logician and advocate. He spent much of the 1930s writing the biography of his famous ancestor John Churchill, the Duke of Marlborough, and was undoubtedly interested in presenting a favorable portrait of a man who received mixed reviews from other historians. The prolific American historian Henry Steele Commager abridged the biography (from six volumes to three) and wrote in an introduction to the massive work:

> "*Marlborough* is an argument for the defense all the way; but an argument not fabricated by cleverness or insinuated by chicanery, or imposed by violence, but grounded on the solid rock of evidence. It is balanced, temperate, and fair; it carries conviction.
>
> "It cannot fairly be said that Churchill is blind to the weaknesses and the flaws in Marlborough's character, but it can be said that he regards the weaknesses as venial and the flaws as superficial, and when he casts up the balance of weakness and strength, he is content with the result. He is a skillful attorney for the defense, and if he does not convince us that Marlborough is blameless, he does persuade us that a blameless Marlborough would be uninspiring."[19]

This is an important lesson from the greatest historian/statesman of our age—persuasion prevails in the end not through artifice but through the **persuasive use of truth**. Your brief, in all its sinews and fibers, must, like Churchill's *Marlborough*, be an "argument" for your client, but not an

---

[19] Winston S. Churchill, *Marlborough, His Life and Times* xxx (Commager abridgment 1968).

argument "fabricated by cleverness or insinuated by chicanery" but, rather, one "grounded on the solid rock of evidence." If it is "balanced, temperate, and fair," and uses the truth persuasively, your brief will carry conviction and increase your odds of winning.

B. *Make the Bad Facts Work For You*

In *The "How-To-Win" Trial Manual*, I explain how to make the bad facts work for you during the trial. You must do this at the appellate level as well. Later, when we analyze the briefs in the actual cases, we'll see some concrete ways to do this. But for now, I offer two examples—one from a pivotal moment in history, one from a current controversy that may also be pivotal for our society.

In describing William of Normandy's invasion of England in 1066, Winston S. Churchill tells us in Volume One of his *History of the English-Speaking Peoples* that William "fell flat on his face as he stepped out of the boat. 'See,' he said turning the omen into a favourable channel, 'I have taken England with both my hands.'"

On Friday, November 5, 1999, district court judge Thomas Penfield Jackson issued his long-awaited findings of fact in the *Microsoft* antitrust case. The findings surprised no one, of course, because it was clear that Judge Jackson had used the bench trial to fill in the blanks for which a prior appellate court ruling had reversed him. Amid the resulting Sturm und Drang, *The Wall Street Journal* put its editorial finger on the effective-advocacy aspect of the case:

> "We also see the failure of Microsoft's strategy, which was to deny the meaning of its own actions, lest those actions retroactively be found illegal because the court pins the label "monopoly" on it. That was unfortunate. Microsoft had a strong case to make that it had behaved in the only way any rational competitor could have.
>
> "Microsoft should have argued that we have a monopoly because our customers want us to have one. There is a great deal more software in the world than there would otherwise be, because software designers can invest in creating products knowing there is an installed base of compatible operating systems that won't soon be displaced. And consumers know they can lay out a thousand bucks or more for

a PC without taking a Betamax-vs.-VHS gamble that their investment will be rendered obsolete."[20]

In every appeal, you must be able to find the thread that turns the stumbling blocks in your case into stepping stones—to, as Churchill penned it, divert those bad facts into a "favourable channel."

C. *Question Presented.*

The *Question Presented* part of the appellate brief is your first shot at the appellate judge (and law clerk). This is your first chance to successfully argue your case. Your questions must, accordingly, be framed with care. They *must*:

- be concise
- be clear
- be fairly stated

and, most important:

- *compel* the answer you want.

Examples:

In a hypothetical automobile-accident case, the jury found that Mary Jones, the defendant-driver of a car, negligently damaged Roger Smith's van, when she drove into it after, according to her testimony, she swerved to avoid a pickup truck that had veered into her lane. Mary Jones's appeal centers on the trial court's failure to give the "emergency" instruction. Compare the persuasive force of the following "questions presented":

For the Defendant-Appellant (Mary Jones):

1. "Did the trial court commit error by failing to give the emergency instruction?"

OR

---

[20] *The Wall Street Journal* A50 (November 8, 1999).

2. "Mary Jones testified that she was driving slower than the speed limit when a pick-up truck suddenly swerved in front of her, forcing her to steer to the right to avoid colliding with the truck. Should the trial court have instructed the jury about Mary Jones's duty of care when faced with an emergency?"

Number 1 is the dry, vanilla type of question presented. It fairly and accurately states the question presented to the appellate court for review, but it is lifeless and bleached of all persuasion. Its weakness is that the reader has no clue as to what the answer to the question *should be*.

Number 2, on the other hand, is filled with enough facts (Mary Jones was not speeding; the pickup truck "swerved"; the truck swerved in front of her; the swerve was "sudden") so that the reader is moved to wonder why the trial judge did *not* given the instruction. Stated another way, the question leaves the reader with an initial view that: 1) Mary Jones faced a sudden and surprising event, which, in common parlance, folks would call an "emergency"; and 2) that Mary Jones did not create the emergency.

For Plaintiff-Respondent (Roger Smith):

1. "Did the trial court commit error by failing to give the emergency instruction?"

OR

2. "In an automobile accident case, did the trial court abuse its discretion by instructing the jury:

— that the jury should not find the defendant negligent if she exercised the same degree of care and caution as would a reasonable driver under the same or similar circumstances, and

— that the jury should consider all of the facts they found to be properly proven by the evidence

even though the trial court did not specifically use the word 'emergency' or give the form instruction on 'emergency'?"

Here again, the first question presents the issue in a neutral, bland, vanilla way. The reader has no inclination what the answer should be. On the other hand, the second way of presenting the issue for the appellate court's review breaks out of the box to present the issue in a way that the appellate court will see that, on the whole, the jury was fairly and accurately instructed. In essence, the appellee is arguing: "Gee, maybe in a perfect world the trial judge would have given the emergency instruction (although we persuaded her not to), but there was no harm done because the jury was given an accurate statement of the law, which permitted them to decide the case fairly." Stated another way, if the jury believed Mary Jones's version of the accident, then that sudden swerving by the truck was a "circumstance" that they could consider in determining whether Jones was negligent.

Some lawyers believe that the "question presented" should always be phrased so that the desired answer is "yes." I disagree. It is a general rule in the law that the party wanting to have a court reach a certain result has the burden of proof on that issue. Here, the *appellant* can only win her appeal if she persuades the court that the trial court erred in not giving the instruction. Moreover, she had the burden of persuading the trial court *to give* the instruction in the first place. The defendant neither had the burden before the trial court nor has the burden on appeal. Yet, the subtext of a "question presented" that is structured so that "yes" is the desired answer places a burden of persuasion on him. Watch (I give two different ways the desired answer is "yes"):

> "In an automobile accident case, did the trial court not abuse its discretion by instructing the jury:
>
> — that the jury should not find the defendant negligent if she exercised the same degree of care and caution as would a reasonable driver under the same or similar circumstances, and
>
> — that the jury should consider all of the facts they found to be properly proven by the evidence
>
> even though the trial court did not specifically use the word 'emergency' or give the form instruction on 'emergency'?"

Yes, the "not abuse its discretion" is clumsy. Let's try a different formulation:

> In an automobile accident case, did the trial court appropriately instruct the jury:

— that the jury should not find the defendant negligent if she exercised the same degree of care and caution as would a reasonable driver under the same or similar circumstances, and

— that the jury should consider all of the facts they found to be properly proven by the evidence

even though the trial court did not specifically use the word 'emergency' or give the form instruction on 'emergency'?"

The latter two examples (especially the second one, which abandons the helpful "abuse of discretion" standard) load the appellee with some of the burden that the recommended example (the one numbered "2.") does not. In short, it is to the appellee's advantage to have the court respond "Of course not!" after reading the appellee's "question presented"—that is, that the appellant has not satisfied the appellant's burden of showing trial-court error.

Strategy:

☞ Although the "but even if" *concept* is used in the framing of the second of the hypothetical questions presented on behalf of Roger Smith, the *phrase* "but even if", should ***not*** be used. You should ***not*** begin the question presented by, as most lawyers would: "Even if the trial court erred in not giving the 'emergency' instruction, was the error harmless because ... " Using the phrase "but even if" concedes the error—something that you do not have to do.

☞ When loading a "question presented" with facts or concepts, as I've done in Number 2 above, use typography to make the question easy to follow. Don't make the mistake of running together a series of complicated sentences.

The important point to remember is that the arguments should *support one another*, not conflict.

D. *Pick Your Issues With Care*

You should restrict your arguments to your most powerful; do not throw in everything and, as we used to say, the kitchen sink. Again, Judge Wald's comments are instructive:

> "Confident counsel should almost always go for broke and rely on their one or two best arguments, abandoning the other 9–10 wish-list entries. There is, of course, always some small risk of dropping an argument that might appeal to one or two judges, but I can assure you in the vast majority of cases that possibility is theoretical only, and *the fewer arguments you make the more attention they will get from us in preparing and disposing of your case*."[21]

The Seventh Circuit Handbook makes a similar point: "Except in unusually complicated cases,a brief that treats more than three or four matters runs a serious risk of becoming too diffused and giving the overall impression that no one claimed error can be very serious."[22] This is also the advice of John C. Goldbold, who, in his long career as a federal appellate judge, served as Chief Judge of both the United States Court of Appeals for the Fifth Circuit and, later, when part of the Fifth Circuit was split off, the Eleventh Circuit:

> "The mind of an appellate judge is habitually receptive to the suggestions that a lower court committed error. But receptiveness declines as the number of assigned errors increases. Multiplicity hints at lack of confidence in any."

Lawyers all over the country throw in every possible issue because they are afraid that if they lose the appeal someone will criticize them; they hear the following "footsteps": "Oh, you should have argued such and such ..." or "Why didn't you argue this and that ... ?" In a very real sense, these lawyers are committing malpractice out of the fear that others will think they have committed malpractice.

Strategy:

☞ Grasp the nettle of your convictions; argue only those issues that: 1) are your best; and 2) that are consistent with one another.

E. *Summary of Argument*.

The *Summary of Argument* part of the appellate brief is your chance to boil down your argument to is most powerful essence. This is the "bird's-eye

---

21 PATRICIA M. WALD, 19 TIPS FROM 19 YEARS ON THE APPELLATE BENCH, 1 *The Journal of Appellate Practice and Process* 11 (1999). (Emphasis added.)

22 PRACTITIONER'S HANDBOOK FOR APPEALS 86.

view" of your appeal. After reading the summary of your argument, the appellate judge (and law clerk) should have the distinct belief that you deserve to win. As with the *Questions Presented* part of the brief, formulation of the *Summary of Argument* requires significant thought and care.

- Must be long enough to be effective—but short enough to be appealing.
- The facts should be intertwined with the law so that the summary powerfully compels the answer you seek.
- Unless prohibited by court rule, it should contain brief, but forceful, references to controlling legal authority.
- Discrete thoughts should be in paragraphs that are separately numbered.
- Avoid unsupported rhetoric.

The last point needs emphasis, and applies to every part of your brief and, indeed as we will see when we discuss effective oral argument, to that aspect of you appeal as well: *Avoid unsupported rhetoric*. What do I mean? Lawyers love emotion-laden arguments. But rhetoric must be earned by facts. Rhetoric that is not supported by facts is like a meringue—all form, very little substance, and loaded with air. You will persuade the judges before whom you appear *only* by showing them that your client deserves to win. That can only be done with *facts*—organized and presented in their most persuasive way.

Strategy:

☞ The *Summary of Argument* is a powerful tool of persuasion and should be used even when the court rules do not require it. But here, as elsewhere, you must avoid naked rhetoric.

Example:

An excerpt from Mary Smith's appellate brief in our hypothetical automobile-accident case:

Summary of Argument

> It is settled law that it is an abuse of discretion for a trial court not to instruct the jury on an issue properly raised by the evidence. [citation] Here, there was uncontradicted evidence that:
>
> — Mary Jones was driving under the speed limit,
>
> — Mary Jones was cut off by a speeding red pickup truck that swerved in front of her.
>
> This a classic example of a driver being confronted with an "emergency" not of her own doing. [citation] Although the trial court did instruct the jury with the pattern instruction on negligence, the trial court refused to instruct the jury on what, under the law, constituted an "emergency." This left the jury free to speculate about what an "emergency" was. This left twelve jurors free to apply their own and, possibly, different definitions. As a result, Mary Jones's trial counsel could not adequately argue the "emergency doctrine" because the jury did not have the central, critical, legal definition.
>
> This Court has specifically held that the 'emergency' instruction should be given when that issue is fairly raised by the evidence. [citation] The trial court's failure to instruct the jury on an issue critical to Mary Jones's defense in this case was based on its erroneous view of the law that the standard jury instruction on negligence was, in its word, 'adequate' [R:24:3 (Transcript of Instructions Conference)] The trial court thus abused its discretion. [citation].

This "summary of argument" builds on facts, and shows the judges *why* you *should* win—rather than, in the case of mere rhetoric, only that you *want* to win. The following two examples may crystallize this point:

> 1) The police violated the defendant's Fourth Amendment rights by searching him without probable cause. Accordingly the trial court erred by not suppressing the cocaine they found in Smith's pockets.

Yes, this is a summary of the defendant's argument, but is mere rhetoric (albeit rhetoric that is not screaming) because there are no facts from which a reader can assess the truth or falsity of the statement.

> 2) Sam Smith, the defendant was walking through the mall on his way to one of the stores to buy his sister a present. All of a sudden three plain-clothes detectives surrounded him, threw him up against the wall, and rifled his pockets. In doing this, the detectives violated Smith's Fourth Amendment rights, and the trial court erred by not suppressing the cocaine they found in Smith's pockets.

We will see real-life examples of mere rhetoric when we analyze the briefs in both the civil and criminal cases.

F. *Statement of Facts.*

This is the chance to show the appellate judge (and law clerk or staff attorney) that you *deserve to win.* Many an appeal is won or lost in the statement of facts. Perhaps Justice Louis J. Brandeis put it best when he is reported to have said: "Let me write the statement of facts, and I care not who writes the law."[23] But, your statement of facts must not be overtly argumentative. The Handbook published by the United States Court of Appeals for the Seventh Circuit alerts counsel that the statement of facts must be "concise and objective" and "must be a fair summary without argument or comment."[24]

Use some of the same techniques that you use in your opening statement to the jury—this *is* your *opening statement* to the appellate court.

- **Your Brief Must Have One Central Theme**

As noted, lawyers taking an appeal often make the mistake of larding their briefs with every conceivable error that they believe the trial court has made. Pick your field of battle—the issue or issues in which you have the greatest confidence. Moreover, once you pick the issue, find a way to tie them together so they work synergistically. Thus, for example, if you represent a criminal defendant appealing his or her conviction, your theme might be that the trial judge's errors deprived your client of a fair trial—that is, a trial in whose verdict reasonable persons would be confident. If, on the other hand, you

---

[23] Quoted in Brown, *Legal Training as a Qualification for Modern Diplomacy*, 10 YALE L. REP. 23 (Spring 1964), *cited in* Michael R. Fontham, *Written and Oral Advocacy* 53 (1985).

[24] PRACTITIONER'S HANDBOOK FOR APPEALS 84.

represent the prosecution on appeal, your theme might be that the defendant *did* have a fair trial and either the trial judge's rulings were within the ambit of the judge's discretion or that, in the context of the trial as a whole, did not make the verdict untrustworthy.

- **Your Statement of Facts Must Resonate With Your Theme**

In every appeal, there are zillions of facts. Indeed, setting out all the "facts" could take nearly as many pages as the transcripts and exhibits. You must pare the facts that you present to those that are essential to the most persuasive presentation of your arguments. Thus you must, as Judge Wald suggests, omit facts that are "extraneous." Frankly, most of the briefs that I read are larded with facts that are wholly irrelevant to the issues presented for review.

Lawyers load briefs with extraneous facts for two main reasons. First, it is easier to put everything in, rather than take the time to analyze and eliminate. It reminds me of George Bernard Shaw's famous letter to a friend: "Please excuse the length of my letter; if I had more time it would be shorter." Second, lawyers have the mistaken idea that this is the way it *should* be done. After all, they see the same thing in appellate decisions—sometimes festooned with extraneous facts galore! But judges don't have to persuade anyone; their livelihood or success does not depend on whether anyone reads their decisions (advancement up the judicial hierarchy depends on other less esoteric and cerebral matters). *You*, however, *want* the appellate judges (and their clerk staff) to read your brief with pleasure, rather than with despair. You must craft every part of your brief, especially the statement of facts, with care. As the Seventh Circuit Handbook says:

> "Great care should be taken that the facts are all marshalled and stated. If this is done, the facts themselves will often develop the relevant and governing points of law. *An effective statement summarizes the facts so that the reader is persuaded that justice and the precedents both require a decision for the advocate's client.*"[25]

---

25 PRACTITIONER'S HANDBOOK FOR APPEALS 84–85 (emphasis added).

▸ **Build "Argument" Skeleton First**

An effective and efficient way to assess what facts are important to your appeal is to build a skeleton of your argument first. Indeed, try writing the Argument section of your brief first, and then go back to write the Statement of Facts. Then you will not only know what facts to plug in, but you will also be able to arrange those facts in their most persuasive order. This way you can assure that your facts —all of them—will resonate with your theme, and that these facts will not be lost in a sea of fog. After you do this, you can fine-tune your argument section, and, then return to fine-tune your Statement of Facts.

Strategy:

☞ Write your Argument section first, then write your Statement of Facts.

▸ **Infuse Theme With High Value**

An appellate court will not reverse a trial judge merely because of some (or even many) technical errors. The errors must have had a substantial impact in either prejudicing the appellant's case or screwing-up the law. Your statement of facts must hit the judges be like a bolt of lightning: If you are the appellant—justice has not been done; if you are the respondent—the appeal itself, though perhaps not "frivolous" in the technical sense, is a waste of time.

- **Quick Hook — Get Appellate Judge (and law clerk or staff attorney) to *root for your client.***

As with an opening statement to a jury, your first few sentences are *crucial.* Make them count!

- **Do not use a chronological or witness-by-witness approach. Rather, tell the story in its most persuasive way.**

I know that it is *easier for you* to write a statement of facts using a witness-by-witness approach—that's the way the transcript is set out: witness 1, witness 2, etc. Chronology, no matter how easy, is hardly the most interesting *or* persuasive way.

In the early days of the Associated Press, its reporters stuck to a chronological style. Thus, the following AP dispatch, written by reporter Lawrence Augustus Gobright, and reprinted in the *New York Daily Tribune* of Saturday, April 15, 1865:

> "President Lincoln and wife, with other friends, this evening visited Ford's Theater, for the purpose of witnessing the performance of the 'American Cousin.'
>
> "It was announced in the papers that Gen. Grant would also be present, but he took the late train of cars for New Jersey.
>
> "The theater was densely crowded, and everybody seemed delighted with the scene before them. During the third act, and while there was a temporary pause for one of the actors to enter, a sharp report of a pistol was heard, which merely attracted attention, but suggested nothing serious, until a man rushed to the front of the President's box, waving a long dagger in his hand, and exclaiming, 'Sic semper tyrannis,' and immediately leaped from the box, which was on the second tier, to the stage beneath, and ran across to the opposite side, making his escape amid the bewilderment of the audience, from the rear of the theater, and mounting a horse, fled.
>
> "The screams of Mrs. Lincoln first disclosed the fact to the audience that the President had been shot, when all present rose to their feet, rushing toward the stage, many exclaiming, 'Hang him, hang him.'
>
> "The excitement was of the wildest possible description, and of course, there was an abrupt termination to the theatrical performance."

No journalist would write that way today, lashed to the mast of chronology. Don't you. Rather you must arrange your facts in their most persuasive, intriguing, order, so that, as Judge Wald has noted in a passage quoted earlier, and as the Seventh Circuit Handbook also says, the court's answer to the issue presented will be in your favor once the court has read your statement of facts. Stated another way, you must make the judge *want* you to win. If you make the judge want you to win, he or she will find a way, and will use the same tools that jurors use, rationalization and denial, *plus* the millions of judicial decisions.

- **Use Visual Aids**
  - ▸ Diagrams
  - ▸ Photographs
  - ▸ Tables
  - ▸ Charts

There are two types of visual aids that you can use in your brief:

1) Those visual aids that are already in the record—either as evidentiary or demonstrative exhibits.

   — An "evidentiary" exhibit is one received into evidence and is part of the substantive appellate record: the jury was allowed to consider it as proof of some fact necessary for its verdict.

   — A "demonstrative" exhibit is shown to the jury to help it understand the evidence, but is not itself evidence.

   An example of a demonstrative exhibit is a diagram that the trial lawyer used in closing argument to demonstrate an intersection collision—drawing the diagram as he or she recounted the testimony for the jury.

   An "evidentiary" exhibit is one, for example, drawn by a witness to an accident that describes what she saw—it is an extension of her oral testimony, rather than something created by someone else to help the jury understand that witness's testimony.

You can put in your brief reproductions of both evidentiary and demonstrative exhibits. Thus, as we have seen, Rule 32(a)(1)(C) of the Federal Rules of Appellate Procedure provides that: "Photographs, illustrations, and tables may be reproduced by any method that results in a good copy of the original; a glossy finish is acceptable if the original is glossy."

2) Those visual aids that are not in the appellate record, but that you prepare for your appellate brief. You use these pictures or

diagrams to explain concepts that are hard to grasp from the mere written word.

For example, if the appeal is about an automobile accident, and, for whatever reason, the appellate record does not have a diagram of the accident, draw one for the judges so they can visualize more easily what happened. You must, however, *alert the reader that you are including it to explain the testimony that* <u>*is*</u> *in the record.* The following is one way how to do this:

> "Mrs. Knight testified that she was stopped at the corner of Main and Elm, waiting for the red light to turn green. [R 7:3 (Transcript of Mrs. Knight's testimony)] She was headed north. [R 7:3] The light turned green. [R 7:4] Mrs. Knight entered the intersection. [R 7:4] Before she was half-way through the intersection, a car driven by the defendant, Mr. Weeks, hit her on the passenger side of her car. [R 7:4–5] He was going from east to west. [R 7:5] So we can better see what happened as Mrs. Knight described it in her testimony, we have drawn a diagram of the intersection of Main and Elm, and have put it at the bottom of this page. Mrs. Knight's car is marked with the letter "*K*," and the car of the defendant, Mr. Weeks, is marked with the letter "*W*." Mr. Weeks's course of travel is shown with a heavy dotted line. Although this diagram is not part of the appellate record, we believe that it accurately and fairly represents a visualization of Mrs. Knight's testimony, and we include it here for the court's convenience."

It is much easier to grasp abstract concepts from diagrams than it is to distill them from words alone. The dynamics of a scene shown in a diagram can be grasped instantly. In contrast, a reader trying to picture something from a verbal description must do the transformation in his or her head; your diagram does the job for the reader and helps the judge "see" what happened.

- **Give Record References for *Every* Statement You Make.**

There is an old saying that a tree makes no noise if it falls in a remote forest where there is no one to hear the crash. That or may not be true, depending upon your philosophical or metaphysical bent. What *is* true, however, is that if you do not give a record reference, the event or testimony or evidence that you describe never happened. Rarely will judges or staff do *your* job and scour the file or boxes of files to find support for some statement that you make. Anything you say in a brief that does not have support in the record will be ignored—appellate judges may not go outside the record; anything that you say in a brief that does not have a record-reference citation will, similarly, be ignored. Thus, Rules 28(a)(7) and 28(b) of the Federal Rules of Appellate Procedure, as with the rules of most if not all jurisdictions, require that statements of facts have "appropriate references to the record."

When you cite to the record, make your citations clear. Generally, the appellate record will be numbered: The summons will be "1," the complaint "2," etc. Most lawyers, then, citing to page 2 of the complaint will cite [R 2:2]. That is fine as it goes. But remember, your job is to make it easy for the appellate judges. Thus, for example, unless the judge has just looked at record document "48," he or she will not know that your citation is to the testimony of the defendant's accountant. True, occasionally the document to which reference is made is clear from the context of the sentence, as in: "The defendant's accountant testified that ..." More often than not, however, the referenced document is not clear, and *it may make a difference*. Surely, the weight that an appellate court will give to a statement will vary, depending upon whether the statement comes from a self-serving affidavit submitted in opposition to a motion for summary judgment by the party who now quotes the statement in his or her appellate brief, or whether it comes from the testimony of an opposing party. Thus, in your record-reference cites, give the reference in full, as in: [R 2 (complaint): 2] or [R 37 (transcript of 1/9/97) (testimony of James Peterson, M.D., plaintiff's medical expert) 76]. Putting the reference in brackets permits the reader to skip over it if that information is not important at the moment; making the reference complete lets the reader evaluate the statement to which the record cite is attached. One further suggestion: avoid using "***Id.***, at 17" or some variance; generally the first reference to that the document was on another page, sometimes many pages earlier. By using "***Id.***, at 17" you're forcing the reader to go back and look for the first time that document was cited. Indeed, I am typing this sentence on a Sunday evening; this afternoon, I read a brief that used "***Id.***, at ___" throughout. At one point it was important for me to know *where* in the record I could find the reference. I had to search through several pages to find the first time the document referred to as "***Id.***" was mentioned. The additional thirty seconds or so may not seem like much time, but it interrupted the flow of my reading and was annoying. Don't annoy the folks who will decide your case.

• Quote or Reproduce Crucial Portions of the Record—Do Not Merely Paraphrase, But Paraphrase *and* Quote.

Judges are always suspicious. After all, both sides claim that right and justice and truth is on their side, not to mention the "controlling law." One side, and possibly both, is, at best, putting a spin on his or her position. Thus, judges read briefs with great skepticism. This means that when you say something in a brief that purports to reflect the record (or the law—we'll discuss this later), you must be punctiliously accurate, or risk admonition or worse.

Several years ago, a prominent criminal-defense lawyer in Milwaukee filed an appellate brief on behalf of a client who was convicted of several drug crimes. The lawyer argued on appeal that the prosecution violated ***Brady v. Maryland***, 373 U.S. 83, 87 (1963), which held that "the suppression by the prosecution of evidence favorable to an accused upon request [*sic*] violates due process where the evidence is material either to guilt or to punishment," by not giving the defendant recordings of a conversation the defendant had with a fellow jail inmate, during which the defendant allegedly denied possessing the drugs. ***State v. Lass***, 194 Wis.2d 591, 603, 535 N.W.2d 904, 908 (Wis. Ct. App. 1995). The brief did not reveal, however, that the defendant's trial lawyer told the trial court that he *was* given the tape, which was worthless: "They also gave me a tape and which I listened to, which was clearly inaudible. I can't hear anything on the tape, just because of the noise in the jail and whatever have you." ***Id.***, 194 Wis.2d at 604, 535 N.W.2d at 908. The tape could not have been both "clearly inaudible" *and* exculpatory. Moreover, anything the defendant said while he was in jail would have been hearsay and not admissible into evidence if offered by him. Arguments like this destroy a lawyer's credibility. But this was not all; the lawyer also misrepresented what the trial court did in connection with another of the defendant's assertions on appeal.

The defendant's trial was scheduled to start on a Monday. He claimed that the prosecutor violated his rights by turning over to him on the Friday before that Monday some three-hundred pages of documents that allegedly concerned the defendant's "wealth." His brief on appeal claimed, without citation to the record, that this "wealth" evidence was crucial to the case; that the trial judge denied the defendant's motion to exclude the evidence; and that the trial judge denied him a continuance to review the material. This was all not true. First, the three-hundred pages were *not* used at the trial. Second, the trial judge did not deny the defendant a reasonable opportunity to review the material, and, in fact, the trial judge had told the parties that it would "at least consider an adjournment" if the defendant's trial lawyer needed one to review the documents. ***Id.***, 194 Wis.2d at 605, 535 N.W.2d at 908, 909. Additionally, the prosecutor said that if the defendant's lawyer needed an adjournment, he "certainly could not object to that." ***Ibid.***

The defendant's lawyers on appeal either deliberately lied to us, or, at the very least, were negligent in preparing the appeal. We admonished them by name in the published decision. ***Ibid.***

An assistant United States Attorney in California was equally disingenuous with a United States district court judge and the United States Court of Appeals for the Ninth Circuit. Two persons were tried on serious drug charges, arising out of an alleged conspiracy with a third person, Krikor Nourian, whom the defense surmised was cooperating with the government. During the trial, the government did not call Nourian as a witness, but, rather, introduced his statements under Rule 801(d)(2)(E) of the Federal Rules of Evidence, which admits as substantive evidence against members of a conspiracy statements made by any of them during the course of and in furtherance of the conspiracy. The government also refused to give the defense lawyers access to Nourian. The defense asked the jury to infer that Nourian's testimony would have hurt the government's case against the defendants because although it could have called him as a witness, it did not. The assistant United States Attorney responded:

> "The government can't force someone to talk. They have to agree to talk after they've been arrested.
>
> "Well, you can figure out defendant Nourian was arrested. He has Fifth Amendment rights. *He has the right to remain silent*. The government can't force anyone to talk. It is against their Fifth Amendment rights. *Don't be misled that the government could have called Nourian.*"

United States v. Kojayan, 8 F.3d 1315, 1317–1318 (9th Cir. 1993) (emphasis by the court).

This was not true, and the government lawyer did nothing during subsequent colloquy before the district court, and a motion for a new trial, to correct his false statement. ***Id.***, 8 F.3d at 1318–1319. But there is more. In its appellate brief before the Ninth Circuit, the government argued that the prosecutor's comments "were all supported by the record before the jury." ***Id.***, 8 F.3d at 1319. During oral argument, and only when pressed by insistent questioning, did the prosecutor finally admit that the government had a cooperation agreement with Nourian. *Id.*, 8 F.3d at 1320. Even more astounding was the government's argument in its brief before the Ninth Circuit. In the words of the court of appeals, the government argued that because "defense counsel had done something improper by asking the jury to infer that Nourian was available to the government, ... it was therefore 'fair advocacy' for the prosecutor to assert the contrary, even if he knew it was false." *Id.*, 8 F.3d at 1319.

The court of appeals, of course, recognized that the government's argument was both spurious and dangerous:

> "As we note below, there was nothing at all wrong with what defense counsel said and did. See pp. 1320-21 *infra*. More significantly, we're taken aback by the government's assertion that it is ever 'fair advocacy' for a lawyer to make false statements in court. Even had defense counsel made a factual misstatement, even had he committed an impropriety, this surely would have given opposing counsel no license to do the same. The claim of impropriety should have been addressed to the court, not remedied through self-help."

Ibid.

Kojayan was written by Circuit Judge Alex Kozinski, one of this nation's brightest and most articulate jurists. Its opening paragraphs are a classic in American jurisprudence:

> "In many ways this is a run-of-the-mill case. A misdeed was committed, and the wrongdoers did their best to keep from being found out. When their actions were questioned, they denied any impropriety and pointed the finger at others. Eventually forced to own up, they did so only partially and grudgingly, 'minimiz[ing their] involvement in the ... conduct and ... not fully accept[ing] responsibility.' *United States v. Yanez*, 985 F.2d 371, 376 (7th Cir.1993).
>
> "A run-of-the-mill case in many ways, but with a twist."

Id., 8 F.3d at 1316. And so it was. But the "twist" became even more grotesque. The government lawyers, who are given the awesome power to prosecute in the name of the United States of America, learned nothing from this justifiably severe chastisement. In a motion to "depublish" the opinion or, in the alternative, to delete the name of the assistant United States Attorney, Jeffrey S. Sinek, from the opinion, Terree A. Bowers, the United States Attorney excused Sinek's misrepresentations as "the unfortunate result of errors of judgment, driven, in Mr. Sinek's case, by his failure to fully understand the unique and special ethical obligations of prosecutors." *Motion For Depublication, Or, In The Alternative, Modification of Opinion* (September 22, 1993) (uppercasing and underlining omitted). Interestingly, the UNITED STATES ATTORNEY'S MANUAL reminds prosecutors that: "In dealing with the grand jury, the prosecutor must always conduct himself or herself as an officer of the court whose function is to ensure that justice is done and that guilt shall not escape nor innocence suffer."[26] Prosecutors have no less a responsibility to the courts in which they appear as representatives of the United States.

One need not be a "prosecutor," of course, to know that *all* lawyers have an ethical obligation to our system of justice that requires that they be scrupulously honest in their representations to judicial tribunals. Thus Rule 3.3 of the Model Rules of Professional Conduct reiterates the requirement that has regulated our profession since its inception:

> "RULE 3.3 CANDOR TOWARD THE TRIBUNAL
>
> "(a) A lawyer shall not knowingly:
>
> "(1) make a false statement of material fact or law to a tribunal;"

The official Comments explain:

> "[A]n assertion purporting to be on the lawyer's own knowledge, as in an affidavit by the lawyer or in a statement in open court, may properly be made only when the lawyer knows the assertion is true or believes it to be true on the

---

[26] U.S. ATTYS. MAN. 9-11.010. The line is cribbed from *Berger v. United States*, 295 U.S. 78, 88 (1935) ("The United States Attorney is the representative not of an ordinary party to a controversy, but of a sovereignty whose obligation to govern impartially is as compelling as its obligation to govern at all; and whose interest, therefore, in a criminal prosecution is not that it shall win a case, but that justice shall be done. As such, he is in a peculiar and very definite sense the servant of the law, the twofold aim of which is that guilt shall not escape nor innocence suffer.").

> basis of a reasonably diligent inquiry. There are circumstances where failure to make a disclosure is the equivalent of an affirmative misrepresentation."

Rule 3.3 Comment [2].

Lawyers skate on thin ice when they try to mislead—even slightly—or when their briefs give the appearance of being misleading. They not only violate their ethical obligations, but they also hurt their client's cause; a lawyer known for sharp practices is not an effective advocate. One way to let the court know that you are being scrupulously accurate is to quote from the record—using quotes to *validate* your paraphrase of the testimony or other evidence. This not only puts the judges at ease—you show contemporaneously that your paraphrase is not taking liberties with the record—but it also allows you to *repeat the good stuff*. Just as repetition is the parent of learning, it is also the parent of persuasion. Thus, the lesson:

- **Quote or Reproduce Crucial Portions of the Record—Do Not Merely Paraphrase, But Paraphrase *and* Quote.**

Strategy:

☞ The quotes (or reproductions) *corroborate* your paraphrasing—this enhances your personal credibility and personal advocacy.

☞ Paraphrase first, and then quote. This permits you to repeat the good points for greater impact.

☞ Actual reproduction of exhibits in the record is better than quoting from them.

<u>*Example*</u>:

An excerpt from Mary Smith's appellate brief in our hypothetical automobile-accident case:

> "Mary Smith testified that as she drove north on West 35th Street and was going the speed limit, a red pickup truck passed and then swerved in front of her car:

'Q How fast were you going just before the accident?

'A About thirty-five.

'Q What's the speed limit on that street?

'A Thirty-five.

'Q So you were going the speed limit?

'A Yes.

'Q Were vehicles passing you?

'A Yes, some.

'Q Did a pickup truck pass you?

'A Yes.

'Q And what color was the pickup truck?

'A Red.

'Q Did it pass you fast or slowly?

'A Fast. It swerved right into me.

'Q Were you expecting the pickup truck to swerve into you?

'A No. I had to steer to the right to avoid a collision.'

[R:20:13-14 (Transcript of Jones's testimony)] Samantha Wayland, an accident reconstruction engineer [R17:2-3 (Transcript of Wayland's Testimony)], testified that Jones's car was going no more than thirty miles an hour when it hit Mr. Smith's van. [R17:21]"

- **The *Statement of Facts* prepared by the respondent (appellee) should *not* follow the order of the Appellant. Rather, the respondent should set the order of his or her *Statement of Facts* to be its most persuasive.**

All too often, the respondent or appellee gives away his or her chance to influence the reader with the justness of the client's cause by not taking the time to craft a persuasive statement of facts. You should *never* adopt your opponent's statement of facts.

Strategy:

☞ If your opponent's statement of facts says something that is helpful to you, quote it (with the appropriate citation to the opposing brief) in addition to your paraphrase:

> No one disputes that the contract between the plaintiff, Rogers Manufacturing Company, and the defendant, Line-Lite, Inc., required that Line-Lite do a weekly analysis of internet traffic on Rogers's server. [R 5:3–4 (contract); 7:16; and 7:49 (testimony of James DeBella, Rogers's President & CEO)]. Indeed, the Line-Lite in its brief before this court concedes this: 'Line-Lite undertook to survey the internet usage of Rogers's customers.' [Line-Lite's brief, p. 7.]

This permits you to get double-duty from a fact that is helpful to you—you get to say it twice.

☞ If you are appealing from a trial court's adverse judgment entered after a bench trial, be alert that it is almost impossible to overturn a trial court's findings of fact—they must be "clearly erroneous," that is, an appellate court will overturn a trial court's findings of fact only if there is *no* evidence, when looked at in light most favorable to the winning side, that either directly or inferentially supports that finding. Under this rigorous, almost-impossible-to-meet standard of review, you will rarely get an appellate court to reverse a trial court's bench-trial judgment unless you can show that the trial court erred on some legal issue. Thus, if you are arguing that the trial court *did* err on a legal issue, it is good strategy to *adopt* the trial court's findings of fact *verbatim*—so the appellate court understands that you are not basing your appeal on any quarrel with the trial court's findings. Suggestion:

> "After a three-day bench trial, the trial court issued its findings of fact and conclusions of law. We do not dispute any of the trial court's findings of fact; indeed, we adopt them *in toto* as our own on this appeal. Accordingly, we set out below, as our Statement of Facts, those facts found by the trial court in its written decision of September 14, 1999."

If there are facts in the record that will help you persuade the appellate court that right and justice is on your side, but the trial court did not incorporate them into its formal findings, you can preface your adoption of the trial court's findings with those facts. The key, however, is to alert the appellate court that you are not asking them to overturn the trial court's findings of fact. Suggestion:

> "The Rogers Manufacturing Company was founded in 1888 by Samuel Rogers, then a recent immigrant from England. [Record Reference] Over the years, the company grew from its early beginnings as a maker of hoes and scythes, into this area's largest farm-implement manufacturer. [Record Reference] Before the problem with Line-Lite, it employed more than three-thousand workers—in this community and in three other cities in this state. [Record Reference] Then, as the trial court found, Line-Lite's failure to monitor Rogers's internet server, caused catastrophic mixups with not only Rogers's huge customer base, but also with their internal operations. [Trial Court's Findings, ¶¶ 17, 19] There is no dispute about this, and we expressly adopt the trial court's findings of fact as our own on this appeal.
>
> "The only dispute on this appeal is whether the trial court's limiting Rogers's to its contractual remedies against Line-Lite, and its rejection of Rogers's tort claim against Line-Line, which effectively will put Rogers out of business, was an erroneous application of established legal principles. For the reasons set forth in the *Argument* section of this brief, we believe that the trial court misapplied the law. We have no quarrel, however, with any of the trial court's findings of fact, and set them out in toto here as our own:"

G. *Statutes Involved.*

Whether this is required by your jurisdiction or not, *your* brief should reprint the pertinent statutes in their entirety. Briefs submitted by the respondent (appellee) should reprint the statutes even though the appellant has already done so. The statutes should be set out in full in the *Statutes Involved* part of your brief and, also, every place where the statute is discussed. You want to make things as easy as possible for the tribunal that will decide whether you win or lose.

Strategy:

☞ It is not enough to have the relevant statutes in a separate part of the brief or in the appendix. Quote the pertinent part of the statute on the page or pages where you discuss it; don't make the judges flip pages to find it.

☞ Contemporaneously corroborate your spin on the statute with supporting case law (or other authority—such as a respected treatise).

To show how this works, I give you several hypothetical examples from an *Argument* part of a brief. In each example, I show the usual, but wrong, way, and a right way.

WRONG:

The only document submitted to the trial court in opposition to our motion for summary judgment was a conclusory affidavit signed, "on information and belief," by Line-Lite's in-house lawyer. This is not competent to raise a genuine issue of material fact that would preclude the granting of a motion for summary judgment. *See* F.R.C.P. 56(e); ***Automatic Radio Mfg. Co., Inc. v. Hazeltine Research, Inc.***, 339 U.S. 827, 831 (1950).

RIGHT:

The only document submitted to the trial court in opposition to our motion for summary judgment was a conclusory affidavit signed, "on information and belief," by Line-Lite's in-house lawyer. By law, this cannot raise a genuine issue of material fact to prevent the granting of a motion for summary judgment. Specifically, Rule 56(e) of the

> Federal Rules of Civil Procedure requires that: "Supporting and opposing affidavits shall be made on personal knowledge, shall set forth such facts as would be admissible in evidence, and shall show affirmatively that the affiant is competent to testify to the matters stated therein." This has long been the law. ***Automatic Radio Mfg. Co., Inc. v. Hazeltine Research, Inc.***, 339 U.S. 827, 831 (1950) (That part of an affidavit "made upon information and belief ... does not comply with Rule 56(e) of the Federal Rules of Civil Procedure."). Simply put, as in ***Automatic Radio***, the lawyer's affidavit here does not comply with Rule 56(e).

Note several things about the right way to do it:

First, I have not abbreviated "Federal Rules of Civil Procedure." You should rarely, if ever, abbreviate. Yes, I know many of you who love acronyms will say that federal judges, who will be reading the brief, know what "F.R.C.P." means. Sure. But it is *easier* to read the words than the letters: we can scan the words "Federal Rules of Civil Procedure" without forcing the mind to translate "F.R.C.P."—even when the abbreviation is fairly routine. But what about, for example, the following: "EMTALA" versus "Emergency Medical Treatment and Active Labor Act." It is easier to read "the Act" (or, if several statutes are involved, "the Medical Treatment Act") than "EMTALA" any day. Perhaps "IRS" can stand alone. But "ADA" when you mean "Anti-Discrimination Act" cannot stand alone—many judges, especially older judges appointed by democrats, will also see "ADA" as "Americans for Democratic Action." And does "IRA" stand for "Individual Retirement Act" or the "Irish Republican Army"? How about "CIA": "Central Intelligence Agency" or "Culinary Institute of America"? I guess it depends on your penchant—spies or food. It is no answer to say "you can tell from the context." Sure, but for an instant, the judge's mind is distracted—something that you do not want.

Second, I coupled with the statute a supporting case. This puts the judge's mind at ease that your spin on the statute is not from left field. In the Rule 56(e) example, the case is probably not needed—I present it as a template. But in the following example, a case is needed. And notice that I quote from the case, rather than requiring the reader to take my paraphrased word for it. Most of the time, the quotes can be in parentheticals, as in the Rule 56(e)/***Automatic Radio*** example. Other times, you will want to break it out, as in the following example, which shows a right and wrong way to handle a more complicated statute. First, the way most lawyers do it:

WRONG:

> Although EMTALA requires hospitals to give patients coming to their emergency departments an "appropriate medical screening examination," it does not create a cause of action for medical malpractice. *See* 42 U.S.C. § 1395dd(a); ***Marshall v. East Carroll Parish Hospital Service District***, 134 F.3d 319, 322 (5th Cir. 1998).

This was fairly straightforward. It is clear and accurate. Yet, what's wrong? What's wrong is that supporting citations do not *contemporaneously* corroborate the argument. Briefs written this way force the reader to go to the material cited. Compare the above with:

RIGHT:

> The Emergency Medical Treatment and Active Labor Act requires hospitals to give patients coming to their emergency departments an "appropriate medical screening examination." The statute provides:
>
>> "In the case of a hospital that has a hospital emergency department, if any individual ... comes to the emergency department and a request is made on the individual's behalf for examination or treatment for a medical condition, the hospital must provide for an *appropriate medical screening examination* within the capability of the hospital's emergency department, including ancillary services routinely available to the emergency department, to determine whether or not an emergency medical condition ... exists."
>
> 42 U.S.C. § 1395dd(a) (emphasis added). This clause is designed to prevent hospitals from turning away patients who need emergency medical treatment; it does not set a standard of care, and does not create a cause of action for medical malpractice. Thus, as the United States Court of Appeals for the Fifth Circuit recently recognized:
>
>> "We agree with the other courts which have interpreted EMTALA [The Emergency Medical Treatment and Active Labor Act] that the statute was not intended to be used as a federal malpractice statute, but instead was enacted to prevent 'patient

> dumping,' which is the practice of refusing to treat patients who are unable to pay."

Marshall v. East Carroll Parish Hospital Service District, 134 F.3d 319, 322 (5th Cir. 1998). Thus, an "'appropriate medical screening examination' is not judged by its proficiency in accurately diagnosing the patient's illness, but rather by whether it was performed equitably in comparison to other patients with similar symptoms." ***Ibid.***

In this example, the argument is supported by authority presented so the reader does not have to lift his or her eyes from the page (or reach for a book, or log on to a computer, or walk down the hall) to see that the argument accurately reflects the authority. Doing it this way makes it easy for the reader to see that you are being honest and forthright.

Note also the following:

1) That when the court uses the acronym, I put the full name in brackets—again, this makes it easier for the reader.

2) "***Ibid.***" is OK when the reference is within the same paragraph—the reader will not have to search for the citation. If, however, the last citation to ***Marshall*** was further back, I would have cited the second cite not as "***Ibid.***" (or ***Id.***, as some lawyers and courts are using even when the citation is on the same page as before), but as: ***Marshall***, 134 F.3d at 322. This gives to the reader the pin citation and doesn't force the reader to flip back, perhaps through several pages, looking for the volume (as would "***Id.***, at 322").

3) When you are quoting a statute to give the context of a phrase that you have pulled from the statute, italicize the phrase as it sits in the statute so the reader's eye will be drawn to it immediately; this avoids forcing the reader to scan the statute, which might be quite long, in an attempt to find the particular phrase you are discussing. Again, all of this is designed to make it easy for the judges, law clerks and staff attorneys who will be deciding, or influencing the decision in, your appeal.

H. *Argument.*

This is the place to give the appellate judges and their staff the tools to find in your favor. If you've done your job up to this point, the court is eager to discover a way for you to win. As Judge Wald has said, the essence of the argument section of the brief is to show the appellate court that "the law *allows*" the result you want.[27] As we have already mentioned, almost by definition, any civil case that is appealed can go either way—it simply does not pay to appeal a case that is a clear win for the other side.

Although, as Judge Posner tells us, it may be "common" for appellate judges to slant the facts in favor of a desired outcome, appellate judges rarely have to slant the *law* to do what they think is right. There are so many cases out there that there at least one to support almost any proposition—just as there are legal maxims to support almost any point:

- Statutes in derogation of the common law will be strictly construed.
- Statutes in derogation of the common law that are remedial in nature will be liberally construed. (*Every* statute that changes a common-law rule is "remedial"!)[28].

Thus, you know that the Pennsylvania Supreme is reaching when it cites and relies on a 1964 opinion by the Supreme Court of South Dakota, and *vice versa.*

The key to effective appellate advocacy is to marshall your forces in their most persuasive formations. Although you *must* cite legal authority for your propositions, your arguments will not be effective unless they are also *founded on reason and common sense*. Judges understand that any moderately intelligent lawyer can find cases to support an argument, and they all have young, bright, energetic law clerks who can do the same for them. The smart, successful advocate goes *beyond* rote citation, and, indeed, this is precisely

---

[27] PATRICIA M. WALD, 19 TIPS FROM 19 YEARS ON THE APPELLATE BENCH, 1 *The Journal of Appellate Practice and Process* 12 (1999) (emphasis by Judge Wald).

[28] Karl N. Llewellyn collected these dueling maxims in his famous *Remarks on the Theory of Appellate Decision and the Rules of Canons About How Statutes Are to Be Construed*, 3 VAND. L. REV. 395, 401–406 (1950). *See also* Llewellyn, *The Common Law Tradition* 521–535 (1960).

what the Seventh Circuit recommends. In fact, this is such good advice, that I am going to reprint it in large, bold type:

> **"Where possible, the emphasis should be on reason, not merely on precedent, unless a particular decision is controlling. A few good cases on point, with a sufficient discussion of their facts to show how they are relevant, are preferred over a profusion of citations."**[29]

Now, let's look at some of the mechanics, with an eye to making it easy for the appellate judge to go your way:

- The Headings in Each Subsection of Your Argument Should Track Your *Questions Presented*.

<u>*Example*</u>:

If your *Question Presented* is

> "Mary Jones testified that she was driving slower than the speed limit when a pick-up truck suddenly swerved in front of her, forcing her to steer to the right to avoid colliding with the truck. Should the trial court have instructed the jury about Mary Jones's duty of care when faced with an emergency?"

You might phrase your subsection heading this way:

> "The trial court should have instructed the jury on a driver's duty of care when faced with an emergency, in light of Mary Jones's uncontradicted testimony that she was driving slower than the speed limit when, all of a sudden, a pickup truck swerved in front of her car and forced her veer to the right in order to not hit that truck."

- **You must cite legal authority. Arguments that are made without the citation of supporting legal authority will generally be disregarded.**

---

29 PRACTITIONER'S HANDBOOK FOR APPEALS 85

- Marshall the legal authority in your favor.
- Acknowledge, but distinguish, legal authority that does not support your position.
- Quote the actual language from the opinions you cite.

Example: Let's look at several hypothetical paragraphs from our emergency-instruction appeal:

When someone faces an emergency that he or she did not create, that person is not negligent if he or she does things the way a normally prudent person would do them—even if in hindsight it seems that he or she has not made the "wisest choice" of possible alternatives. ***Lane v. Brown***, 328 Or. 42, 46–47, 970 P.2d 206, 208 (1998) (quoting Uniform Civil Jury Instruction No. 20.08). Thus, Uniform Civil Jury Instruction No. 20.08 provides:

> "People who are suddenly placed in a position of peril through no negligence of their own, and who are compelled to act without opportunity for reflection, *are not negligent if they make such a choice as a reasonably careful person placed in such a position might make, even though they do not make the wisest choice*."

Ibid. (emphasis added). This is the law, and juries should be so told—otherwise they might use hindsight to hold someone forced to react to an emergency to the higher standard of care that applies in non-emergency situations. *See* ***Wiles v. Webb***, 329 Ark. 108, 115, 946 S.W.2d 685, 689 (1997) (In giving the emergency instruction, "the trial court informs the jury that due to an emergent circumstance, the defendant is not as responsible for what occurred as he might otherwise have been.")

Here, Mary Jones testified that she was driving slower than the speed limit of thirty-five miles per hour when a pickup truck suddenly swerved in front of her, forcing her to veer to the right avoid the truck. [R 17:21 (Transcript of Jones's testimony)] As a result, she hit the plaintiff's van, which was parked on the street. [R 17:24] This testimony was neither refuted nor rebutted.

Although he was not there, and produced no witnesses at the trial to so testify, the plaintiff claims that there was no truck and that Mary Jones hit his van because she lost control of her car. [R 16: 45–47 (Transcript of Smith's testimony)] As we have seen, the jury found that Mary Jones was negligent. [R 8 (Verdict)] Admittedly, even though Mary Jones testified without contradiction by anyone that she was cut off by the pickup truck, and had to react quickly to that emergency in order avoid what could have been a very serious collision with the pickup truck, the jury could have disregarded her testimony. *See* ***State ex rel. Reynolds v. Aldridge***, 107 Ill.App.3d 679, 681, 437 N.E.2d 1268, 1270, 63 Ill.Dec. 346, 348 (1982) ("jury is not required to believe a witness' statement merely because it is unrebutted"). But, of course, the converse is also true: the jury could have—and most likely did, given the fact that her testimony was not disputed by any witness or evidence—believed her. There was thus strong evidence before the jury: 1) that Mary Jones faced an emergency not of her doing; and 2) that she had to react suddenly to avoid the danger created by that emergency. Nevertheless, the trial court refused to instruct the jury—in the words of ***Wiles*** quoted earlier—that Mary Jones was not as "as responsible for [the accident] as [s]he might otherwise have been," because of that emergency. This was an error of law because it permitted the jury to — wrongly — hold Mary Jones to a higher standard of care than the law permits, even if they believed her unrefuted testimony. *See* ***Wiles***, 329 Ark. at 115, 946 S.W.2d at 689 (emergency instruction "informs the jury that due to an emergent circumstance, the defendant is not as responsible for what occurred as he might otherwise have been").

Let's analyze this example.

1) All the cases cited have quotes relevant to the argument—either stand-alone quotes or within parentethicals. This assures the reader that you are being forthright in your citation of authority. Do this routinely—even for non-controversial legal points (as with the point that juries are not bound by even uncontradicted testimony); it helps to build a bond of trust between you and the judges who are reading your brief.

2) We acknowledge that even though Mary Jones's testimony was not disputed, the jury could have disregarded her testimony. Often, lawyers make the mistake of not acknowledging, or glossing over, matters that are inconvenient or harmful to their position. Don't let your opponent make that point for you, putting his or her spin on it. For example, if Mary Jones's lawyer had written:

> Although he was not there, and produced no witnesses at the trial to so testify, the plaintiff claims that Mary Jones sideswiped his parked van because she lost control of her car. [R 16: 45–47] As we have seen, the jury found that Mary Jones was negligent, even though her testimony that she faced a sudden emergency was not controverted. [R 8] The trial court's refusal to instruct the jury—in the words of ***Wiles*** quoted earlier—that Mary Jones was not as "as responsible for [the accident] as [s]he might otherwise have been," because of that emergency. This was an error of law because it permitted the jury to — wrongly — hold Mary Jones to a higher standard of care than the law permits. *See* ***Wiles***, 329 Ark. at 115, 946 S.W.2d at 689 (emergency instruction "informs the jury that due to an emergent circumstance, the defendant is not as responsible for what occurred as he might otherwise have been").

The defendant's lawyer could have argued in the reply brief:

> The fatal flaw in the plaintiff's argument is that her testimony was not disputed by any other witness. Thus, she seems to argue that the jury had to accept her testimony without analysis or suspicion. Well, how could her testimony have been disputed by anyone? She was the only person there at the time—except for the alleged "driver" of this phantom truck that she claims cut her off. She never produced this

"driver." The jury understood that she was free to say anything she wanted about why she sideswiped Mr. Smith's parked van. Simply put, the jury did not have to believe her story about the phantom truck. *See* ***State ex rel. Reynolds v. Aldridge***, 107 Ill.App.3d 679, 681, 437 N.E.2d 1268, 1270, 63 Ill.Dec. 346, 348 (1982) ("jury is not required to believe a witness' statement merely because it is unrebutted"). The jury obviously did not believe her.

3) I give pin cites to all the reporters in which the cases appear. Some judges might have one reporter and not another.[30] Again, you want things to be easy for the persons who will decide whether you win or lose. Don't make it difficult for the judge to find the specific the authority you cite.

- Your legal argument must be internally consistent and consistent with the facts proven by the record.
  - Inconsistent arguments weaken your personal credibility with the court.
  - Avoid making arguments *seem* inconsistent, even though they are not.

Strategy:

☞ Craft your brief so the arguments appear to be wholly consistent with one another. Contrast the following two versions:

WRONG: "There was no consideration and, therefore, no contract. But, even if there was a valid contract, the plaintiff breached it."

RIGHT: "There was no consideration, and, moreover, the plaintiff did not even do what he says the contract obligated him to do."

---

[30] Thus, in my court, the Wisconsin Court of Appeals, some of the judges use the official Wisconsin Reports (cited as Wis.2d) while other judges use West's Northwest Reports (cited as N.W.2d). Starting with cases decided in January of 2000, lawyers appearing before the Wisconsin courts will have to not only cite to the two reporters, but also to a vendor-neutral citation that is slowly spreading across the country: referencing the case by the year and its sequential number; any pin cites will be the decision's numbered paragraphs.

- Weave together the facts, properly proven by the record, and the law.

    - As with the *Statement of Facts*, you must give record references for *every* statement of fact, *every time*—even if you have already done so.

      – Again, make it easy for the court. Don't force the judges to search through your statement of the facts to find that record reference.

    - As with the *Statement of Facts*, you should quote from the record, rather than merely paraphrase.

- *Unlike* the *Statement of Facts*, the respondent (appellee) *should* follow the appellant's order of argument. Thus, if the appellant argues "consideration" in Part I of the *Argument* portion of her brief, so should the respondent. Many appellate judges will read each side's *Argument* sections in tandem—make it easy to do, and don't hide your response in a place where it will be difficult to find. Certainly don't hide it in a footnote. *See* ***United States v. Restrepo***, 986 F.2d 1462, 1463 (2d Cir.1993) ("We do not consider an argument mentioned only in a footnote to be adequately raised or preserved for appellate review.")

  If you are the appellee and you disagree with the way the appellant has phrased the issue in its heading, you must still follow the appellant's order, but indicate why you believe the issue has not been stated fairly. The following is an example:

  Assume that the appellant has framed the subsection heading as we have earlier:

  > "The trial court should have instructed the jury on a driver's duty of care when faced with an emergency, in light of Mary Jones's uncontradicted testimony that she was driving slower than the speed limit when, all of a sudden, a pickup truck swerved in front of her car and forced her veer to the right in order to not hit that truck."

You might want to phrase your subsection heading this way:

> "The trial court did not abuse its discretion in not using the word 'emergency' in instructing the jury that it should not find Mary Jones negligent if she, in the trial court's words, "exercised the same degree of care and caution as would a reasonable driver under the same or similar circumstances," and, additionally, that it should consider "all of the facts" they found to be "properly proven by the evidence."

Note: The "issue" is the same, although the phrasing is different. You can then point put that the jury was thus free to consider, if it believed her testimony, Mary Jones's version of the collision.

- **Do Not Use Uppercase Words In Any Heading—Whether a "statement of facts" or an "argument."**

As we will see when we look at the briefs in the appeals that we analyze in the next part of this book, anything written in uppercase—all capitals—words is very hard to read. Don't do it.

- **Nonpublished Decisions**

We've seen how the appellate courts throughout the country are swamped with cases. One of the results is the nonpublished decision. With few exceptions (such as where the nonpublished decision is cited as the "law of the case" or for *res-judicata* or collateral-estoppel purposes), nonpublished decisions generally may not be cited within their jurisdictions.[31] Sometimes this rule leads to anomalous results. Thus, in Wisconsin, decisions by the state trial courts are rarely published by the commercial reporters (Commerce Clearing House will, for example, occasionally, publish specialized decisions (anti-trust, tax, etc.) of the Wisconsin state trial courts in one of their focused

---

[31] Check your appellate court's local rules. For example, nonpublished decisions of the United States Court of Appeals for the Fifth Circuit Court that were released before January 1, 1996, "are precedent." Fifth Circuit Rule 47.5.3. Nonpublished decisions in the Fifth Circuit released after January 1, 1996, although not precedent, "may, however, be persuasive" and may, accordingly, be cited. Fifth Circuit Rule 47.5.4.

looseleaf volumes). Nevertheless, those decisions may be presented to the Wisconsin state appellate courts as persuasive authority, but nonpublished decisions of the Wisconsin Court of Appeals may not be. But this does not mean that nonpublished decisions cannot help you.

Nonpublished decisions, which are generally available on either WestLaw or Lexis, are helpful in two ways. First, a nonpublished decision from a court outside of your jurisdiction may, depending upon the wording of your jurisdiction's appellate-court rules, be cited to your appellate courts. Second, the nonpublished decisions in your jurisdiction can be valuable research sources, and perhaps give an inkling of the views of either a particular court or a panel of that court.

Strategy:

☞ Do not shun nonpublished decisions from other jurisdictions. Depending on rules of the appellate courts in your jurisdiction, you may be able to cite those decisions to your courts.

☞ Do not shun nonpublished decisions from your own jurisdiction. You can get two things from them:

1) Research help

2) Perhaps a mirror that reflects the views of your court or a panel of that court. *Caveat:* Occasionally, nonpublished decisions will conflict with each other, even if those decisions come from the same court. This may be an example of changed direction or even a situation where the proverbial left hand does not know what the right hand is doing.

I. *Procedural History*.

This section of the brief is designed to succinctly tell the appellate court about the case's history: when it was commenced, when the answer was filed, when the motions that are of dispute on appeal were decided, etc. It is often, however, a largely incomprehensible jumble of dates and technical terms. Effective appellate lawyers use typography to make this easier reading.

Example:

An excerpt from the brief in our hypothetical automobile-accident case:

January 9, 1990 . . . . Roger Smith filed summons and complaint.

January 27, 1990 . . Summons and complaint served on the defendants.

February 14, 1990 . . . . Mary Jones filed answer.

May 14, 1992 . . . . Jury trial began.

May 19, 1992 . . . . Jury trial ended.

July 7, 1992 . . . . Trial court entered judgment on the verdict.

August 17, 1992 . . . . Notice of Appeal timely filed.

Arranging the procedural history this way, rather than as a confusing narrative, permits the judges and staff reading your brief to see at a glance the specific aspect of that history that may be of interest. Again, and I know this has become a refrain by now, *make it easy!*

J. *Conclusion.*

The *Conclusion* part of the appellate brief should be a short, plain statement of relief requested. In our hypothetical ***Smith v. Jones*** automobile-accident case, Mary Jones would ask that the judgment be reversed and the matter remanded for a new trial. Roger Smith, on the other hand, would ask that the judgment be affirmed. Avoid the temptation to re-argue your case. The "Conclusion" section of the brief is to let the judges know precisely what type of relief you are seeking: new trial, new trial on liability only, new trial on damages only, remand for an evidentiary hearing, affirmance, etc. You would be surprised how many lawyers do not spell out clearly the relief they are seeking. Don't join them! Again, make it easy! Make it clear!

K. *The Appendix.*

The appendix is a very important part of the parties' submission. Every jurisdiction has differing requirements as to what the appendix must have. Remember, however, that many appellate judges read briefs while they are at home or are otherwise away from chambers. Thus, often briefs will be read, and tentative conclusions reached, when the judge does not have access to either the record, the case reports, or even his or her law clerk. Remember, making life easy for the tribunal that decides your case (be it a jury, judge, or an appellate court), is the hallmark of effective advocacy. Thus, every appendix should have, in addition to the materials required by the rules, the following:

- The trial court's decision, whether oral or written.

Often, the first thing we will look at is the trial judge's opinion; after all, it gives his or her reasons. Moreover, the trial judge's opinion, whether oral or written, will often give a fairly neutral and quick summary of the case, the parties, what is in dispute, as well as his or her reasons for the decision. Additionally, appellate judges are ever alert to the standards of review that control what we can or cannot do. As we will see in greater detail in the section of this book headed "Standards of Review—Gold Mines and Mine Fields," factual findings by either a judge or a jury are almost invulnerable to attack on appeal. On the other hand, a trial judge's legal conclusions are, essentially, subject to *de novo* review. Reading the trial judge's opinion helps us put the various aspects of the decision into the appropriate compartments:

- findings of fact

A trial court's findings of fact will not be disturbed on appeal unless they are "clearly erroneous"—the trial court is in a much better position to evaluate the witnesses and their testimony.

- conclusions of law

An appellate court will analyze *de novo* legal issues without giving the trial court deference.

- intertwined questions of law and fact

The more a trial court's analysis of the legal issue depends on its evaluation of those things that are best observed by the trial judge (the demeanor of witnesses, for example), the greater deference to that analysis the appellate court will give.

We read the briefs against this mosaic.

- The entries from the docket or judgment roll.

This gives us the complete time line of the case. It differs from the procedural aspects of the case set out in the *Procedural History* because it is complete; the *Procedural History* part of your brief only has those things that are relevant to the appeal. Occasionally, however, the judges or law clerks will want to see a bird's-eye view of the entire case.

- The order or judgment from which the appeal is taken, and the notice of appeal.

These are the specific documents that give the appellate court jurisdiction over your appeal. Make it easy for the appellate judge or appeals-court staff to find.

- Extensive passages from the trial testimony or trial exhibits so the excerpts reprinted in the main portion of the brief can be examined in their context.

Including these passages in your appendix is very important. Make certain that the *entire* context is given. Don't make the mistake of one lawyer who filed an appendix in a case on whose appellate panel I sat where the appendix was a jumble of pages from the trial transcript, which, although numbered sequentially in the appendix, omitted the transcript page numbers. For some reason the lawyer thought that it was OK to just give disjointed parts of testimony that were cut off, often in mid-sentence, when the very next page in the appendix dropped the reader into the middle of some other witness's testimony! It was awful! Don't make the same mistake.

- Photocopies of critical case law.

Yes, we have law books. Yes, most of us have access to WestLaw or Lexis, or both. But, as I mentioned before, many of us read briefs away from chambers. If there is a case or two upon which you believe your appeal rests, put it in the appendix! Use the technology we have to help you win your appeal; to help your clients get the justice to which they and you believe they are entitled.

- Photocopies of the complete text of the statutes involved.

Here again, as with the critical case law, if the appeal involves the application of statutes, ordinances, or rules, reprint those statutes, ordinances, or rules in their entirety. Judges like to see context. If you omit the context the judge may believe that you are hiding something.

Strategy:

> ☞ Unless prohibited by court rule, highlight, preferably with a yellow highlighter, those portions of lengthy documents (testimony, exhibits, statutes, or cases) that you want the court to read. Yes, this *will* take the time of a secretary, paralegal, or, perhaps, even one of your children; it can, however, be very effective in directing the busy appellate judge to the critical points. You highlighted cases in law school because it helped you to go right to the point in which you were interested; give the same help to the judges who will decide your appeal.

L. *The Reply Brief.*

In about thirty-percent of the appeals that are assigned to me the appellant does not file a reply brief. For the life of me, I do not know why. Perhaps along the way the lawyer heard advice similar to that given by an acquaintance of mine, Mike Fontham, a lawyer with a sterling reputation and, I assume, ability, who is a partner in a major law firm in New Orleans. In his 1985 book on appellate practice, *Written and Oral Advocacy*, Mike gives this advice:

> "The appellee always has the chance to make a direct response to the opposition's contentions in the appellee's brief. The appellant, on the other hand, has a choice of whether to file a reply brief. The decision involves a weighing of the need to reply to points not covered in the initial brief versus the desire to avoid repetition and added cost. Generally, if the appellee raises no points that are not covered, and therefore blunted, in the initial brief, a reply is unnecessary. A reply should not be made solely to rehash arguments. However, if new points are raised, new authorities cited, or erroneous factual claims made, a reply is usually essential. The attorney should not leave it to the judges to think of answers to opposition contentions."[32]

---

[32] MICHAEL R. FONTHAM, WRITTEN AND ORAL ADVOCACY 45 (1985).

As I write this, I've been an appellate judge for twelve years, and was a trial judge for nine years before that. With all due respect to Mike Fontham, his advice to "generally" not submit a reply brief is suicidal.

First, how likely is it that *every* argument that you make in your appellant's brief-in-chief will anticipate every counter-argument and all their nuances? Perhaps if you or your client is a mystical seer—like Kreskin the mind-reader who dominated the early days of television variety shows—your appellate brief-in-chief will anticipate and persuasively dispose of all the arguments that your opponent will raise in his or her brief. Even then, however, it is golden to have *the last word*. I am not advocating mindless repetition—I *am* advocating that you take the arguments your opponent makes in the appellee's (respondent's) brief and turn them to your advantage by demonstrating that they have little or no support either in the appellate record or in the law. In every jurisdiction, failure to do so is taken as a concession. You *must* counter your opponent's spin, whether or not "new points are raised, new authorities cited, or erroneous factual claims made."

Second, the "cost" of filing a reply brief is *de minimis* compared to the money and time that you and your client have already spent. Fontham's concern about cost reminds me of some folks whom I know who went to Hawaii but refused to eat some of the delicious naturally ripened and fresh native fruits because they were a dollar or so more than those fruits cost in a Milwaukee supermarket! My advice to lawyers, as well as travellers: spend the dollar and enjoy the freshly picked pineapple. Do not fall into the trap of false economy characterized by the derisive: "Penny-wise and pound-foolish."

The only statement in Fontham's advice on whether to file a reply brief with which I agree is his last: "The attorney should not leave it to the judges to think of answers to opposition contentions." If you follow *that* advice, you will ignore his other advice and *always* file a reply brief.

Strategy:

☞ Use your reply brief to respond *specifically* to the arguments the appellee makes. First quote the part to which you are responding. Then point out the error. To separate the quoted portion from your response, use either a different font or size or both.

Example:

> On page 17 of Roger Smith's brief, he says:
>
> > "There was no need for the trial judge to give the 'emergency instruction' because the instructions that the judge did give told the jury that they were to consider 'all of the facts and circumstances in the case' in reaching their verdict. Thus, the jury was fully apprised that they could consider Ms. Jones's testimony, if they believed her, that she was cut off by a pickup truck."
>
> We disagree. By not telling the jury how the law defines an "emergency," each of the jurors was free to apply his or her own layperson's view. Thus, some jurors might have imposed a higher threshold of suddenness and danger than the law requires, and may have assumed that one vehicle cutting off another on the road was just one of the normal hazards of driving. Those jurors that applied this higher standard could have found Ms. Jones negligent even though if they had been properly instructed they would have found her free from negligence. Thus, contrary to Mr. Smith's assertion, which we have quoted above, an instruction telling the jurors to consider all the facts and circumstances of the case is *not* sufficient without *also* telling them how to properly evaluate those facts and circumstances. Stated another way, the jurors could have believed Ms. Jones's testimony that she was driving under the speed limit and was cut off by the truck, and still have found her to be negligent because they applied a higher threshold as to what constitutes an emergency than the law allows. Accordingly, the trial court's refusal to give the "emergency instruction" was prejudicial error.

One final, but extremely important, thought on the reply brief. You must never, never, make an argument for the first time in your reply brief. That does not mean that you cannot add new authority to support arguments already made; but you may not raise a new issue in a reply brief. Courts everywhere will ignore it. So, what do you do if there is something critical to your case that, for some reason, you forgot or were unable to argue in your brief-in-chief (and, presumably, before the trial court—see Part VI. Preserves and Toast). You must, of course, do something. I suggest that you be frank with the court. If you have a reply brief that asserts the new matter send it with a motion or a letter (depending upon the rules and practice of your jurisdiction) that says essentially the following:

> We understand that a reply brief may not raise an issue or make an argument that was not raised or argued in the brief in chief. [citation] Since we filed our brief in chief, however, [set forth what has happened that leads you to want to make the new argument in your reply brief]. It is critical to the fair resolution of this appeal that the court consider all of the matters discussed in our reply brief—including the new matter. Accordingly, we respectfully move the court to accept and consider this reply brief in its entirety, and that the court also give [opposing party] any amount of time deemed appropriate to respond, and that with [opposing party]'s response the briefing be closed and that the court either schedule oral argument or take the case as submitted on the briefs.

If you do this or something similar, you will have accomplished three things:

1) The judges will recognize that *you* understand the rule about not putting new matter in a reply brief. This enhances your credibility with the court. I can tell you that a lawyer who puts new matter in a reply brief and does not acknowledge that he or she is doing something that should not be done, is eviscerating his or her persona as a knowledgeable, skillful lawyer. The syllogism that the judges will apply is: "If the lawyer doesn't know this simple and universal rule of appellate briefing, how can we trust that lawyer to accurately argue the law or the facts of record?"

2) You are alerting the judges that not only is your appeal important, but that the new matter that you want to bring to their attention is also important. By asking them to exercise their discretion in the interest of "fairness" you are tacitly asserting that "fairness" requires a decision favorable to your client.

3) By asking the court to give the other side an opportunity to respond, you assure the court that you are not attempting to sandbag your appointant, and that you are being fair.

The important thing to remember here, as with all of your advocacy: Be honest, sincere, direct, and forthright. You will attract more flies with the honey of honesty than you can with the vinegar of sharp practice.

IV.
ORAL ARGUMENT.

I believe that oral argument is generally essential to the appellate process. Nevertheless, more and more courts are dispensing with oral argument in many—or, for some courts, most—of their cases. Although some have suggested that a request for—or refusal to waive—oral argument is a sign of weakness, I disagree. Many a case has been won on oral argument—some that appeared on a first-reading of the briefs to be losers. Oral argument gives the advocate a chance to put out the small fires of doubt before they become raging infernos that consume his or her case in the judges' decision conference. They also give the appellate judge the invaluable opportunity to clarify a troubling matter that has chafed at his or her analysis like a pebble in the shoe.

As a preliminary matter, you should do three things:

1) Find out whether the appellate court is a "hot" bench; that is, whether the judges read the briefs before argument. Although a generation ago, many courts were "cold"—that is, the judges did not read the briefs before argument—most courts today are "hot." This means that they know your case, and will have questions. Don't assume that you are writing on a clean slate; you are not.

2) If possible, sit in on oral arguments before the panel that will hear your case. This will give you a feel for the judges and how they act at oral argument. Some judges like to toy with the lawyers, trying out all sorts of far-fetched hypotheticals to see how far the lawyer will push the logic upon which his or her appellate position rests. Other judges will not ask any questions; they will sit like inscrutable potentates—almost daring you to read their minds. Still other judges will use the lawyers as foils to argue a position to the other members of the panel. You will be better able to represent your client if you know who does what and for what reason. Additionally, you will lessen the chance of being taken by surprise *in front of your client* if faced with a particularly aggressive judge.

3) Most important, if oral argument is discretionary with your appellate court, try to reflect on why the court has asked for it. Does the case present an issue of first impression? Is there something in the briefs that may not be clear? Is there disagreement on the court or panel—that is, does setting the case for oral argument signal an ideological or other split for which you must be prepared?

A good appellate argument is a conversation, not an oration. As with effective trial advocacy, the "true art" of appellate advocacy is in keeping the art hidden. This is how Justice Felix Frankfurter described the oral-advocacy skills of a former law clerk—skills every appellate lawyer should try to emulate:

> "When he appeared at the lectern, erect and handsome, with an agreeable voice, serene rather than self-confident, tactful but firm, and always master of his case, the Court increasingly was assured of an argument that gave pleasure as well as enlightenment."[33]

An advocate such as Frankfurter described certainly increased the odds of victory for his clients. I offer the following additional tips:

- After the brief, obligatory introductory material, your first two or three sentences to an appellate panel should be as carefully thought-out as the first two or three sentences of your opening statement to the jury; these are critical moments of your advocacy.[34] Don't fall back on a dull, non-persuasive recitation of the procedural history or chronology. Get to the heart of the matter:

Example:

> May it please the court. My name is Carol Cantrell, and I represent Mary Jones. She was sued by Roger Smith,who sought to recover for damage to his van. The jury found Ms. Jones to be negligent. We're appealing from the judgment because the trial

---

[33] F. Frankfurter, *Of Law and Men*, 321 (1956).

[34] The Handbook published by the United States Court of Appeals for the Seventh Circuit, for example, provides:

> "Counsel should introduce themselves in their opening statements. Appellant's counsel should normally tell the court in the first few words how the case got to the court of appeals, the nature of the case, the issue, and the relief requested. A statement that counsel intends to save a portion of the allotted time for rebuttal is unnecessary and inappropriate. Whether time for rebuttal is saved depends entirely on how much time the opening consumes. It is counsel's own responsibility to watch the time."

PRACTITIONER'S HANDBOOK FOR APPEALS 105.

> court refused to instruct the jury on the standard of care under an emergency.
>
> At the trial, Mary Jones testified without contradiction that she was driving slower than the speed limit on a city street when all of a sudden a pickup truck from the left-hand lane suddenly swerved in front of her, forcing her to steer quickly to the right to avoid an accident. That's when she hit Mr. Smith's van. In anyone's parlance, she faced an emergency. Yet, the trial judge refused to tell the jury that a person when faced with an emergency that he or she did not create does not have to react to that emergency with perfection. As a result, the jury was allowed to hold her to the non-emergency standard of care and thus found that she was negligent in striking the plaintiff's parked van.

This is much better than the traditional:

> May it please the court. My name is Carol Cantrell, and I represent Mary Jones, the appellant. This case is here because on September 14, 1999, a jury found that my client was negligent in the operation of her vehicle. Etc. etc.

- Do *not* read your argument.

You want the judges to have faith in you and your cause. Truth-givers do not read; they don't have to read because the verity of what they say wells up within them. While an appellate panel will be more sophisticated than most jurors, and will not view you necessarily as a truth-giver *per se*, they *will* be moved by your perceived belief in the justness of your cause. After all, you are more familiar with the case than they are—or will ever be—even if you did not try it. They will be more likely to accept what you say if your argument rings with unalloyed sincerity. This is also the advice of the Seventh Circuit Handbook:

> "Never read your argument; points are more forcefully made by speech that has at least the appearance of spontaneity. When counsel reads an argument, a veil is created between the court and the advocate."[35]

---

35 PRACTITIONER'S HANDBOOK FOR APPEALS 107.

Politicians know that truth-givers do not read, which is why they all use teleprompters—to give everyone the impression that they are not reading—what the Seventh Circuit calls the "appearance of spontaneity."

Lawyers tell me that they read their oral arguments because they are afraid that they will forget important points if they do not read, and because they want to say everything just right. These are not reasons; they are excuses by lawyers who are either reluctant or afraid to make the effort to do their job properly. Moreover, in most appellate courts, the judges will ask questions right from the get-go; if you are reading from a prepared script you will be less able to respond properly to those questions.

The first excuse that lawyers use to justify reading their opening statements is that they are afraid that they will forget some of their points. This problem is solved—as it is when you are standing before a jury to give your opening statement or your closing argument—by having, either on the podium or on three-by-five index cards (which you can keep in one of those nifty leather pocket-sized holders), the points you wish to cover in tidy bulleted paragraphs, as in the following example.

- Faced emergency
    - truck swerved
    - avoid collision
    - avoid serious injury
    - testimony not disputed
- Emergency Instruction
    - purpose
    - what happens if not given
    - that's what jury did

Stand at the podium, look the judges in the eye, and tell them why you must prevail on the appeal. Do not be afraid to let the judges see you think. You are the truth-giver, not an actor either reading or remembering a prepared script. As I point out in *The "How-To-Win" Trial Manual* when discussing an opening statement before a jury, Mary Wisewell has noted: "There is no music in a rest, but there is music's making." For the lawyer in the courtroom, a pause is not only the prelude to meaning, it can be meaning in and of itself.

The second excuse lawyers use to justify reading their oral arguments is that, as with lawyers who read their opening statements or closing arguments to a jury, they want to use precisely the right words. Would these same lawyers read a prepared statement while they were having a critical discussion with a significant other, even though each word there *could* be crucial and a wrong word could destroy the relationship? Of course not. Reading an oral argument to an appellate panel affects the judges them in the same way as reading a prepared statement to a significant other affects that person—it casts doubt on your sincerity.

- Explain to the court why you *should* win:
  - The specific facts of your case;
  - The general welfare of society;
  - Controlling legal principles.
- Do not get entangled in a thicket of detail: cut to the heart of your case and why the court should either affirm or reverse.
  - Pare analysis of the facts of your case to its essential elements.
  - Do not get bogged-down in either extensive citations or the attempt to distinguish cases either from one another or from your case.
- If asked a question, answer it *immediately*; do not say: "I will get to that in a moment, Your Honor."
- Know your record cold. Be prepared to give record references in support of your statements.

- Know the facts of each and every case you cite and those cited by your adversary.

    - Be prepared for "hypotheticals" from the judges based on those facts.

    - Be prepared for the "outlandish" hypothetical, designed to test the outer limits of your argument.

    Have your lawyer friends "moot-court" you—pepper you with questions and challenge your arguments. Every good lawyer serious about his or her argument before an appellate court will do this.

- Do not rely on rhetoric.

    In one recent oral argument, a lawyer went on and on with flights of rhetorical fancy—even relying on the Declaration of Independence as a reason why an award of punitive damages to his client should be affirmed. When asked for a case citation that supported the underlying legal argument, the lawyer replied: "I'm a rhetoric man." He then pointed to his co-counsel, who shared the oral-argument presentation, saying: "He's the case man."

Although the lawyer's oration might have made good newspaper copy, it was wholly wasted on us. And it would be wasted on any court. Indeed, Karen Donovan, a reporter for *The National Law Journal*, made a similar observation about the September 21, 1999, closing arguments in the federal government's antitrust lawsuit against Microsoft, which although presented to a judge presiding over a bench trial, was the functional equivalent of oral argument before an appellate panel:

> "Both sides urged U.S. District Judge Thomas Penfield Jackson to focus on the 'real world' but then, as lawyers will do, ignored the other's strongest legal points and pieces of evidence . . .
>
> "The government's lead lawyer, David Boies, never confronted the trove of documents on America Online Inc.'s $10 billion buyout of Netscape Communications Corp., the Internet rival whose business the government claims was crushed by Microsoft's predatory conduct. The documents suggest that Netscape's Web browser business is robust and that AOL has big

> plans for its future.
>
> "Likewise, John L. Warden, of New York's Sullivan & Cromwell, avoided the contents of damaging e-mail on Microsoft's campaign against Netscape that form the backbone of the government's case.
>
> "The vast ceremonial courtroom where the closing argument took place swallowed up the parties' rhetoric. The government compared Microsoft to the emperor with no clothes. Mr. Warden, feisty in the end, slammed the government's claims as 'baloney' and 'nuts.' It's hard to imagine that this will make much of a difference when the judge and his law clerk, David McIntosh, a 1998 Harvard Law graduate, sort through the massive record in this historic case."[36]

Boies, the former senior litigator of Cravath, Swain & Moore, and Warden are both pre-eminent lawyers with superb reputations. Yet, they too, fell into the trap that law schools and mentoring lay for even the brightest of would-be advocates. To paraphrase Edward Gibbon's observation in his *Decline and Fall of the Roman Empire*, rhetoric has little efficacy except on those already persuaded.[37]

The lawyer's client, of course, is the most convinced by the justness and righteous of his or her cause. Accordingly, that client is a ready and highly appreciative audience for the lawyer's flights of fanciful rhetoric. Although the rhetoric may cement the lawyer-client relationship, it does little to advance the client's cause where that cause is most in the balance: in court. As I've pointed out in *The "How-To-Win" Trial Manual*, rhetoric does little to win trials. It also does little to win appeals.

- Be direct, forthright, and candid.
  - Never exaggerate or misstate.

---

[36] Karen Donovan, MICROSOFT CASE CLOSES STRANGELY, 22 *The National Law Journal* #6 at 1, 7 (October 4, 1999).

[37] Gibbon observed that "that the power of instruction is seldom of much efficacy, except in those happy dispositions where it is almost superfluous." 1 Edward Gibbon, THE DECLINE AND FALL OF THE ROMAN EMPIRE 66 (Heritage Press ed. 1946).

- Turn the "stumbling blocks" in your case into "stepping stones"—*don't ignore them.*

- If asked a question the answer to which you do not know, admit it, and offer to submit a supplemental response.

<u>Example</u>:

"The answer to that question escapes me for the moment, Your Honor. If the court has no objection, I will find the answer and submit a letter to the court within five days, with a copy to opposing counsel."

- Never fight with the court; it is the tribunal you are trying to persuade.

- Use visual aids where appropriate. A large chart showing the accident intersection, a schematic diagram of the assembly line where the worker was injured, the words of the applicable statute, a photocopy of the pivotal clause of the contract, etc. This not only lets the judges see what you're talking about, it breaks the general tedium that pervades much of oral argument.

- Give as much thought to your closing two or three sentences as you do to ones with which you started.

V.
STANDARDS OF REVIEW—GOLD MINES AND MINE FIELDS.

As the title to this section indicates, standards of review provide both opportunities for and dangers to the appellate lawyer. First, standards of review can be used by the skillful appellate lawyer to prevail on a close question that would, if a different standard of review applied, go the other way. Second, they can ensnare the less-skilled appellate lawyer into making an argument that cannot win. Ruggero J. Aldisert, former Chief Judge of the United States Court of Appeals for the Third Circuit tells us in his handbook for judges and law clerks, that he has "seen competent lawyers completely nonplussed when we ask them [during oral argument] to state the standard of review."[38] Of course, Judge Aldisert is being too kind—the lawyers who do

---

[38] RUGGERO J. ALDISERT, OPINION WRITING 53 (1990).

not know the standard of appellate review applicable to the issues are hardly "competent."

For example, appellate courts universally look at the findings of fact made by the trial court as being almost invulnerable. In the words of Rule 52(a) of the Federal Rules of Civil Procedure:

> "Findings of fact, whether based on oral or documentary evidence, shall not be set aside unless clearly erroneous, and due regard shall be given to the opportunity of the trial court to judge of the credibility of the witnesses."

The United States Supreme Court has equated the "clearly erroneous" standard with an inquiry as to whether the trial judge has abused his or her discretion: "[T]he abuse-of-discretion and clearly erroneous standards are indistinguishable." ***Cooter & Gell v. Hartmarx Corp.***, 496 U.S. 384, 401 (1990). This seems to me to be even more deferential than the Court's earlier, oft-quoted, formulation that a finding will be held to be "clearly erroneous," even if there is evidence in the record to support it, if the appellate court has "the definite and firm conviction that a mistake has been committed." ***United States v. United States Gypsum Co.***, 333 U.S. 364, 395 (1948).

Some appellate courts do give less deference to a trial court's finding of fact when that finding is based solely on documentary evidence than when it is based on the testimony of witnesses. Indeed, that was the law in the federal courts before a 1985 amendment to the Federal Rules of Civil Procedure added "documentary evidence." *See* ***Bull's Corner Restaurant v. Director of the Fed. Emergency Management Agency***, 759 F.2d 500, 502 (5th Cir.1985) ("[T]he degree of deference to be accorded a district court's findings of fact is lower when the case is submitted wholly on documents than in the situation where the evidence is presented by witnesses appearing before the district court.") If you are arguing an appeal in federal court, you must be alert to the change. The older standard-of-review cases that apply the less-deferential standard when the trial court's findings rest on a documentary evidence are no longer good law.

The skillful appellate lawyer recognizes the extreme deference given to the trial court's findings of fact, and will shape his or her argument accordingly. The less-skilled, or less-experienced, appellate lawyer will attempt to charge the windmills of the trial court's findings, and, essentially, re-argue the facts in his or her appellate brief. Again, Judge Aldisert: "It makes no sense for lawyers to dress up a closing speech to a jury in the form of a brief to an appellate court that simply repeats the trial lawyer's recitation of a litigant's best *evidence* instead of addressing the *facts* found by the fact finder." Aldisert, *Opinion Writing* at 53.

Hardly a month goes by that I don't read a brief submitted by a well-meaning lawyer who tries to persuade us that the trial court's findings of fact do not have support in the evidence—even though those findings are backed by the testimony of one or more witnesses. These mis-directed efforts have about as much chance of success as would an attempt to scamper up an oil-slicked slide at an amusement park. They not only waste the precious pages in the lawyer's appellate brief, they squander the lawyer's credibility—a lawyer who is ignorant of so basic a standard of review that it is codified in the rules cannot be trusted to perceptively analyze, and argue from, more complex legal issues.

It is well beyond the scope of this book to give a treatise on the standards of review used by appellate courts to sift decisions of the trial courts and of the administrative agencies. Suffice it to say, that the distinctions can become quite dicey, where only those metaphysicians with the skill of Erasmus might be able to divine *any* real distinction between the formulations—except those that might lurk within the judges' preconceived views on the substantive matter that comprises the appeal. Consider this explanation of the various degrees of deference given by the Wisconsin courts to the interpretations of statutes by administrative agencies:

> "There are three distinct levels of deference that we afford an agency's interpretation: great weight, due weight or *de novo*. We afford "great weight" to an agency's interpretation when the following conditions are met: (1) the agency was charged by the legislature with the duty of administering the statute; (2) that the interpretation of the agency is one of long-standing; (3) that the agency employed its expertise or specialized knowledge in forming the interpretation; and (4) that the agency's interpretation will provide uniformity and consistency in the application of the statute. When we afford great weight deference, we will sustain that agency's reasonable interpretation even if there is a more reasonable interpretation available. We afford "due weight" to an agency's interpretation when it "has some experience in an area, but has not developed the expertise that necessarily places it in a better position to make judgments regarding the interpretation of the statute than a court." When we afford "due weight," we will not overturn an agency's reasonable interpretation that comports with the purpose of

> the statute unless we determine that a more reasonable interpretation is available. Finally, we review an agency's statutory interpretation *de novo* when the issue before the agency is clearly one of first impression, or when the agency's position on the issue has been so inconsistent so as to provide no real guidance."

Madison Newspapers, Inc. v. Wisconsin Department of Revenue, 599 N.W.2d 51, 57–58 (Wis. Ct. App. 1999) (internal citations, paragraph breaks, and introductory material omitted). This reminds me of Chief Justice William Rehnquist's plaintive lamentation about the inability of discerning minds to parse a difference between the various standards of review applicable when reviewing legislation that imposes classification-distinctions between various groups:

> "I would think we have had enough difficulty with the two standards of review which our cases have recognized—the norm of 'rational basis,' and the 'compelling state interest' required where a 'suspect classification' is involved—so as to counsel weightily against the insertion of still another 'standard' between those two. How is this Court to divine what objectives are important? How is it to determine whether a particular law is 'substantially' related to the achievement of such objective, rather than related in some other way to its achievement? Both of the phrases used are so diaphanous and elastic as to invite subjective judicial preferences or prejudices relating to particular types of legislation, masquerading as judgments whether such legislation is directed at 'important' objectives or, whether the relationship to those objectives is 'substantial' enough."

Craig v. Boren, 429 U.S. 190, 220–221 (1976). As "diaphanous and elastic" as the many standards of review may be, and may become, you must be aware of them, and use them to advance the interests of your client's appeal.

Courts use standards of review for several reasons. First, it accommodates and gives deference to the expertise of the various components of our governmental system.

- Trial judges are more expert in evaluating the evidence than are appellate judges because the trial judge sees and hears the witnesses and is also privy to the dynamics and ambience of the trial. Thus, not only are trial judge's findings of fact fairly invulnerable to reversal on appeal, but, also, a trial judge's decision to overturn or let stand a jury verdict is given great deference by the appellate court.

- Great deference is also given to jury verdicts, both in civil cases and in criminal cases, where, of course, a verdict of acquittal is final. Jurors are presumed to be able to assess the credibility of the witnesses and analyze the evidence, and a jury verdict will not be overturned unless there is no evidence in the record to support it.

- Appellate judges, because they sit in panels of three, five, seven, or nine, are deemed to have more *collective* wisdom and experience than a single trial judge. Moreover, appellate panels have greater resources for reflection and research than do trial judges, who are often forced to make decisions at the moment—without weeks or months of reflection, research, and analysis. Thus, appellate courts give very little or no deference to a trial judge's legal conclusions—those legal conclusions that are not inextricably intertwined with facts adduced at a trial or hearing. Additionally, deference to a trial judge's legal conclusions might very well lead to a balkanization of the law—judges in different court rooms reaching different legal conclusions, all affirmed on appeal (as they would be if the appellate panel gave deference to the judge's legal opinions). This is especially important in the area of constitutional criminal law; protections afforded by our constitutions and our laws should not vary with the court room in which a defendant may appear. Indeed, the very real disparity in the exercise of sentencing discretion—to which appellate courts generally give great deference—was the impetus for the enactment of the Federal Sentencing Guidelines, which have essentially removed most of the federal trial judge's sentencing discretion, and have resulted in significant second-guessing by the federal appellate courts.

- Administrative agencies deal every day with the complex matters within their purview, and they are generally given broad berth by reviewing courts, whose judges have less expertise in those matters. Thus, courts give significant deference to the administrative agency both in connection with the agency's factual determinations and the agency's application of the law—the degree of deference varying with the agency's experience.

Standards of review also serve another purpose: by giving appellate courts fairly limited areas within which to operate, the standards of review eliminate a significant amount of work. This is, in essence, judicial triage. Imagine how much time and effort (and how many more judges would be needed) if every jury trial, if every bench trial, if every determination by an administrative agency—no matter how complex—was subject to *de novo* review by the appellate courts. Trial and administrative-agency transcripts would have to be studied in detail, not—as at present—to see if an error was made, but, rather, to weigh and assess and analyze.

The lesson for the appellate practitioner is clear: never take an appeal, never outline your brief, never write your brief, unless you know the standard of review that applies to each of your issues. Thus, the Federal Rules of Appellate Procedure require that the brief set out "for each issue, a concise statement of the applicable standard of review (which may appear in the discussion of the issue or under a separate heading placed before the discussion of the issues)."[39] As another example, the Connecticut Rules of Appellate Procedure provide: "The argument on each point shall include a separate, brief statement of the standard of review the [appellant] [appellee] believes should be applied."[40] Most other jurisdictions also have similar requirements. Even if yours does not, put it in. You will not only help the judges analyze your issues, but you will also help yourself frame your argument. Simply put, a lawyer cannot write an effective, persuasive appellate brief without a *thorough* and *comprehensive* understanding of the applicable standards of review.

VI.
PRESERVES AND TOAST

As we have seen, "standards of review" circumscribe the scope of the appellate court's inquiry into possible error by the trial court or by an administrative agency. Closely related to this is the general rule that an appellate court will not consider an issue or argument that is raised or asserted for the first time on appeal—except when consideration of that issue or argument is results in an affirmance (trial court will be affirmed if it reaches the right result, albeit for the wrong reason). There are three reasons, founded in both fairness and efficiency.

First, if the point was not argued to the trial court, the opposing party could not have made whatever record would be necessary to support its argument on appellate review.

---

39 Rule 28(a)(9)(B) of the Federal Rules of Appellate Procedure.

40 Connecticut Rules of Appellate Procedure §§ 67-4(d), 67-5(d).

Second, asserting an issue on appeal that was not presented to the trial judge reeks of sandbagging—both of the judge and of the opponent.

Third, considering an argument that is asserted for the first time on appeal also weakens "finality"—if considered, the appellate court might need to remand the case to the trial court for an evidentiary hearing (or even a new trial before a jury) that could have been avoided if the issue had been presented to the trial court or agency to begin with.

Although appellate courts will consider an issue presented for the first time on appeal if that leads to an affirmance, and will *occasionally*, in the extraordinary "plain error" situations, reverse on an issue or argument not made to the trial court, the lesson for the appellate lawyer is clear.

Strategy:

> ☞ If you must assert an issue or make an argument on appeal that was not raised or argued before the trial court, recognize that you are asking the appellate court to do something that it rarely does—come up with compelling reasons why it should do so in your case.

If you do not, and the point was not preserved before the trial court, you will be toast. (I know that "preserves and toast" is probably a bit too "cute" for some of you. But the point is, I hope, now indelibly fixed in your mind. And that is why I chose the image.)

VII.
GET RID OF THE CLUTTER.

Clutter is the bane of most briefs. It is almost as if lawyers take a course on how to clutter a brief with stuff that detracts from a forceful presentation. The simple fact is that clutter in a brief, like static on a radio or snow on a television screen, interferes and obscures. Rather than help the reader move through the material, it slows the reader down.

The folks that run our major consumer-focused businesses recognize this (although probably not in their internal memoranda) and go to extraordinary lengths to remove even milliseconds of clutter. Thus, as James Gleick tells us in his recent book *Faster* (1999), when you call directory assistance to get a listing, computer software removes the clutter from your speech: If you say in response to the prompt asking for the listing you want, "Uh ... Dominos Pizza," special software removes the pause and "uh" in passing your request to the operator—all to save a second or two. Make your briefs easier and faster to read; eliminate the clutter. The following are some examples:

1. *The "(Hereinafter referred to as ...)."*

There are several things wrong with this. First, why would anyone use the word "hereinafter"? To sound like a lawyer? To impress a significant other?

Second, even those of you who omit the "hereinafter" do put how you will refer to the party or person or company in parentheses, as in: "Melvin Koopersmith ('Koopersmith')" or "General Motors ('GM'). " Think about it; how many Koopersmiths are you writing about? How many General Motors? Will any judge not know about whom you are writing when you refer to Mr. Koopersmith as "Koopersmith" or General Motors as "GM" even if you do not use the parenthetical? Of course not. The parentheticals just take up space. Leave them out.

2. *The acronyms or abbreviations.*

I touched upon this, but it bears repeating. With the exception of a few, universal acronyms (IRS or US), which everyone will recognize and absorb without even a millisecond of thought, other acronyms require the reader to *process* the letters before the brain is able to know what they mean. Thus, to give you another example: "GI"—even in a medical-malpractice case, the brain first skims past the fleeting association with "soldier." Other acronyms are even more difficult to parse. Consider this example—the first two paragraphs of a recent decision of the Wisconsin Supreme Court:

> "Defendants, James R. Klauser, Secretary of the Wisconsin Department of Administration, and Charles P. Smith, State Treasurer, seek review, and the plaintiffs, the State Engineering Association (SEA), the Wisconsin Retired Teachers Association (WRTA), and the Wisconsin Education Association Council (WEAC), seek cross-review, of a published decision of the court of appeals. The court of appeals' decision affirmed in part and reversed in part a decision of the circuit court for Dane County, Angela B. Bartell, Judge.
>
> "At issue is the constitutionality of 1987 Wis. Act 27, §§ 436m, 684r, and 688km, under which Wisconsin Retirement System (WRS)

> trust funds were used to pay a "Special Investment Performance Dividend" (SIPD) to certain WRS annuitants. We conclude that Act 27 and its implementation constitute a taking of the plaintiffs' property without just compensation, in violation of Article I, § 13 of the Wisconsin constitution. Accordingly, we order the Administration Defendants, in their official capacities, to replenish the WRS fixed annuity reserve account in an amount equal to all funds paid out of the account pursuant to Act 27, plus interest at the effective rate. See Wis.Stat. § 40.02(23) (1987-88). We also conclude that the ETF Defendants did not breach their fiduciary duties by implementing Act 27. Finally, we determine that the plaintiffs are entitled to reasonable attorney fees to be paid out of the recovery under the "common fund" doctrine."

Wisconsin Retired Teachers Ass'n., Inc. v. Employe Trust Funds Bd., 207 Wis.2d 1, 7–9, 558 N.W.2d 83, 86–87 (1997) (footnotes and internal citation to decision of the court of appeals omitted) (The Wisconsin statutes and some judges spell the word "employee" with one "e" at the end of the word: "employe."). In these first two paragraphs the opinion confronts us with six acronyms: SEA, WRTA, WEAC, WRS, SIPD, and ETF. Five are defined for us with parentheticals; the definition of one is not given, and the reader is relegated to the title to determine that ETF means "Employe Trust Funds." The opinion is long; what reader is going to remember what WRTA or SIPD means without going back and looking it up? When you write your briefs, don't make it difficult for the reader. Instead of SEA, what's wrong with "State Engineering Association" or "the Engineering Association"? Or "the Performance Dividend" rather than "SIPD"? It is a lot quicker and easier to read "The Engineering Association" and "the Performance Dividend" than it is "SEA" and "SIPD." The acronyms require additional steps of cognition, the words—albeit taking up more space and ink—do not.

3. *Citations.*

As I mentioned before, citations to authority and the record are there for one purpose: to let the reader find the thing to which you refer. The citations should be written so they make the reader's job easy, not difficult. Thus, "***Id.***, at 173" tells us absolutely nothing *unless* we know what "*Id.*" refers to. If the last time the case name and volume number appeared was not on the same page, the reader will have to flip back to find both the name of the case and the volume of whatever reports to which the page citation refers. How much easier for the reader is: ***Jones***, 117 U.S. at 173. Do it that way, and make it easy for the judges who will decide your appeal.

The same holds true for record references. We've already discussed how [R 17 (Transcript of Dr. Rogers's testimony) 19] is better and, indeed, easier to read and understand than is the more commonly used [R 17:19].

4. *Simple Words.*

Lawyers are like other professionals: they love to use the jargon they learned in professional school when that jargon seemed like the key to admission. After all, if you *sound like* a (lawyer) (doctor) (engineer) you are closer to being one. It reminds me of Herman Melville's comment, which I also quote in *The "How-To-Win" Trial Manual*:

> "A man of true science uses but few hard words, and only when none other will answer his purpose; whereas the smatterer in science thinks that by mouthing hard words he proves that he understands hard things."

But doctors and engineers don't have to persuade others (except when they are seeking venture capital for their ideas); lawyers do. Use simple words—even in an appellate brief, which are written for other lawyers (and the client, of course). In the next part, we will analyze briefs in a Ninth Circuit case involving a computer game and claims of copyright infringement. The lawyers use the term "audiovisual" throughout when referring to the images and sounds produced by the game. Yes, "audiovisual" is a perfectly good word, but it is a five-dollar word. Additionally, the word goes by too fast. And if you want the eye to linger so you can make your point that both *sounds* and *images* are involved, use those words. When you review the drafts to your briefs, make sure that you do not use the five-dollar words, except in those rare cases, as Melville noted, "when none other will answer" your purpose.

Why do lawyers clutter their briefs with buzz words, acronyms, abbreviations, five-dollar words, and hard-to-use citations? The simple answer is because they've been taught to do so, through the generations: teacher to mentor to student. As I point out in *The "How-To-Win" Trial Manual* that's the same reason most people fall down when they are shot: They think they should.[41]

---

[41] "Although the popular belief that many people fall down upon being shot is generally accurate, experts have determined that this occurs not for physiological reasons, but as a learned response. People who have been shot believe they are supposed to fall immediately to the ground, so they do." David Simon, HOMICIDE 413 (1993).

VIII.
ADVOCACY IN THE REAL WORLD

The only way to learn how to tie one's shoe laces is to do it. Very few adults, not to mention youngsters who are routinely able to master the task, would be able to tie shoe laces if they had to rely on a manual with the various steps set out in sequence ("First, take the left lace in your left hand ..."). Law schools recognize this, and now sprinkle their curricula with "practical" courses on how to try a case and how to write an appellate brief. As I've pointed out in *The "How-To-Win" Trial Manual*, however, most of the trial-advocacy techniques taught in law school are suicidal to effective advocacy. Indeed, in my view, that is why so very few lawyers *look forward* to trying cases. After all, the usual excuses: "it's too hard" or "trials take too much time" or "it's just a roll of the dice" could also be said of baseball. The average baseball player gets a hit in less than one-third of his times at bat; and of the *really good* baseball players none has consistently gotten hits even four times out of ten at bats since Ted Williams. Yet, they *love* to play their game.

Although there are some—the very successful trial lawyers—who love *their* game of trying cases, most lawyers do not. Perhaps it is because they recognize, either on a subliminal or overt level, that the techniques they've been taught and use run counter to the common sense they had when they entered law school. In fact, a lawyer in Oklahoma City told me after participating in one of my full-day, large-group trial-advocacy programs that "the trouble with law schools is that they make you check your common sense when you walk in and they don't give it back when you leave."

Law schools also leach common sense from appellate advocacy. Why else would someone writing a brief where the defendant was named Klinkowitz make the first reference to her this way: "Lorna Klinkowtiz (hereinafter 'Klinkowtiz' or 'the defendant')"? We have seen how many of the routine practices of lawyers writing an appellate brief stand in the way of effective appellate advocacy. But it is one thing to set out what should and what should not be done, and it is another thing to apply those principles to real-life situations. That is what we're going to do now.

We're going to analyze two actual appeals, a civil case and a criminal case, and see what was done right, what was done wrong, and what could have been done to make the briefs forceful, persuasive tools. And, in the process, we're going to learn how to view the issues the way the appellate judges do.

These are real cases, real briefs, and the appeals led to published appellate-court opinions. I have made suggestions as to how I would have framed the arguments, together with my reasons. I have not tried to conform those suggestions to the courts' ultimate decisions, but, rather, in a way that I believe would have been most effective to get a favorable decision. Thus, you may see some of my suggested arguments echoed in the decisions that you read, and you may see other of my suggested arguments either ignored or rejected.

This exercise will, if you devote the time and effort the analysis requires, be an interesting and enlightening journey. But it will take work—work, however, that will pay dividends for the investment.

Analyze the briefs in a two-step process:

> 1) What you would like to see, and what would persuade you, if you were the judge hearing the appeal; and, therefore
>
> 2) How you would make the briefs better.

This is the type of analysis you should make with all of your cases. Join me as we explore advocacy in the real world.

The first case is, admittedly, complex. The second case, a criminal case, will present issues that, on the surface at least, are relatively straight forward.

I'm starting with the complex case because you will not be able to successfully represent your clients in *any* case unless to can take the *hard* case and make it clear. There is a story about Richard Feynman, the physics Nobel laureate, who lamented over his inability to explain one of his theories to his students. Feyman realized that this meant that he did not really understand that theory himself. Simply put, you must master your case, and if you cannot explain it to the judges, it means that you do not understand it yourself.

Your first task with any case, especially the complex case, is to boil it down to its essential elements, and figure out how to explain those elements so each makes sense to someone who is not particularly knowledgeable in that field.

1. *Computer-game Mayhem.*

What happens when the publisher of a successful computer game encourages its customers to create new game-scenarios that can be played on the game, and also encourages those customers to share their creations with not only their friends but also the world *via* internet postings, and another company compiles the internet-posted game scenarios and sells the compilation? If the computer-game publisher complains and tries to stop the compiler from selling the compilation, who wins?

This was the question presented in a case that comes from the federal district court in Los Angeles: *Micro Star v. FormGen, Inc.* FormGen owned rights to the game; Micro Star was selling the compilations on a compact disk. The case was started by Micro Star, which sought a declaration that it could continue to sell the disk. FormGen counterclaimed seeking an injunction against Micro Star. Although there were other, collateral, issues (essentially, in addition to a dispute about discovery, whether Micro Star violated FormGen's copyright by depicting scenes from the copyrighted game on its packaging, and including with the compact disk screensavers using the FormGen characters), we will limit our analysis to the issue of whether Micro Star could sell the compilations. Let's see how the district court handled that issue (I'm including all of the district court's discussion of that issue as well as its recitation of the general background, but am omitting the court's discussion of the collateral issues—the district court concluded that Micro Star's packaging and the screen savers on the Micro Star CD violated FormGen's copyright). The full decision is reported at 942 F. Supp. 1312.

The District Court's Decision:

Defendants/counterclaim plaintiffs Formgen, Inc. and Apogee Software, Ltd. d/b/a 3D Realms Entertainment (together, "Movants") on August 9, 1996 filed an application for a Preliminary Injunction pursuant to Federal Rule of Civil Procedure 65. Movants, the manufacturers and distributors of the video CD-ROM game "Duke Nukem 3D" (hereinafter Duke 3D) allege that the video CD-ROM game "Nuke It," manufactured and distributed by plaintiff Micro Star, infringes upon the creative works protected by Duke 3D's copyright and trademark registrations. Movants seek an order to enjoin any further distribution and production of Nuke It, and to compel Micro Star to recall all existing copies of Nuke It.*

---

* **This is not a book about decision writing. I will therefore let pass, other than this brief note, how cluttered and confusing this opening paragraph is. Don't ever do this in *your* writing—although it might look like that of some judges and other lawyers, and (continued)**

After reviewing the papers and the law, and hearing oral argument on September 23, 24, and 26, 1996, the court finds that good cause exists to partially grant movants' request for a preliminary injunction. Specifically, the court finds that Nuke It's depiction of scenes from Duke 3D on its packaging, as well as its offering of screen savers from Duke 3D, is an infringing use of movants' copyrighted creative works. As to the actual CD-ROM itself, and as to the trademark claims brought under the Lanham Act, the court denies movants' request for injunctive relief. Consequently, the court has issued a preliminary injunction, dated September 26, 1996, which orders Micro Star to: (1) immediately cease from using screen scenes on Nuke It's packaging which infringe upon Duke 3D's copyrighted material; (2) recall all existing Nuke It packages which depict copyrighted Duke 3D screen scenes; (3) immediately cease from including any DN3D screen savers in its Nuke It products; and (4) make its best efforts to remove or cover over any Nuke It packaging on the market which makes reference to Duke 3D screen savers.

BACKGROUND

Movants are the makers and distributors of the computer game "Duke Nukem 3D". As to their copyright, movants registered "Duke Nukem 3D, Shareware Version" with the Copyright Office on August 8, 1996, six days after Micro Star filed a claim for declaratory judgment that it was not infringing on movant's copyrights or trademarks.

As purchased in stores, the Duke Nukem 3D ("Duke 3D") game has 29 levels through which players advance, killing monsters and other evil creatures. In order to continue to generate interest in the game, the movants included in the software the option and ability for players to create "new" levels themselves, which is done through an editor called BUILD.EXE. Through this editor and other tools provided, users can create files with the extension .MAP, which they can play in addition to, or instead of, the levels that come with the game. However, to play any of the new .MAP levels, users must own a registered copy of Duke 3D. Whenever a player exits the Duke 3D game, a message appears on his screen which tells him about tools which are included and can be used to build new levels. This same message additionally informs the user that once he creates his own new level, "you can then pass to your friends, or upload to other Dukers on-line."

One of the main issues before this court is the fact that the packaging for Nuke It contains 30 scenes from the Duke 3D game, depicting such original art work as the Cycloid, Emperor, Battlelord, Assault Trooper, Ripper Chaingun, Octabrain, and Enforcer. In addition, a version of Nuke It released in July of 1996 contained 25 screen savers, described as "wallpaper," that depicted scenes and audiovisual elements from the Duke 3D game. Finally, an earlier version of Nuke It also contained at least

---

(continued)
your significant other might be wowed by your ability to write complex, almost incomprehensible sentences, your briefs will not be clear, concise, or persuasive.

two levels that were identical to those found on Duke 3D, the zoo.map and the E1L1Weap.map; these levels have been voluntarily removed by Micro Star. Accordingly, this court must determine if whether by granting permission for authorized users of the product to pass on or trade their new levels, movants have waived any or all rights to copyright protection for commercial exploitation of their creative expression.

Duke 3D contains a copyright notice on both its packaging and on its screen. The opening screen for the build editor indicates that the build editor and associated tools may not be re-packaged and sold, and finishes by stating "Please refer to LICENSE.DOC for further information on levels created with BUILD.EXE." This LICENSE.DOC file contains several restrictions, including that there can be no commercial sales of any new levels created and that all rights are granted back to movants.

Micro Star downloaded 300 of these new user created levels that were available on the Internet, and packaged them as "Nuke It." As these are just new "levels," Nuke It can only be utilized by users who already own a registered copy of Duke 3D. The "Nuke It" cover states "Over 300 New Levels for Duke Nukem 3D(TM)," and in small print in the corner of the cover contains a disclaimer that states "Requires registered version of Duke Nukem 3D(TM)--Duke Nukem 3D(TM) is a registered trademark of 3D Realms Entertainment. This product is not associated with nor will it be supported by 3D Realms Entertainment." After movants first complained to Micro Star that Nuke It was infringing upon their trademark and copyright marks, Micro Star requested a license, which was denied. Thereafter, Micro Star added a red sticker ("red sticker disclaimer") to the cover of Nuke It which states "These levels were independently created by 3rd parties not affiliated with 3D Realms, creator of Duke Nukem 3D(TM)."

There is some dispute over whether these stickers have been placed on all copies of Nuke It being offered for sale, as movants offer a declaration which says that as of August 3 and August 7, 1996, at three different stores in the New York area there were Nuke It packages without the red sticker disclaimer. Additionally, on September 25, 1996 movants offered another declaration which stated that as of that date several stores in the Dallas area were also selling Nuke It packages that did not contain the red sticker disclaimer. However, as it was not until the end of July that Micro Star agreed to put the red sticker disclaimers on Nuke It, it is possible that there are still some packages in stores which have not yet been stickered. Micro Star informed the court that as of this date, over 61,000 copies of Nuke It have been sold.

DISCUSSION

Preliminary injunctive relief is available if the party meets one of two tests: "(1) a combination of probable success and the possibility of irreparable harm, or (2) serious questions are raised and the balance of hardship tips in its favor." *Arcamuzi v. Continental Air Lines, Inc.*, 819 F.2d 935, 937 (9th Cir.1987). "These two formulations represent two points on a sliding scale in which the required degree of irreparable harm increases as the probability of success decreases." *Id.* Under both formulations, however, the party must demonstrate a "fair chance of success on the merits" and a "significant threat of irreparable injury." *Id.*

On a claim for copyright or trademark infringement, the test for whether preliminary injunctive relief is warranted is the same: (1) a combination of probable successes on the merits and the possibility of irreparable injury or (2) serious questions going to the merits and a balance of hardships tipping sharply in movants favor. *See Triad Sys. Corp. v. Southeastern Express Co.*, 64 F.3d 1330, 1334 (9th Cir.1995), *cert. denied,* ___ U.S. ___ (1996).

Likelihood of success on the merits is by far the most important factor in intellectual property cases. "In a property infringement claim, a showing of a reasonable likelihood of success on the merits raises a presumption of irreparable harm." *Johnson Controls, Inc. v. Phoenix Control Systems*, 886 F.2d 1173, 1174 (9th Cir.1989).

A. Copyright Claims

Movants claim that they have a valid copyright in the Duke 3D game and its elements that extends to derivative works created by others. Micro Star responds that there has been no infringement of any rights granted by the copyright act, that Nuke It is permissible under the "fair use" doctrine, and that even if these two arguments fail, movants have waived or abandoned their rights to limit the creation and distribution of MAP files. Micro Star additionally alleges that LICENSE.DOC is not a valid licensing agreement.

To establish copyright infringement, movants must demonstrate (1) that they own a valid copyright; and (2) that Micro Star violated their alleged right to distribute derivative works. *Feist Publications Inc. v. Rural Telephone Service Co.*, 499 U.S. 340, 361-63 (1991).

1. Infringement of Rights Granted By Copyright Act

In *Lewis Galoob Toys, Inc. v. Nintendo of America, Inc.*, 964 F.2d 965 (9th Cir.1992), *cert. denied* 507 U.S. 985 (1993), the Galoob company sold the "Game Genie" which was designed to use Nintendo's console to control Nintendo's games. Inserted between a game cartridge and the Nintendo system, the Game Genie allowed a player to alter up to three features of the Nintendo game, such as increasing the number of lives, increasing the character's speed, or giving the character more strength. As such the Game Genie did not alter data that was stored in Nintendo's game cartridges, but the changes would be displayed on the TV screen for the duration of the game. *Id.* at 967.

The court held that the Game Genie did not create a derivative work, as it only enhanced the audiovisual displays originating in the Nintendo cartridge. The court justified its holding by stating that a derivative work must "incorporate a protected work in some concrete or permanent form ... we cannot ignore the actual source of the Game Genie's display." *Id.* at 969.

Micro Star argues that Nuke It is really just a more sophisticated Game Genie. Micro Star points out that like the Game Genie, Nuke It does not supplant the demand for Duke 3D, as Nuke It is useless unless used with Duke 3D. Micro Star also argues that all of the copyrightable elements of Duke 3D observed on the screen while playing Nuke It are contained on the Duke 3D program files, and that the data on the MAP files contained on Nuke It is generic data and not programming.

As to the Nuke It CD-ROM itself, and the programming it contains, the court is not convinced that the movants have shown that the data sequence in the Nuke It MAP files is subject to copyright protection. Furthermore, the court finds that Micro Star has shown that the audiovisual elements which appear on the screen while playing Nuke It originate from Duke 3D, and not from Nuke It. Therefore, the court finds that movants have not shown a valid copyright in the data sequence contained in the Nuke It MAP files, and consequently denies the injunctive relief requested as to the Nuke It CD-ROM itself.

* * *

In summary, as the court has concluded that the MAP files do not constitute copyright infringement but the packaging does, Micro Star remains free to re-package and continue to sell the Nuke It CD-ROM, so long as the product does not infringe upon Duke 3D's protected creative works.

— — —

The district court decision relied heavily on a Ninth Circuit decision it believed was directly on point: *Lewis Galoob Toys, Inc. v. Nintendo of America, Inc.*, 964 F.2d 965 (9th Cir.1992), *cert. denied* 507 U.S. 985 (1993). We reprint *Galoob* here because it helps us to analyze the briefs submitted to the Ninth Circuit in the *Micro Star* appeal.

Lewis Galoob Toys, Inc. v. Nintendo of America, Inc.:

FARRIS, Circuit Judge:

Nintendo of America appeals the district court's judgment following a bench trial (1) declaring that Lewis Galoob Toys' Game Genie does not violate any Nintendo copyrights and dissolving a temporary injunction and (2) denying Nintendo's request for a permanent injunction enjoining Galoob from marketing the Game Genie. *Lewis*

Galoob Toys, Inc. v. Nintendo of America, Inc., 780 F. Supp. 1283 (N.D. Cal. 1991). We have appellate jurisdiction pursuant to 15 U.S.C. § 1121 and 28 U.S.C. §§ 1291 and 1292(a)(1). We affirm.

FACTS

The Nintendo Entertainment System is a home video game system marketed by Nintendo. To use the system, the player inserts a cartridge containing a video game that Nintendo produces or licenses others to produce. By pressing buttons and manipulating a control pad, the player controls one of the game's characters and progresses through the game. The games are protected as audiovisual works under 17 U.S.C. § 102(a)(6).

The Game Genie is a device manufactured by Galoob that allows the player to alter up to three features of a Nintendo game. For example, the Game Genie can increase the number of lives of the player's character, increase the speed at which the character moves, and allow the character to float above obstacles. The player controls the changes made by the Game Genie by entering codes provided by the Game Genie Programming Manual and Code Book. The player also can experiment with variations of these codes.

The Game Genie functions by blocking the value for a single data byte sent by the game cartridge to the central processing unit in the Nintendo Entertainment System and replacing it with a new value. If that value controls the character's strength, for example, then the character can be made invincible by increasing the value sufficiently. The Game Genie is inserted between a game cartridge and the Nintendo Entertainment System. The Game Genie does not alter the data that is stored in the game cartridge. Its effects are temporary.

DISCUSSION

1. *Derivative work*

The Copyright Act of 1976 confers upon copyright holders the exclusive right to prepare and authorize others to prepare derivative works based on their copyrighted works. *See* 17 U.S.C. § 106(2). Nintendo argues that the district court erred in concluding that the audiovisual displays created by the Game Genie are not derivative works. The court's conclusions of law are reviewed de novo. *See Rozay's Transfer v. Local Freight Drivers*, Local 208, 850 F.2d 1321, 1326 (9th Cir.1988), *cert. denied*, 490 U.S. 1030 (1989). Its findings of fact are reviewed for clear error. *See id.*

A derivative work must incorporate a protected work in some concrete or permanent "form." The Copyright Act defines a derivative work as follows:

> A "derivative work" is a work based upon one or more preexisting works, such as a translation, musical arrangement, dramatization, fictionalization, motion picture version, sound recording, art reproduction, abridgment, condensation, *or any other form in which a work may be recast, transformed, or adapted.* A work consisting of editorial revisions, annotations, elaborations, or other modifications which, as a whole, represent an original work of authorship, is a "derivative work."

17 U.S.C. § 101 (emphasis added). The examples of derivative works provided by the Act all physically incorporate the underlying work or works. The Act's legislative history similarly indicates that "the infringing work must incorporate a portion of the copyrighted work in some form." 1976 U.S.Code Cong. & Admin. News 5659, 5675. *See also Mirage Editions, Inc. v. Albuquerque A.R.T. Co.*, 856 F.2d 1341, 1343-44 (9th Cir.1988) (discussing same), *cert. denied*, 489 U.S. 1018 (1989).

Our analysis is not controlled by the Copyright Act's definition of "fixed." The Act defines copies as "material objects, other than phonorecords, in which a work is *fixed* by any method." 17 U.S.C. § 101 (emphasis added). The Act's definition of "derivative work," in contrast, lacks any such reference to fixation. *See id.* Further, we have held in a copyright infringement action that "[i]t makes no difference that the derivation may not satisfy certain requirements for statutory copyright registration itself." *Lone Ranger Television v. Program Radio Corp.*, 740 F.2d 718, 722 (9th Cir.1984). *See also* Paul Goldstein, Derivative Rights and Derivative Works in Copyright, 30 J. Copyright Soc'y U.S.A. 209, 231 n. 75 (1983) ("the Act does not require that the derivative work be protectable for its preparation to infringe"). *Cf. Kalem Co. v. Harper Bros.*, 222 U.S. 55, 61 (1911) (finding the movie "Ben Hur" infringed copyright in the book Ben Hur even though Copyright Act did not yet include movies as protectable works). A derivative work must be fixed to be protected under the Act, see 17 U.S.C. § 102(a), but not to infringe.

The argument that a derivative work must be fixed because "[a] 'derivative work' is a work," 17 U.S.C. § 101, and "[a] work is 'created' when it is fixed in a copy or phonorecord for the first time," id., relies on a misapplication of the Copyright Act's definition of "created":

> A work is 'created' when it is fixed in a copy or phonorecord for the first time; where a work is prepared over a period of time, the portion of it that has been fixed at any particular time constitutes the work as of that time, and where the work has been prepared in different versions, each version constitutes a separate work.

Id. The definition clarifies the time at which a work is created. If the provision were a definition of "work," it would not use that term in such a casual manner. The Act does not contain a definition of "work." Rather, it contains specific definitions: "audiovisual works," "literary works," and "pictorial, graphic and sculptural works," for example. The definition of "derivative work" does not require fixation.

The district court's finding that no independent work is created, *see Galoob*, 780 F.Supp. at 1291, is supported by the record. The Game Genie merely enhances the audiovisual displays (or underlying data bytes) that originate in Nintendo game cartridges. The altered displays do not incorporate a portion of a copyrighted work in some concrete or permanent form. Nintendo argues that the Game Genie's displays are as fixed in the hardware and software used to create them as Nintendo's original displays. Nintendo's argument ignores the fact that the Game Genie cannot produce an audiovisual display; the underlying display must be produced by a Nintendo Entertainment System and game cartridge. Even if we were to rely on the Copyright Act's definition of "fixed," we would similarly conclude that the resulting display is not "embodied," see 17 U.S.C. § 101, in the Game Genie. It cannot be a derivative work.

Mirage Editions is illustrative. Albuquerque A.R.T. transferred artworks from a commemorative book to individual ceramic tiles. *See Mirage Editions*, 856 F.2d at 1342. We held that "[b]y borrowing and mounting the preexisting, copyrighted individual art images without the consent of the copyright proprietors ... [Albuquerque A.R.T.] has prepared a derivative work and infringed the subject copyrights." *Id.* at 1343. The ceramic tiles physically incorporated the copyrighted works in a form that could be sold. Perhaps more importantly, sales of the tiles supplanted purchasers' demand for the underlying works. Our holding in *Mirage Editions* would have been much different if Albuquerque A.R.T. had distributed lenses that merely enabled users to view several artworks simultaneously.

Nintendo asserted at oral argument that the existence of a $150 million market for the Game Genie indicates that its audiovisual display must be fixed. We understand Nintendo's argument; consumers clearly would not purchase the Game Genie if its display was not "sufficiently permanent or stable to permit it to be perceived ... for a period of more than transitory duration." 17 U.S.C. § 101. But, Nintendo's reliance on the Act's definition of "fixed" is misplaced. Nintendo's argument also proves too much; the existence of a market does not, and cannot, determine conclusively whether a work is an infringing derivative work. For example, although there is a market for kaleidoscopes, it does not necessarily follow that kaleidoscopes create unlawful derivative works when pointed at protected artwork. The same can be said of countless other products that enhance, but do not replace, copyrighted works.

Nintendo also argues that our analysis should focus exclusively on the audiovisual displays created by the Game Genie, i.e., that we should compare the altered displays to Nintendo's original displays. Nintendo emphasizes that " '[a]udiovisual works' are works that consist of a series of related images ... *regardless of the nature of the material objects ... in which the works are embodied*." 17 U.S.C. § 101 (emphasis added). The Copyright Act's definition of "audiovisual works" is inapposite; the only question before us is whether the audiovisual displays created by the Game Genie are "derivative works." The Act does not similarly provide that a work can be a derivative work regardless of the nature of the material objects in which the work is embodied. A derivative work must incorporate a protected work in some concrete or permanent form. We cannot ignore the actual source of the Game Genie's display.

Nintendo relies heavily on *Midway Mfg. Co. v. Artic Int'l, Inc.*, 704 F.2d 1009 (7th Cir.), *cert. denied*, 464 U.S. 823 (1983). *Midway* can be distinguished. The defendant in *Midway*, Artic International, marketed a computer chip that could be inserted in Galaxian video games to speed up the rate of play. The Seventh Circuit held that the speeded-up version of Galaxian was a derivative work. *Id.* at 1013-14. Artic's chip substantially copied and replaced the chip that was originally distributed by Midway. Purchasers of Artic's chip also benefited economically by offering the altered game for use by the general public. The Game Genie does not physically incorporate a portion of a copyrighted work, nor does it supplant demand for a component of that work. The court in *Midway* acknowledged that the Copyright Act's definition of "derivative work" "must be stretched to accommodate speeded-up video games." *Id.* at 1014. Stretching that definition further would chill innovation and fail to protect "society's competing interest in the free flow of ideas, information, and commerce." *Sony Corp. of America v. Universal Studios, Inc.*, 464 U.S. 417, 429 (1984).

In holding that the audiovisual displays created by the Game Genie are not derivative works, we recognize that technology often advances by improvement rather than replacement. *See* CHRISTIAN H. NADAN, NOTE, A PROPOSAL TO RECOGNIZE COMPONENT WORKS: HOW A TEDDY BEARS ON THE COMPETING ENDS OF COPYRIGHT LAW, 78 CAL.L.REV. 1633, 1635 (1990). Some time ago, for example, computer companies began marketing spell-checkers that operate within existing word processors by signalling the writer when a word is misspelled. These applications, as well as countless others, could not be produced and marketed if courts were to conclude that the word processor and spell-checker combination is a derivative work based on the word processor alone. The Game Genie is useless by itself, it can only enhance, and cannot duplicate or recaste [*sic*], a Nintendo game's output. It does not contain or produce a Nintendo game's output in some concrete or permanent form, nor does it supplant demand for Nintendo game cartridges. Such innovations rarely will constitute infringing derivative works under the Copyright Act. *See generally* NADAN, *supra*, at 1667-72.

2. *Fair use*

"The doctrine of fair use allows a holder of the privilege to use copyrighted material in a reasonable manner without the consent of the copyright owner." *Narell v. Freeman*, 872 F.2d 907, 913 (9th Cir.1989) (citations omitted). The district court concluded that, even if the audiovisual displays created by the Game Genie are derivative works, Galoob is not liable under 17 U.S.C. § 107 because the displays are a fair use of Nintendo's copyrighted displays. "Whether a use of copyrighted material is a 'fair use' is a mixed question of law and fact. If the district court found sufficient facts to evaluate each of the statutory factors, the appellate court may decide whether defendants may claim the fair use defense as a matter of law." *Abend v. MCA, Inc.*, 863 F.2d 1465, 1468 (9th Cir.1988), *aff'd sub nom. Stewart v. Abend,* 495 U.S. 207 (1990).

Section 107 codifies the fair use defense:

> In determining whether the use made of a work in any particular case is a fair use the factors to be considered shall include--
>
> (1) the purpose and character of the use, including whether such use is of a commercial nature or is for nonprofit educational purposes;
> (2) the nature of the copyrighted work;
> (3) the amount and substantiality of the portion used in relation to the copyrighted work as a whole;
> (4) the effect of the use upon the potential market for or value of the copyrighted work.

The factors are nonexclusive, *see Fisher v. Dees*, 794 F.2d 432, 435 (9th Cir.1986), and section 107 does not indicate how much weight should be ascribed to each.

Much of the parties' dispute regarding the fair use defense concerns the proper focus of the court's inquiry: (1) Galoob or (2) consumers who purchase and use the Game Genie. Nintendo's complaint does not allege direct infringement, nor did it try the case on that theory. The complaint, for example, alleges only that "Galoob's marketing advertising [sic], promoting and selling of Game Genie has and will *contribute to* the creation of infringing derivatives of Nintendo's copyrighted ... games." (emphasis added). Contributory infringement is a form of third party liability. *See*

Melville B. Nimmer & David Nimmer, 3 Nimmer on Copyright § 12.04[A][2], at 12-68 (1991). The district court properly focused on whether consumers who purchase and use the Game Genie would be infringing Nintendo's copyrights by creating (what are now assumed to be) derivative works.

Nintendo emphasizes that the district court ultimately addressed its direct infringement by authorization argument. The court concluded that, "[b]ecause the Game Genie does not create a derivative work when used in conjunction with a copyrighted video game, Galoob does not 'authorize the use of a copyrighted work without the actual authority from the copyright owner.' " *Galoob*, 780 F.Supp. at 1298 (quoting *Sony*, 464 U.S. at 435 n. 17). Although infringement by authorization is a form of direct infringement, this does not change the proper focus of our inquiry; a party cannot authorize another party to infringe a copyright unless the authorized conduct would itself be unlawful.

Nintendo disputes this conclusion. According to Nintendo, a party can unlawfully authorize another party to use a copyrighted work even if that party's use of the work would not violate the Copyright Act. Nintendo's argument is unpersuasive. In *Sony*, 464 U.S. at 449, for example, the Court considered whether consumers were using the Betamax for a commercial or noncommercial purpose even though Sony itself obviously was acting in its own commercial self-interest. Professor Nimmer similarly concludes that, "to the extent that an activity does not violate one of those five enumerated rights [see 17 U.S.C. § 106], authorizing such activity does not constitute copyright infringement." 3 Nimmer on Copyright § 12.04[A][3] [a], at 12-80 n.82.

The district court concluded that "a family's use of a Game Genie for private home enjoyment must be characterized as a non-commercial, nonprofit activity." *Galoob*, 780 F.Supp. at 1293. Nintendo argues that Game Genie users are supplanting its commercially valuable right to make and sell derivative works. Nintendo's reliance on *Harper & Row Publishers, Inc. v. Nation Enters.*, 471 U.S. 539, 562 (1985), is misplaced. The commercially valuable right at issue in *Harper & Row* was the right of first publication; Nation Enterprises intended to publish the copyrighted materials for profit. *See id.* at 562-63. *See also Sony*, 464 U.S. at 449 ("If the Betamax were used to make copies for a commercial or profit-making purpose, such use would presumptively be unfair."). Game Genie users are engaged in a non-profit activity. Their use of the Game Genie to create derivative works therefore is presumptively fair. *See Sony*, 464 U.S. at 449.

The district court also concluded that "[t]he [Nintendo] works' published nature supports the fairness of the use." *Galoob*, 780 F.Supp. at 1293. Nintendo argues that it has not published the derivative works created by the Game Genie. This argument ignores the plain language of section 107: "the factors to be considered shall include ... the nature of the copyrighted work." The argument also would make the fair use defense unavailable in all cases of derivative works, including "criticism, comment, news reporting, teaching ..., scholarship, or research." 17 U.S.C. § 107. A commentary that incorporated large portions of For Whom the Bell Tolls, for example, would be undeserving of fair use protection because the incorporated portions would constitute an unpublished derivative work. This cannot be the law.

The district court further concluded that the amount of the portion used in relation to the copyrighted work as a whole "cannot assist Nintendo in overcoming the presumption of fair use." *Galoob*, 780 F.Supp. at 1293. The video tape recorders at issue in *Sony* allowed consumers to tape copyrighted works in their entirety. The Supreme Court nevertheless held that, "when one considers ... that [video tape recording] merely enables a viewer to see such a work which he had been invited to witness in its entirety free of charge, the fact that the entire work is reproduced does not have its ordinary effect of militating against a finding of fair use." 464 U.S. at 449-50 (citations omitted). Consumers are not invited to witness Nintendo's audiovisual displays free of charge, but, once they have paid to do so, the fact that the derivative works created by the Game Genie are comprised almost entirely of Nintendo's copyrighted displays does not militate against a finding of fair use.

Nintendo would distinguish *Sony* because it involved copying copyrighted works rather than creating derivative works based on those works. In other words, the consumers in *Sony* could lawfully copy the copyrighted works because they were invited to view those works free of charge. Game Genie users, in contrast, are not invited to view derivative works based on Nintendo's copyrighted works without first paying for that privilege. *Sony* cannot be read so narrowly. It is difficult to imagine that the Court would have reached a different conclusion if Betamax purchasers were skipping portions of copyrighted works or viewing denouements before climaxes. *Sony* recognizes that a party who distributes a copyrighted work cannot dictate how that work is to be enjoyed. Consumers may use a Betamax to view copyrighted works at a more convenient time. They similarly may use a Game Genie to enhance a Nintendo Game cartridge's audiovisual display in such a way as to make the experience more enjoyable.

"The fourth factor is the 'most important, and indeed, central fair use factor.' " *Stewart*, 495 U.S. at 238 (quoting 3 Nimmer on Copyright § 13.05[A], at 13-81). The district court concluded that "Nintendo has failed to show any harm to the present market for its copyrighted games and has failed to establish the reasonable likelihood of a potential market for slightly altered versions of the games at suit." *Galoob*, 780 F.Supp. at 1295.

Nintendo's main argument on appeal is that the test for market harm encompasses the potential market for derivative works. Because the Game Genie is used for a noncommercial purpose, the likelihood of future harm may not be presumed. *See Sony*, 464 U.S. at 451. Nintendo must show "by a preponderance of the evidence that *some* meaningful likelihood of future harm exists." *Id.* (emphasis supplied).

Nintendo's argument is supported by case law. Although the Copyright Act requires a court to consider "the effect of the use upon the potential market for or value of the *copyrighted work*," 17 U.S.C. § 107(4) (emphasis added), we held in *Abend* that "[a]lthough the motion picture will have no adverse effect on bookstore sales of the [underlying] novel--and may in fact have a beneficial effect--it is 'clear that [the film's producer] may not invoke the defense of fair use.' " 863 F.2d at 1482 (quoting 3 Nimmer on Copyright § 13.05[B], at 13-84). We explained: " 'If the defendant's work adversely affects the value of any of the rights in the copyrighted work ... the use is not fair even if the rights thus affected have not as yet been exercised by the plaintiff.'" *Id.* (quoting 3 Nimmer on Copyright § 13.05[B], at 13-84 to 13-85 (footnotes omitted)). The Supreme Court specifically affirmed our finding that the motion picture adaptation "impinged on the ability to market new versions of the story." *Stewart*, 495 U.S. at 238.

Still, Nintendo's argument is undermined by the facts. The district court considered the potential market for derivative works based on Nintendo game cartridges and found that: (1) "Nintendo has not, to date, issued or considered issuing altered versions of existing games," *Galoob*, 780 F.Supp. at 1295, and (2) Nintendo "has failed to show the reasonable likelihood of such a market." Id. The record supports the court' findings. According to Stephen Beck, Galoob's expert witness, junior or expert versions of existing Nintendo games would enjoy very little market interest because the original version of each game already has been designed to appeal to the largest number of consumers. Mr. Beck also testified that a new game must include new material or "the game player is going to feel very cheated and robbed, and [the] product will have a bad reputation and word of mouth will probably kill its sales." Howard Lincoln, Senior Vice President of Nintendo of America, acknowledged that Nintendo has no present plans to market such games.

The district court also noted that Nintendo' assertion that it may wish to re-release altered versions of its game cartridges is contradicted by its position in various other lawsuits:

> In those actions, Nintendo opposes antitrust claims by using the vagaries of the video game industry to rebut the impact and permanence of its market control, if any. Having indoctrinated this Court as to the fast pace and instability of the video

> game industry, Nintendo may not now, without any data, redefine that market in its request for the extraordinary remedy sought herein.... While board games may never die, good video games are mortal.

Galoob, 780 F.Supp. at 1295. The existence of this potential market cannot be presumed. *See Sony*, 464 U.S. at 451. *See also Wright v. Warner Books, Inc.*, 953 F.2d 731, 739 (2d Cir.1991) (affirming district court's finding of no reasonable likelihood of injury to alleged market because "[p]laintiff has offered no evidence that the project will go forward"). The fourth and most important fair use factor also favors Galoob.

Nintendo's most persuasive argument is that the creative nature of its audiovisual displays weighs against a finding of fair use. The Supreme Court has acknowledged that "fair use is more likely to be found in factual works than fictional works." *Stewart*, 495 U.S. at 237. This consideration weighs against a finding of fair use, but it is not dispositive. *See Sony*, 464 U.S. at 448 (fair use defense is an "equitable rule of reason"). The district court could properly conclude that Game Genie users are making a fair use of Nintendo's displays.

3. *Temporary and permanent injunction*

Galoob has not violated the Copyright Act. Nintendo therefore is not entitled to a temporary or permanent injunction.

AFFIRMED.

RYMER, Circuit Judge, concurring in the judgment:

I concur in the judgment for reasons stated by the district court, *Lewis Galoob Toys, Inc. v. Nintendo of America, Inc.*, 780 F.Supp. 1283 (N.D.Cal.1991).

— — —

The issue in the *Micro Star* appeal that we will be considering is, as phrased by the district court, whether "Micro Star violated [FormGen's] alleged right to distribute derivative works" in the copyrighted game. Relying on *Galoob*, the district court found that "that Micro Star has shown that the audiovisual elements which appear on the screen while playing Nuke It originate from Duke 3D, and not from Nuke It," and that, accordingly, FormGen did not have "a valid copyright in the data sequence contained in the Nuke It MAP files."

Against this background, we are now ready to see how the parties handled the appeal. As I already mentioned, I'm going to limit our analysis to one issue: whether Micro Star should be stopped from selling its compilation of the game levels or scenarios posted on the internet by fans of the "Duke Nukem 3D" computer game. Thus, for our purposes, we will be treating FormGen's cross-appeal as the appeal. We therefore start with the presentation and argument of this issue in FormGen's cross-appeal brief in-chief.

Before we look at the briefs, however, let's analyze the issue from the appellate court's standpoint. This is something you must always do before you even start your research; you want to be able to see the forest of public policy before you get bogged down in the branches and leaves of the applicable law. As we've pointed out before, the applicable law in most appeals can support either side. This is clear by not only the plethora of reported decisions—you can find a case that stands for almost any proposition—but also that: 1) reversals mean that reasonable judges view the law differently; 2) split appellate decisions mean that reasonable judges view the law differently. So you must start with the public policy considerations that will drive the judge to want to decide in your favor. As an advocate, you have to recognize what they are, and how the judges before whom you appear will analyze those considerations.

Strategy:

☞ *Evaluate* the *competing* public-policy arguments.

As in most cases that end up on appeal, there are public-policy considerations in our computer case that support both sides of the argument.

Here there are two:

First, and this favors FormGen's appeal, society has a strong interest to both reward and protect creativity. Few would devote their energies and talents in an attempt to create something useful or entertaining unless there was some mechanism to prevent others from appropriating the fruits, just as few farmers would plant and nurture a crop if that crop could be later stolen by interlopers. This interest is reified in our copyright and patent laws, and judges will generally be sympathetic to an argument that "Gee, I created this. I'm the one who should benefit."

Second, and this favors Micro Star's defense of the district court's ruling, society also recognizes that while protection of intellectual property is important, it is also important to confine narrowly the exclusive rights to that property. As *Ecclesiastes* tells us, "there is no new thing under the sun"—almost every intellectual creation builds on what has gone before. Indeed, one-thousand years before Homer, an Egyptian scribe chiseled the following lament about the rarity of the truly original: "Would I have phrases that are not known; utterances that are strange in new language that has not been used, free from repetition, not an utterance which has grown stale, which men of old have spoken."[29] Being overly protective of intellectual property stifles, not encourages, creativity.

Thus, if we are arguing that Micro Star unfairly appropriated FormGen's property, and that the district court should be reversed, we want to focus on the need to protect the fruits of intellectual property. If, on the other hand, we want the appellate court to affirm, we will argue that the district court gave to FormGen all the protection it needs, and that FormGen itself recognized the utility to not only the public but also to itself by building into "Duke Nukem 3D" the tools with which others could create new game levels. Indeed, we will point out that FormGen encouraged its customers to create new game levels and that FormGen not only invited them to share those new levels with friends but also to post them on the internet where anyone in the world could download them. All Micro Star did, we will argue, was to take what was freely available on the internet and make it easy for Duke Nukem fans to play the new levels without having to endure the delays of downloading each new level.

Strategy:

> ☞ *Use* the public-policy arguments *to win*.
>
> This is the kind of analysis you must do in every case. It will help you with your research—to plug into your analysis supporting authority. I cannot over-emphasize this. It is important that you distill your case to the essence of the *policy arguments* underlying both your client's position and the position of the opponent. Only then will you be able to forcefully and persuasively marshall the authority to convince the judges both that you *should win* and *that the law allows you to win.*

---

[29] Quoted in James Gleick, *Genius: The Life and Science of Richard Feynman.*

Let's see whether the parties have done this, and, if so, how well. Along the way, we will point out the good and bad elements of each brief, and suggest improvements that will help you improve *your* appellate advocacy. My comments will be in brackets and in **Univers Bold**. The footnotes are the briefs'.

One final note before we begin. Some lawyers who read this book before publication told me that although we are limiting the briefs to essentially one issue, the briefs are too long and should be relegated to an appendix. One lawyer told me that he skimmed through much of the briefs of both parties. I chose this case, however, because although it concerns a pop-culture item, the case is complex with much arcane terminology. We will show how the briefs in even this type of a case can be made clear, concise, and persuasive. If you are tempted to skim through portions of the briefs, imagine how such a brief strikes judges who must read many briefs in a day. When you come upon a part that tempts you to skim, try to figure out why. Also, see how you would make that part more interesting, more to the point, and more persuasive. Then, apply that same critical eye to your own briefs. If you do, it is more likely that *they* will be studied, not skimmed.

[Both briefs submitted to the Ninth Circuit started out with an untitled introductory paragraph. In both briefs, it is the first text to greet the judges. Let's look at each to see how the lawyers used this valuable real estate. FormGen's brief has this confusing jumble:]

> Appellees and Cross-Appellants FormGen. Inc. ("FormGen"), GT Interactive Software Corp. ("GTI"), and Apogee Software, Ltd. d/b/a 3D Realms Entertainment ("Apogee") (collectively, "Movants") appeal from the partial denial of their motion for a preliminary injunction in the Second Amended Order Granting in Part and Denying in Part Preliminary Injunction (the "Preliminary Injunction") issued on September 30, 1996 by the U.S. District Court for the Southern District of California (Huff, J.). This Brief also addresses issues raised by Appellant and CrossAppellee Micro Star in its appeal from the relief granted in the Preliminary Injunction.

[First, do the parentheticals add anything to—or, on the other hand, do they subtract from—the clarity of what should be a

simple statement of the procedural status of the case? Second, can this paragraph be made more clear? Let's try:

> **FormGen and the other defendants before the district court appeal from the district court's denial of their motion to enjoin Micro Star, the plaintiff before the district court, from selling computer-game add-ons that FormGen contends infringes on its computer game "Duke Nukem 3D." Micro Star, which also has appealed from aspects of the district court's order, filed its notice of appeal first. Accordingly, FormGen's appeal is a cross-appeal.**
>
> **The chronology of this case is as follows:**
>
> **[at this point, the brief can set out in tabular form, as suggested on page 60 of this book, the chronology of when the summons and complaint were filed, etc.**

Micro Star's introduction is not much better:]

> Appellant and Cross-Appellee Micro Star hereby submits the following Answering and Reply Brief to address issues raised by appellees and cross-appellants FormGen, Inc., ("FormGen"), GT Interactive Software Corp. ("GTI") and Apogee Software, Ltd. ("Apogee")* in their cross-appeal of the partial denial of their motion for a preliminary injunction as set forth in the district court's Second Amended Order Granting in Part and Denying in Part Preliminary Injunction. In addition, this Brief also addresses issues raised by Apogee in its Answering Brief to Micro Star's appeal from the limited injunction granted by the district court.

[The footnote, which, in the original, is a number, reads: "GT Interactive Software Corp., Apogee and Formgen are collectively referred to as 'Apogee' unless a particular discussion requires more specificity." **Huh? What does that mean? The confusion just added another layer. First, FormGen's brief is referring to its group (itself, GT Interactive Software Corp., and Apogee Software, Ltd.) as the "Movants." Now, Micro Star's brief is referring to them as "Apogee," except when it does not. Again, this introduction can be made much simpler, and can begin the task of persuasion without being obnoxious (and improper):**

> **Micro Star submits this brief in reply to FormGen's brief in support of FormGen's cross-appeal—from the district court's denial of FormGen's motion to stop Micro Star from selling Micro Star's compilation of material it lawfully downloaded from the internet. The district court held that Micro Star's compilation did not violate FormGen's copyright.**

Note that I am identifying the parties in a multi-party lawsuit by the way they appear in the caption to the case. The judges see the caption on the covers of the briefs. This case is: *Micro Star versus FormGen.* Why refer to the parties, and to those united in interest with them on the appeal, by any other name? "Apogee" when the caption has FormGen's name first? That doesn't make any sense and is confusing.

Now let's see how each of the briefs phrases the crucial "questions presented." First, FormGen's appellant's brief:]

1) Whether the District Court erred in holding that the reproduction and distribution by sale of user-created levels for a copyrighted computer game that generate an audiovisual display of the game's protected expression do not infringe the copyright in that expression.

2) Whether the District Court erred in failing to recognize, based on undisputed evidence in the record, that the unique structure of the computer files containing the user-created levels constituted independently protected expression infringed by the reproduction and distribution by sale of copies of such files.

[Are these "questions presented" persuasive? Are they clear? Do they start the appellate judge along the road to deciding in favor of the party that submitted them? These are questions that *you* must ask yourself as you frame these critical elements of your brief. If the answer to any of these questions is "no," your questions are not good enough. And remember, when the appellate judge reads these questions, he or she will know very little about the facts of your case. Let's try our hand at these questions from FormGen's point of view:

> **FormGen sells a copyrighted computer game called "Duke Nukem 3D." The object of this game is for the player to advance from lower levels to higher levels—much like climbing the stairs of a skyscraper. A player climbs a level if he or she is able to destroy various creatures that want to block the player from advancing to a higher level.**
>
> **The "Duke Nukem 3D" game comes with twenty-nine levels already built-in. It also comes with a program that permits players to construct additional levels on their own, and encourages them to circulate these levels to other players as long they do so without charge. Micro Star has collected 300 of these levels posted on the internet by "Duke Nukem 3D" players, put them on a CD, and is selling them.**
>
> **The Micro Star CD cannot be used without the "Duke Nukem 3D" game. Micro Star concedes this. FormGen asked the district court to stop Micro Star from selling the CD, contending that the CD infringes FormGen's copyright in the "Duke Nukem 3D" game. The district court denied FormGen's motion.**
>
> **The question presented by FormGen's appeal is whether Micro Star's sale of the CD containing three-hundred levels of "Duke Nukem 3D" play, all constructed by "Duke Nukem 3D" gamers using the copyrighted software that comes with every "Duke Nukem 3D" game, violates FormGen's copyright in the "Duke Nukem 3D" game, when, admittedly, the Micro Star CD cannot be used without the "Duke nukem 3D" game, and uses and displays the game's copyrighted images, sounds, and computer codes in order to work.**

Long? Yes. Most cases will not need this detailed an explanation before the "question presented" makes any sense. In my view, however, this case does. If you were a judge picking up these briefs for the first time without having even read, as of yet, the district court's opinion, which "questions presented" would you find most helpful to your quick understanding of the issue?

Which formulation would tend to get you rowing in favor of FormGen's position?

Now let's look at Micro Star's questions presented in reply:]

1. Whether the District Court abused its discretion or made a clearly erroneous finding of fact that the data files contained on the *Nuke It* CD did not contain any copyrighted audiovisual elements of *Duke Nukem* 3D.

2. Whether the District Court's finding of fact that the functional structure of the user-created add-on levels for *Duke Nukem 3D* were not protected by any *Duke Nukem 3D* copyright is clearly erroneous.

[The first thing that strikes the seasoned appellate judge is that Micro Star may be misstating the applicable standard of review. Although the decision to grant or to deny a preliminary injunction lies within the reasoned discretion of the district court, *Hiller Cranberry Products, Inc. v. Koplovsky*, 165 F.3d 1, 4 (1st Cir.1999), the exercise of that discretion must be based on a correct view of the law, which the appellate court decides *de novo*, *Ocean Spray Cranberries, Inc. v. PepsiCo, Inc.*, 160 F.3d 58, 61 n.1 (1st Cir. 1998). This is the law in the Ninth Circuit as well. *Gorbach v. Reno*. 179 F.3d 1111, 1118 (9th Cir. 1999). Neither of the questions presented by Micro Star seems to recognize the distinctions between the trial court's findings of fact, which are invulnerable on appeal unless "clearly erroneous," *Gorbach*, 179 F.3d at 1118, the underlying legal premises, which are reviewed *de novo*, *ibid.*, and, if the district court's findings and legal analysis pass appellate-review muster, it's ultimate decision as to whether a preliminary injunction is appropriate, which *is* vested in its discretion, *ibid*.

When defending on appeal a ruling by the trial court, you must first look at the trial court's decision to see how you can best frame the question so as to be both fair and persuasive. In the *Micro Star* case, the district court's discussion of the issue presented by FormGen's appeal was quite brief. Indeed, the following is its entire analysis, which I reproduce here for your convenience:]

Movants claim that they have a valid copyright in the Duke 3D game and its elements that extends to derivative works created by others. Micro Star responds that there has been no infringement of any rights granted by the copyright act, that Nuke It is permissible under the "fair use" doctrine, and that even if these two arguments fail, movants have waived or abandoned their rights to limit the creation and distribution of MAP files. Micro Star additionally alleges that LICENSE.DOC is not a valid licensing agreement.

To establish copyright infringement, movants must demonstrate (1) that they own a valid copyright; and (2) that Micro Star violated their alleged right to distribute derivative works. *Feist Publications Inc. v. Rural Telephone Service Co.*, 499 U.S. 340, 361-63 (1991).

1. Infringement of Rights Granted By Copyright Act

In *Lewis Galoob Toys, Inc. v. Nintendo of America, Inc.*, 964 F.2d 965 (9th Cir.1992), *cert. denied* 507 U.S. 985 (1993), the Galoob company sold the "Game Genie" which was designed to use Nintendo's console to control Nintendo's games. Inserted between a game cartridge and the Nintendo system, the Game Genie allowed a player to alter up to three features of the Nintendo game, such as increasing the number of lives, increasing the character's speed, or giving the character more strength. As such the Game Genie did not alter data that was stored in Nintendo's game cartridges, but the changes would be displayed on the TV screen for the duration of the game. *Id.* at 967.

The court held that the Game Genie did not create a derivative work, as it only enhanced the audiovisual displays originating in the Nintendo cartridge. The court justified its holding by stating that a derivative work must "incorporate a protected work in some concrete or permanent form ... we cannot ignore the actual source of the Game Genie's display." *Id.* at 969.

Micro Star argues that Nuke It is really just a more sophisticated Game Genie. Micro Star points out that like the Game Genie, Nuke It does not supplant the demand for Duke 3D, as Nuke It is useless unless used with Duke 3D. Micro Star also argues that all of the copyrightable elements of Duke 3D observed on the screen while playing Nuke It are contained on the Duke 3D program files, and that

> the data on the MAP files contained on Nuke It is generic data and not programming.
>
> *As to the Nuke It CD-ROM itself, and the programming it contains, the court is not convinced that the movants have shown that the data sequence in the Nuke It MAP files is subject to copyright protection. Furthermore, the court finds that Micro Star has shown that the audiovisual elements which appear on the screen while playing Nuke It originate from Duke 3D, and not from Nuke It.* Therefore, the court finds that movants have not shown a valid copyright in the data sequence contained in the Nuke It MAP files, and consequently denies the injunctive relief requested as to the Nuke It CD-ROM itself.

(Emphasis added.) The crux of the district court's decision is in the next-to-the-last two sentences, which I have italicized for your convenience. In my view, the most sustainable of the two is the second sentence, the elements of which can fairly be characterized as findings of fact; moreover, that the images and pictures that appear on the computer screen when someone uses the Micro Star CD to play the "Duke Nukem 3D" game originate from "Duke Nukem 3D" and not Micro Star's CD is not disputed. This is a good place to begin framing the question presented.

> **The "Duke Nukem 3D" computer game encourages, and provides the requisite software for, players to build additional levels of computer-game play. FormGen also encourages the gamers to share these new levels with the world at large, with out charge and without having to pay any fee to FormGen.**
>
> **"Duke Nukem 3D" gamers have created many additional levels for the game, and many have posted those levels on the internet, where they are available free-of-charge by anyone who wants to download them on to their own computers. Micro Star has selected three-hundred of these new levels, lawfully downloaded them from the internet, and has collected them on an easy-to-use, *virus-free* CD disk. It sells the disk, both to recoup its costs in collecting and checking for viruses, which can be endemic on parts of the internet, the three-hundred levels and to make a profit.**

This court has held previously in *Lewis Galoob Toys, Inc. v. Nintendo of America, Inc.*, 964 F.2d 965 (9th Cir.1992), *cert. denied* 507 U.S. 985, that temporary add-on effects to a computer-game system that do not alter the data of the underlying copyrighted game do not infringe the copyright in that game. *Id.*, 964 F.2d at 967. The district court here found as a fact that the sound and pictures that appear on the computer screen when someone plays "Duke Nukem 3D" with any of the three-hundred levels on Micro Star's CD "originate from Duke 3D" and not the Micro Star CD. We do not understand FormGen to dispute this finding of fact. Moreover, it is also undisputed that use of the Micro Star CD does not alter either the data or any of the underlying computer code of the "Duke Nukem 3D" game.

In light of the district court's findings of fact, the facts that are undisputed, and the law of this circuit as expressed in *Lewis Galoob Toys*, was the district court correct in concluding that the Micro Star CD did not infringe on the "Duke Nukem 3D" game?

You decide which is the better presentation to an appellate judge coming to your brief cold. As I mentioned, although generally judges will read the briefs in sequence, many judges, especially in complex cases, will read the various elements of the briefs (including the appellant's reply brief) in tandem: the questions presented from each brief; the statement of facts from each brief; and the argument section from each brief. This gives us a better overview of the case, and, at the very least, prevents us from reaching a tentative conclusion based on either a deliberate or inadvertent misrepresentation by one of the parties.

Now let's look at the briefs' statements of facts. First FormGen's statements of facts. All bolding, underlining, and other emphasis is by FormGen as are the footnotes.

STATEMENT OF THE CASE

This appeal presents a question of paramount importance to Movants in particular and to the owners of the copyrights in computer games generally: Whether the owner of the copyright in a game that, as a feature of the game, allows users to create additional levels of play for *non-commercial* use will be permitted to exercise the exclusive rights granted authors under § 106 of the Copyright Act, 17 U.S.C. § 101 *et seq.* Unreasonably construing this Court's decision in *Lewis Galoob Toys, Inc. v. Nintendo of Am., Inc., 964* F.2d *965* (9th Cir. 1992), *cert. denied, 507* U.S. *985* (1993), way beyond the rationale suggested by its own facts, the court below held that a competitor -- such as Micro Star -- may simply download from the Internet hundreds of user-created levels of play for Movants' best selling computer game, Duke Nukem 3D ("DN3D"), and sell that compilation at retail, even though it is not disputed that when used by the consumer Micro Star's product, Nuke It, displays the characters, artwork, sounds, and other audiovisual content constituting the protected expression of DN3D. Citing *Galoob,* the lower court based its ruling on the conceded fact that the user-created levels on Nuke It cause certain of the protected expression of DN3D to be displayed by pulling material from an "image library" in DN3D. Nothing in *Galoob* compelled leaping from that technical fact to a result that, at once, defies common sense and eviscerates copyright protection for computer games.

[The statement of the case is supposed to relate the procedural history of the case leading up to the appeal as well as a statement of the relevant facts necessary to an understanding of the appeal. It is not supposed to be overtly argumentative; rather, it should, at best, present the facts in their most persuasive way. This statement is argumentative and will, as a result, rub most appellate judges the wrong way. Indeed, as we have seen, the Handbook published by the United States Court of Appeals for the Seventh Circuit specifically warns counsel that the statement of facts "must be a fair summary without argument or comment."]

A popular feature of computer games is a program -- called, in this case, the Build Editor -- that enables a consumer to create and to share through the Internet additional levels of play. Levels are self-contained scenarios or environments in which a computer game is played, analogous to chapters in a novel or installments in a serial. The creators of DN3D included the Build Editor intending -- as the District Court found for purposes of the Preliminary Injunction -- to permit only noncommercial use of new levels by consumers and to preserve for Movants themselves all commercial exploitation.

Nonetheless, the lower court's ruling has effectively stripped Movants of their rights over the reproduction and distribution by sale of their protected expression, which will irreparably damage the Duke Nukem franchise.

[Again, this is overtly argumentative. This type of rhetoric has to be earned by facts, and, moreover it does not belong in this part of the brief.]

In granting in part the Preliminary Injunction, the District Court properly concluded that all copies of Nuke It then available at retail infringed the DN3D copyright -- requiring an injunction against further sales and a recall of all units in distribution. The court so ruled because Nuke It's packaging contained numerous scenes from user levels ("screen shots") that included the characters and artwork of DN3D and because the original version of the Nuke It CD, still available at some retail outlets, included "screen savers" comprised of such scenes. Memorandum Order at 8 (E.R. 1070).[1] The District Court found that the undisputed commercial use of DN3D's protected expression was not a fair use and that the use of this protected expression to compete with authorized DN3D products would cause irreparable injury to Movants. (E.R. 1071-72.) All of these rulings were plainly correct.

[This relates to that portion of the district court's decision about which we are not directly concerned. FormGen is the appellee on those issues and had filed a separate brief defending the district court's rulings. It mentions those matters again here because it wants to persuade the appellate court that Micro Star is doing something improper, hoping that the infringements found by the district court in connection with those other matters will bleed over to the issue where the district court found no infringement. Again, however, this is too overtly argumentative for this part of the brief.]

However, because of its erroneous belief that *Galoob* compelled a finding that the user-created levels did not embody protected expression, the court declined to enjoin Micro Star from releasing

---

[1] "E.R." citations through p. 1089 refer to Appellant Micro Star's Excerpts of the Record, Vols. I-IV. Cross-Appellants' Supplemental Excerpts of the Record, submitted herewith, are cited as "S.E.R." and are numbered starting at p. 1090.

products similar to Nuke It containing only such levels with all screen savers and screen shots deleted. At the time of the ruling, Micro Star was, in fact, readying such a product, "Nuke It 1000," for October 1996 release.

Micro Star's continued unauthorized commercial exploitation of user-created levels will substantially undermine the market for authorized DN3D add-on products and sequels, thereby impeding Movants' right under § 106 of the Copyright Act to commercial exploitation of their copyright. Because of the District Court's ruling, consumers in the critical holiday season will have before them *authorized* user-created and professionally created level packs from licensees of Apogee matched against the *unauthorized, unlicensed* (and inferior) level packs from Micro Star. Each product to be offered at retail generates additional levels of play containing DN3D protected expression. Unless the provisions and purposes of the Copyright Act are ignored, Movants are entitled to injunctive relief against Micro Star's infringing products.

[Again, this is too overtly argumentative for this part of the brief, and it will rub many appellate judges the wrong way.]

<u>The Facts</u>

A. <u>The Parties</u>

Apogee owns the copyright in DN3D. (E.R. 386: 721-23: 748-49.) FormGen, a subsidiary of GTI, has the exclusive worldwide right to distribute the personal computer version of DN3D, as well as "screen savers" (that is, images used on a video monitor when an application program is not in active use to prevent burn-in) with Duke Nukem motifs, and the right to distribute add-on levels created by Apogee. (E.R. 386-87; 558-59.) Another GTI subsidiary, Wizardware Group, Inc. d/b/a Wizardworks ("Wizardworks"), has been licensed to distribute *authorized* user-created level packs (that is, the type of game that Micro Star has put out without a license). *Id.* GTI itself has the exclusive worldwide right to distribute the dedicated console and video arcade versions of DN3D; it also has been licensed to distribute the next Duke Nukem game, "Duke Nukem Forever," for all media. Rubin Reply Decl. ¶ 3 (E.R. 559). Collectively, GTI and its subsidiaries therefore hold by license what may be termed the "Duke Nukem franchise" -- the rights to commercial exploitation of all Duke Nukem products, subject to the licenses with Apogee.[2]

[This is the mind-numbing stuff, and, worse, it is essentially irrelevant to the appellate issues. Unless there is a dispute about whether one or more of the parties to the appeal have standing, just summarize this material. For example, why not just say: "FormGen, a subsidiary of GT Interactive Software Corp., has the exclusive world rights to distribute the PC version of the 'Duke Nukem 3D' game as well as additional game levels developed by the creator of the 'Duke Nukem 3D' game. Wizardworks, another subsidiary of GT Interactive Software, is licensed by the 'Duke Nukem 3D' owner to sell compilations of levels created by 'Duke Nukem 3D' gamers."]

Micro Star is the distributor of Nuke It. It has elected to proceed with the sale of Nuke It despite having been denied a license and despite receipt of cease and desist letters. (E.R. 577-581.) In assessing Micro Star's conduct, the lower court observed that Micro Star "ran a risk" and "got caught," warranting the imposition on Micro Star of the expense of recalling and correcting its first Nuke It product. (E.R. 932.)

[The district court's "got caught" comment applies to those matters (the screensavers and the package art-work) where the district court sided with FormGen. It is somewhat misleading to interject that comment here, because it implies that the district court was referring to the issue that is the subject of FormGen's cross-appeal, namely whether Micro Star should be allowed to sell its CD compilation of gamer-created levels.]

B. Movants' Copyrighted Game

DN3D consists of three episodes including 29 levels set in a futuristic Los Angeles overtaken by sinister space aliens. The game permits a player to explore this environment, as well as an alien space station, through the eyes of the heavily armed Duke Nukem, who confronts and destroys various types of aliens appearing in different

---

[2] For simplicity, this Brief refers collectively to the rights owned by all Cross-Appellants.

settings -- including towering skyscrapers, deep canyons, and eerie abandoned buildings. (E.R. 55.) All of the artwork for the characters and settings was created by DN3D's designers. The game contains extremely sophisticated graphics and sound effects and is distinguished by a realistic 3-D look in which a player has full mobility within a detailed and lifelike environment. Rubin Decl. ¶ 6 (E.R. 388). DN3D received rave reviews from computer publications for its realistic graphics, sound effects, and overall creativity. It is the best selling computer game of the year, already having sales at retail in excess of 500,000 units. Miller Decl. ¶ 4 (E.R. 18).

[This would be a good place too use the -paraphrase-and-then-quote technique. Let's see a few sentences from the reviews. Perhaps even describe some of the action.]

Numerous unique expressive features are covered by DN3D's copyright, starting with Duke himself and several other visually distinct characters, including Assault Trooper, Octabrain, Protozoid Shiner, Assault Captain, Sentry Drone, and Enforcer. Each of these characters has a distinct physical appearance and history. Blum Reply Decl. ¶¶ 6-7 & Blum Decl. Exh. 2 (E.R. 585-86, 27-31). DN3D's protected expression also includes the unique design of buildings and other physical structures; decorative details including posters and billboards; and various props, including the Medkits, armor, jetpack. and scuba gear used by Duke. Blum Reply Decl. ¶ 6 (E.R. 585-86). The game play is accompanied by action movie style dialogue, heart-pounding music, and dramatic sound effects. The totality of these elements is a unique and distinct product with its own look.

Players who become expert at the game can progress through all of its 29 levels one at a time. The game includes a Build Editor that enables players to create new levels by, in effect, cutting and pasting audiovisual elements from existing levels to create new environments with different combinations of architecture, decoration, and threatening aliens. These new levels, comprised largely if not totally of elements of DN3D's protected expression, are substantially similar to the levels contained in the underlying game and therefore are derivative works under the Copyright Act. Blum Decl. ¶9113-18 (E.R. 58-59); Blum Reply Decl. ¶91 6-13 (E.R. 585-87).

[Quote from the Blum Declaration, which describes the levels and their degree of originality.]

Each of the new levels created for DN3D is stored in a computer data file known as a "MAP file." (E.R. 57.) The MAP files are fixed, permanent computer files that may be stored on a computer's hard drive, copied onto disks, and uploaded onto, or downloaded from, the Internet. (E.R. 882-87.) While Micro Star dismissively describes these MAP files as constituting "mere[] data files" (Micro Star Br. 8), those files embody the protected expression of DN3D in two basic ways.

First, the MAP files include instructions that determine the layout of the level, the selection and placement of characters and architectural elements within the level, and other variables contributing to the look, feel, and narrative flow of the level. Blum Reply Decl. 9116 (E.R. 587). For example. the MAP file determines the specific building interiors or street scenes in which Duke Nukem maneuvers in a particular level and which aliens Duke encounters at which points in that environment. The MAP file interacts with the DN3D game engine to produce the display of DN3D's distinct audiovisual elements. *Id.* Each MAP file thus gives the DN3D player access to a new, self-contained environment in which to play the game. In Micro Star's words, "[e]ach level is a new book with the same character." (E.R. 825.)

[Quote from an example in the record. Show *how* the MAP file does what it does. This is one of the foci—remember, the district court held that the "data sequence" in the MAP files was "subject to copyright protection." Show that they have significant expressive elements. Touch all the bases: first, second, third, and home, and do it sequentially. Take the judges through it sequentially. Remember, they may not be familiar with the arcane world of either computers or computer games. Do not, in A.E. Houseman's line from *The Shropshire Lad,* give them a "brook too broad for leaping." If you do, you're the only one who is in danger of getting wet.]

Second, the MAP files are organized according to a unique and distinctive file structure that also constitutes protected expression entirely apart from the audiovisual displays that the files generate. The unique, creative organization of a computer file is a "non-literal" element of computer software that is independently subject to copyright protection. As explained in detail by Apogee designer Allen H. Blum III (E.R. 54-60, 584-94), the DN3D MAP file structure was created by Apogee's designers and reflects innumerable creative choices embodying the programmer's art rather than the dictates of industry standards or hardware requirements.

[This has to be expanded upon. Take the judges through this step by step, so they can *see* that the MAP files "constitute[] protected expression" and that this "protected expression" is "entirely apart from" the image and sounds that the MAP files display. This paragraph is "rhetoric"—you've got to "show" not "say"!

***Strategy*:**

> ☞ **Paraphrasing = "rhetoric"; Quoting = "proof"]**

As the District Court correctly concluded (S.E.R. 1222-23), Movants have indicated their unequivocal intention to retain all rights to commercial exploitation of DN3D. The DN3D box and printed insert expressly reserve all copyright and trademark rights. (E.R. 62, 64, 75.) In addition, a limited, non-exclusive license comes with the DN3D software package (the "User License") and is referenced on the screen every time a player accesses the Build Editor. (E.R. 19.) In relevant part, the User License requires new levels to be identified with their creators and to indicate that "THIS LEVEL IS NOT MADE BY OR SUPPORTED BY 3D REALMS"; requires that *"the level and any use of it must be offered solely for free* (other than any incidental on-line charges)" (emphasis added); provides that by distributing or permitting the distribution of any new level, its creators "grant back to 3D Realms an irrevocable royalty free right to distribute the level"; and expressly reserves all other rights for Movants. Miller Decl. ¶ 7-9 & Exh. 1 (E.R. 19, 24-25).

[Exercise: Re-write the above paragraph. Here is a start:

> **"The district court found as a fact that .... It wrote '[quote].' This finding is not clearly erroneous for the following reasons ..." etc.**

(continue on your own sheet)

Strategy:

☞ **If you seek to have an appellate court affirm a trial court, be careful not to label a finding of fact as a "conclusion" or even the generic "determination." Findings of fact are given incredible deference by an appellate court—inadvertent mislabeling might weaken the strength of that deference.]**

Movants imposed the restrictions of the User License to prevent the commercial distribution of levels over which they cannot assert quality control as well as to retain solely for themselves the commercial value of exploiting DN3D's popularity through the licensing and marketing of authorized collections of levels, or level packs. (E.R. 19.) Wizardworks has released "Duke! Zone," an authorized pack of user created levels. (E.R. 558-59.) FormGen has developed an add-on game comprised of three new episodes and 10 to 12 newly created levels for DN3D. Rubin Reply Decl. 9110 (E.R. 562).

C. The Infringing Product

Nuke It was introduced by Micro Star in July 1996. Micro Star has consistently admitted that it contributed no original expression for its product; it simply downloaded 300 user-created levels from the Internet, put them on a CD-ROM, and distributed that disk for sale. Moore Decl. ¶ 7-8 (E.R. 414-15). Micro Star's counsel conceded at oral argument below that, without DN3D, Nuke It is a "worthless" product. (E.R. 1000.) Most of the levels included in Nuke It are of amateurish quality. Blum Decl. 9113 (E.R. 57)[3]

---

[3] Micro Star now suggests (Br. 7) that marketing this type of knock-off product is common and accepted. The record reflects, however, the falsity of that argument and shows, *inter alia,* that distribution of a similar product was enjoined by the District Court for the Northern District of California in an unpublished decision and that yet another unauthorized compilation of user-created levels for DN3D was withdrawn in the face of a cease and desist letter (sent at the same time as similar letters to Micro Star). *See* Rubin Reply Decl. ¶¶ 4-6 (E.R. 559-60).

[The brief to which this footnote refers is Micro Star's brief on its appeal.]

[Quote!]

When Nuke It is played according to its instructions, the consumer displays the protected expression of DN3D. Blum Reply Decl. 91 7-13 (E.R. *586).* This is confirmed by the original packaging for Nuke It. Broussard Suppl. Decl. (E.R. 888-92). The box contained some 30 screen shots taken from user levels, and those pictures -- as the District Court found and Micro Star did not contest -- contain characters and artwork lifted from DN3D. (E.R. 839-40.) Nor is there any dispute that the user-created levels on Nuke It are made up of the same elements from DN3D. In its own Emergency Application filed in this Court regarding the recall order (at 5), Micro Star stated that the "screen shots accurately describe the levels that consumers would find *on the Nuke It CD"* (emphasis added).

[Quote after each paraphrase. Show the judges that the record supports your spin.]

For purposes of this appeal, the most pertinent fact is that the user-created levels on Nuke It consist of data structured in a manner designed by Apogee to cause the display of particular DN3D characters at precise locations within defined environments. Blum Reply Decl. ¶ 7-13 (E.R. 586). This method of operation is not disputed. The levels of Nuke It can be played only with DN3D, but when played with DN3D the Nuke It levels -- confirmed by Micro Star's own expert -- draw visuals from the DN3D image library file and determine the placement of those characters and the flow of the narrative. Johnson-Laird Decl. ¶ 15-17 (E.R. 422-23). Whatever the precise technological process by which the screen image is generated, Nuke It gives the consumer access to additional levels with DN3D characters, artwork, and sounds. And that is precisely what

Micro Star is selling: Its packaging proclaimed "OVER 300 NEW LEVELS" for DN3D and -- as noted -- reproduced screen shots showing elements of DN3D. (E.R. 45-49.) Micro Star did not tell consumers what it told the District Court -- that Nuke It consists only of "generic data." (S.E.R. 1143.)[4]

---

[4] In addition to the user-created levels, the original Nuke It disk contained, for use as screen savers, 24 "bit map" files embodying actual screen shots of DN3D game play These bit map files are the equivalent of still photographs taken from a movie. Blum Reply Decl. ¶ 37

(continued)

Micro Star had also begun preparing at the time of the preliminary injunction hearing (for October release) a sequel called "Nuke It 1000" containing additional user-created levels downloaded from the Internet. Rubin Reply Decl. 91 9 (E.R. 561-62).

D. The District Court's Ruling

In the face of cease and desist letters, Micro Star commenced a preemptive declaratory action in the court below seeking a determination that Nuke It did not infringe DN3D's copyright or trademarks. (E.R. 1-12.) The action was filed on August 2. 1996. and the first service of the Summons and Amended Complaint was made on August 5. Four days later, Movants filed counterclaims (E.R. 357-73) alleging copyright and Lanham Act infringements and sought a preliminary injunction (E.R. 13-14; S.E.R. 1090-1114). Under the District Court's local rules, the motion was noticed for September 9 and -- following two continuances sought by Micro Star -- the matter came on to be heard on September 23, as part of the court's motion calendar. After hearing initial argument on September 23 (E.R. 866-81), the court held extended hearings on September 24 (E.R. 760-865) and September 26 (E.R. 989-1063), rendering an oral decision on September 26 (S.E.R. 1205-45) and issuing an initial Order Granting Preliminary Injunction. An amended order, with mechanical corrections, was issued on September 27 together with a Memorandum Order (E.R. 1064-79). Following a further hearing on September 30 (E.R. 918-54), the court issued the Preliminary Injunction (E.R. 906-17).

[This is the procedural material that should be set out in tabular form, under the "statement of the case" part of the brief. This is an example of what I mean:

(continued)
(E.R. 593). Nuke It also contains three additional files (designated "users.com," "defs.com," and "games.com") that are nearly identical copies of files contained in the original DN3D game. These three files are "control files" that are used to customize various elements of DN3D, such as characters, weapons, and other DN3D elements. These three files contain part of the actual source code files for the DN3D game. Blum Reply Decl. ¶ 36 (E.R. 593).

It is not necessary to assess Micro Star's claim (Br. 11 n.8) that "WAD" files for Doom can be converted into MAP files for DN3D, thereby purportedly avoiding infringement of DN3D's copyright, because the record contains no evidence that any of the MAP files compiled and sold on Nuke It originated as Doom files. **[Again, the brief referenced in this footnote is Micro Star's brief on its appeal from the district court's order.]**

Micro Star, having been warned that it was infringing FormGen's copyrights, files a declaratory judgment action in the district court . . . . August 2, 1996

FormGen and the other defendants are served with summons and second amended complaint . . . . August 5, 1996

et cetera.]

The District Court found that Movants had demonstrated a likelihood of success in proving copyright infringement in Micro Star's use of screen savers and screen shots on the CD-ROM and on the packaging.[5] The court further found that there was evidence of irreparable harm (beyond the irreparable harm presumed upon a finding of the likelihood of a copyright infringement); that the balance of equities weighed in favor of Movants: and that the public interest would be served by entry of the Preliminary Injunction. (E.R. 1069-70.) For purposes of entering the Preliminary Injunction, the District Court also found that Movants were the owners of a valid copyright; that this copyright had not been waived or abandoned by permitting consumers to make and distribute user-created levels for non-commercial purposes; and that Micro Star's use of the protected expression in the screen savers and screen shots was not a fair use. (E.R. 1071-74.) The court conditioned the Preliminary Injunction on a $500,000 bond, which was promptly posted. (S.E.R. 1246-51.)

However, the District Court also ruled that, other than the screen savers, the contents of the Nuke It CD did not infringe the DN3D copyright. In its oral decision (S.E.R. 1215-16) and Memorandum

---

[5] Micro Star falsely states (Br. 16 n. 13) that it had deleted screen savers from the Nuke It disk "well before any litigation was contemplated." By July 22, 1996, when Micro Star purports to have issued a version of Nuke It without screen savers (E.R. 415), it had already received a cease and desist letter (E.R. 577-78). Moreover, versions of Nuke It containing screen savers continued to be available for sale even at the time of the preliminary injunction hearing in September. (E.R. 899.) Nor can Micro Star any surprise that its use of the screen shots on Nuke It's packaging might be held to infringe the DN3D copyright. Movants' counterclaims expressly focused on the improper use of the screen shots on the Nuke It disk and, at the hearing on September 24, the District Court made clear that it was focusing as well on the use of protected expression on the packaging and invited supplemental submissions and arguments on that issue for September 26. (E.R. 839-40, 843, 854.) Movants submitted such additional evidence (E.R. 882-97), but Micro Star chose not to do so.

Order, the District Court accepted Micro Star's contention that Nuke It was like the "Game Genie" at issue in *Galoob* because "the audiovisual elements which appear on the screen while playing Nuke It originate from Duke 3D, and not from Nuke It." (E.R. 1069.) Additionally, the lower court was "not convinced that the Movants have shown that the data claim sequence in the Nuke It MAP files is subject to copyright protection." *Id.* It is these parts of the ruling that constitute errors of law and gives rise to Movants' cross-appeal.[6]

[Several things trouble me about this statement of facts. First, as already mentioned, it is argumentative. Statements of facts must be persuasive; they should not, however, be argumentative. Second, it is loaded with static—unnecessary material that distracts from a forceful presentation. Third, the good stuff, the powerful facts that support FormGen's legal arguments, are interspersed helter skelter throughout, without any seeming reason to the order.

If we are to persuade successfully, we must use the tool of "primacy"—what we learn first colors the way we look at what follows; it sets our intellectual or emotional gyroscopes. I've explained the concept at length in *The "How-To-Win" Trial Manual.* Here is another example from history. Following the death of Edward The Confessor, there was a dispute as to who would succeed to the British throne. Apparently, Harold had sworn an oath to accede to William of Normandy's becoming king, but reneged. Winston S. Churchill tells us in his *History of the English Speaking Peoples* how William's forces gained the advantage of "primacy" in the subsequent conflict:

> **"At this very moment, the Almighty, reaching down from His heavenly sphere, made an ambiguous gesture. The tailed comet or 'hairy star' which appeared at the time of Harold's coronation, is now identified by astronomers as Halley's Comet, which had previously heralded the nativity of our Lord: and it is evident that this example of divine economy in the movements for mundane purposes**

---

[6] The District Court did rule that Movants had not shown a likelihood of success on their Lanham Act claims. Because, under the Preliminary Injunction, Nuke It's packaging must be changed due to copyright infringement, Movants do not seek review on appeal of that aspect of the court's decision.

of celestial bodies might have been turned by deft interpretation to Harold's advantage. *But the conquerors have told the tale*, and in their eyes this portent conveyed to men the approaching downfall of a sacrilegious upstart."

(Emphasis added.) [Winston S. Churchill, The Birth of Britian 115-116 (Bantam 1963)] Folks *do* judge books by their covers, people by the first several minutes of that first meeting, and who should win either a trial or an appeal by first impressions, which are hard to overcome.

Thus, in preparing to write your statement of facts, figure out which facts are most helpful to your cause and get them out first. In FormGen's appeal, those facts are:

- Additional levels of the game cannot be created without use of the copyrighted software

- Use of the copyrighted software to create additional levels of the game was specifically conditioned on the non-commercial use of those additional levels

- Micro Star knew this because FormGen repeatedly told Micro Star that it could not use images from the computer game

- The additional levels on the Micro Star CD will not work unless they take, manipulate, and display copyrighted pictures and sounds that are contained in FormGen's game, much like a jukebox will not work unless it can grab a copyrighted record from a stack of records and play it—it may vary the sequence of how the records are played, but the juke box is mute without the copyrighted records. By the same token, Micro Star's CD may vary the sequence of the FormGen copyrighted computer code, but it is mute without FormGen's copyrighted images and sounds and code.

- Micro Star recognized this because the packaging of its CD displayed not the sterile code contained within

the CD, but, rather, the copyrighted images of FormGen's game.

- **The district court found this as a fact when it wrote: "Furthermore, the court finds that Micro Star has shown that the audiovisual elements which appear on the screen while playing Nuke It originate from Duke 3D, and not from Nuke It."**

In my view, these are the critical facts that persuasively argue—in a non-argumentative way—that Micro Star infringed FormGen's copyright. They must be woven together, early in the statement, so that the appellate judges see the logic of the argument upfront. And the facts must be presented in such a way that they are not lost in the verbal equivalent of static hiss.]

Now let's look at Micro Star's statement of facts. Again, the bolding, underlining, and italics are as they are in the original.

<u>STATEMENT OF THE CASE</u>

Micro Star agrees with Apogee that this cross-appeal raises "issues of paramount importance," but Micro Star's formulation of those issues of "paramount importance" is decidedly different: (1) whether the owner of a copyrighted computer application program can use its copyright to prevent any competition by ***compatible,*** not copied, products and (2) whether the copyright holder can retain a copyright interest in data files that it encouraged consumers to create through a hidden license containing provisions "granting back" to the copyright holder a copyright in the consumer's creation.

[These are interesting reformulations of the questions raised by the appeal. They are also loaded unfairly. It is one thing to phrase a question presented to forcefully lead to the conclusion that you seek; it is another thing to have the question pregnant with an assumption that will not be born once the facts are mastered. This is the problem that I see here.

The first question doesn't really describe the issue: the issue is not the "competition" between "compatible" products—as would be the case if the seller of a computer game tried to prevent through legal action based on copyright someone from selling a

more advanced "joystick" with which to play the game. The joystick would be "compatible" with the computer game and might compete with a joystick sold by the game-maker, but the game-maker would not, at least on these limited facts, be able to use the copyright law to prevent those who played it game from using the off-brand joystick.

The second question assumes that the license is "hidden." Apparently, it is partially "hidden"—the gamer is told that it exists, but has to pull it up in order to read it. This distinction should not be covered with "gloss"; a brief-writer must be scrupulously upfront—making weak or bad facts work, rather than attempting to hide them by using words that may be technically honest but are, nevertheless, misleading. Moreover, FormGen is not seeking to lay claim to the 300 levels compiled by Micro Star on its CD; rather, it is attempting to prevent Micro Star from selling a CD that, in its view, appropriates FormGen's copyrighted "Duke Nukem" images, sounds, and computer code.

Misstating the issues by gliding around the core questions bothers seasoned judges, who suspect that the lawyer recognizes that he or she cannot win on a playing field circumscribed by the issues that *are* presented by the appeal. Misstating the issues in this way is especially deadly if done by an appellee—it leads the judges to believe that the trial court's decision cannot be defended head-on. Make certain that when you frame, or reframe, the issues presented by the appeal that you emulate Churchill in his "brief" for the Duke of Marlborough mentioned earlier.

Again the statements of the case and of the facts by both parties here are too argumentative. The statements should lead to the result you want by force of logic—facts built upon facts in the most persuasive way—not rhetoric.]

> The district court properly concluded on the one hand that the allegedly infringing MAP files contained on the *Nuke It* CD "do not contain any copyrightable material" from the *Duke Nukem 3D*

program.[7] Memorandum Order at 12 (Excerpts of the Record ("E.R.") 1074). Nor do the MAP files contain any copyrighted audiovisual elements of *Duke Nukem 3D.* Memorandum Order at 7 (E.R. 1069). Instead, "the audiovisual elements which appear on the screen while playing *Nuke It* originate from Duke 3D, and not from *Nuke It.*" (E.R. 1068).

[With the exception of the word "properly" (which, as being argumentative, does not belong in a statement of facts or of the case), this is good: it sets the factual predicate for Micro Star's argument that *Galoob* requires an affirmance.]

Therefore, contrary to Apogee's assertion that the district court unreasonably construed" this Court's decision in *Lewis Galoob Toys, Inc. v. Nintendo of America, Inc.*, 964 F.2d 965 (9th Cir. 1992), *cert. denied,* 507 U.S. 985 (1993), the trial court correctly made a finding of fact that there was no copying of copyrighted elements of *Duke Nukem 3D* since, among other reasons, *Nuke It* did not "incorporate a protected work in some concrete or permanent form," since the actual source of the displays was *Duke Nukem 3D.* Memorandum Order at 7 (E.R. 1069).

[This, too, is good. It incorporates what the district court looked upon as controlling law, and ties the facts found by the district court to that law. Again, however, there is a blurring of the applicable standards of review, and the phrasing is too argumentative.]

The trial court did not need to reach the second issue. The antithesis of equity, after providing consumers the movie camera, film, sets and editing equipment, as well as urging the consumers to make the movie, Apogee now claims ownership of the movie. After providing the MAP file editor to purchasers of *Duke Nukem 3D* and

---

[7] As discussed in Micro Star's Opening Brief, pp.6-8, *Nuke It* contains 300 additional levels of play for *Duke Nukem 3D.* Those additional levels of play are like new mazes in a maze game or new battles in a "war-type" game. The characters are generally the same or similar, with the same rules of play, but the levels contain different layouts, combinations of elements and/or differing degrees of difficulty. Declaration of Christopher Moore, ¶ 4 (E.R. 412- 413). Because these files have a ".MAP" file extension, they are called MAP files. Johnson Laird Decl., ¶ 8 (E.R. 420). **[The opening brief referred to is Micro Star's brief appealing those portions of the district courts rulings that were adverse to it—the screen saver and the packaging art aspects of the case.]**

urging them to freely create and distribute the MAP files and screen savers throughout the world, Apogee has lost the right to control those creations. Thus, the license and its purported "grant back" provisions are both unenforceable and a separate copyright misuse precluding enforcement of Apogee's copyright.

[This, again, is argumentative. I won't comment on this shortcoming again—I think that I've made my point and that you will be able to recognize it throughout Micro Star's statement of the case, as you were able to recognize it through the statement of the case submitted by FormGen. Don't do it in *your* briefs.]

As discussed in this Court's opinions in both *Galoob* and in *Sega Enterprises, Ltd. v. Accolade, Inc.*, 977 F.2d 1510 (9th Cir. 1992), the Copyright Act forecloses copying, not competition. The district court correctly found that the MAP files distributed on the *Nuke It* CD did not infringe on any *Duke Nukem 3D* copyright. Apogee cannot obtain either a free ride from the purchasers of its own product or use its own inequitable conduct to wrongfully expand its copyright solely for anticompetitive purposes. Under these facts, and the district court's weighing of the parties' disputed contentions of fact, Apogee cannot be entitled to an injunction that the district court in its discretion saw fit to deny.

* * *

[I am deleting material relevant only to Micro Star's appeal, not its reply to FormGen's brief-in-chief on FormGen's cross-appeal from the district court's refusal to enjoin Micro Star's sales of the CD.]

A. Facts.

1. ***Duke Nukem 3D* and *Nuke It***

As discussed in Micro Star's Opening Brief **[on its appeal from the district court's rulings on the screen saver and packaging art]**, the statement of facts of which is incorporated herein by reference, *Duke Nukem 3D* is a "shoot 'em up" computer action game where the player blasts assorted aliens into oblivion with a variety of weapons as the player winds his or her way through mazes consisting largely of different connected hallways and rooms. (E.R. 397-398). These mazes are called "levels." Moore Declaration, ¶ 2 (E.R. 410). Like many other games before it, *Duke Nukem 3D* allowed users of the "registered" or paid-for version to create new levels and play additional levels created by other players. Moore Declaration, ¶ 6 (E.R. 414). Commercial marketing of "add-on" levels is therefore well-established.[8] The availability of "add-on" levels of play for *Duke Nukem 3D* and other computer games maintains the commercial viability of the game long after players have learned how to "survive" through all of the included levels. Moore Decl., ¶ 4 (E.R. 412). *Duke It* contains over 300 user-created add-on levels for *Duke Nukem 3D* (E.R. 397)[9] None of the *Duke It* MAP files can operate independently of *Duke Nukem 3D.* Instead, as fully discussed in Micro Star's Opening Brief at pp. 10-12, the MAP files are only compatible, at least at this time, with *Duke Nukem 3D.* Thus, in order to use the data files on the *Duke It* CD, the purchaser *must* purchase, or already have purchased, the registered version *of Duke Nukem 3D.*

[Does the statement "None of the *Duke It* MAP files can operate independently of *Duke Nukem 3D.* " help of hurt Micro Star? FormGen's complaint is that the Micro Star game commandeers FormGen's copyrighted material. It seems to me that the better tack would be for Micro Star to lay the factual predicate for its argument based on *Galoob,* namely that the use of FormGen's code is transitory and does not result in a "new" creation in any tangible form.]

Although Apogee refused to acknowledge the truth to the district court in its papers filed there, or in its discovery responses

---

[8] In its Brief at p. 10, n. 3, Apogee asserts that add-on products like *Duke It* are neither common nor accepted. However, Apogee has not disputed that "add-on" level products have been marketed for many of *Duke Nukem 3D's* competitors and predecessors, including "Descent," "Hexen," "Heretic," "Doom," "Doom II," 'Warcraft II, " "Command and Conquer," "Sim City," and "Microsoft Flight Simulator." *See* Moore Declaration, ¶ 6 (E.R. 414). Moreover, many of the files on the *Nuke It* CD, if not all of them, are currently available from the *Duke Nukem 3D* area on America Online and Compuserve, where users must pay charges to those services in order to obtain the files. *See* Moore Decl., ¶ 5 (E.R. 413). Thus, Micro Star's characterization is hardly "false."

[9] Apogee has repeatedly stated in its Brief that the *Duke It* MAP files were "inferior quality", (Brief, p. 4) or "amateur-quality" (Brief, p. 10). Despite Apogee's argument to that effect in the proceedings below, the district court declined to make such a finding.

to Micro Star, the MAP files contain neither programming nor any copyrighted elements of the *Duke Nukem 3D* program. Johnson-Laird Decl., ¶¶ 7-18 (E.R. 420-42 3). Instead, the MAP file, which consists of data readable by the *Duke Nukem 3D* program, contains only a reference to a particular element of *Duke Nukem 3D* contained in *Duke Nukem 3D's* image file library —just like a card catalog at the library only contains a reference to a particular book, not the book itself. Johnson Laird Decl., ¶¶ 12-14 (E.R. 421-422). Clearly, the card in a card catalog does not "contain" or "display" the copyrighted book, no more than a citation to a book violates the copyright on the book, which is the logical leap into the abyss that Apogee asks this Court to make.

[The card-catalogue analogy is, in my view, weak. It invites the following response: But Micro Star's game does more than reference the "book" located on the library shelves of the FormGen game, it pulls the "book" from the shelves and uses it *in order to make the Micro Star product commercially viable.* Stated another way, without FormGen's copyrighted images, sounds, and computer code, Micro Star's CD would be a mere circle of plastic, usable, perhaps, as a coaster.]

Weighing the two views of the evidence, the district court made a finding of fact to that effect. Memorandum Order at 7 (E.R. 1 069).[10]

In addition to claiming that the *Duke It* MAP files contained programming or audiovisual elements of *Duke Nukem 3D* when it was clear that the MAP files did not, Apogee claimed for the first time in its Reply papers in support of its motion for a preliminary

---

[10] The district court's finding of fact necessarily weighed the credibility of testimony and credentials of Mr. Alan Blum, Apogee's apparent "expert," a computer programmer for "five years" who "studied" computer science at Cabrillo Community College and University of California at Santa Cruz for three years without obtaining a degree in computer science from either (E.R. 585) with the credibility and qualifications of Micro Star's expert, Mr. Johnson-Laird, a computer programmer for 33 years, qualified as an software expert in several federal district courts, who currently serves as a court-appointed expert, taught software seminars to federal judges at the Federal Judicial Center and is a technical advisor to the U.S. Copyright Office on computer software. (E.R. 418).

injunction that the file "format" of the MAP files was copyrighted.[11] Despite this new claim, Apogee did not make a showing that the MAP file structure was covered by its copyright. *See Duke Nukem 3D* Copyright Registration (E.R. 750-751).[12]

Further undercutting Apogee's "file format" claim, ***Apogee does not dispute that Duke Nukem 3D can play add-on levels created by third parties for Doom.*** Moore Declaration, ¶ 8 (E.R. 414-415). *Duke Nukem 3D's* ability to play add-on levels written for other games show that the MAP file format is merely functional, this "backwards" compatibility is not surprising, given that very little of Duke *Nukem 3D* is actually "original," but instead was itself copied from Id Software's *Doom.*[13] For example, both *Duke Nukem 3D* **[*sic*: the words "and *Doom*" are probably missing]** share the same progression of weapons, i.e., hand combat, pistol, shotgun, chaingun etc. Moore Declaration, ¶ 3 (E.R. 411-4 12). Both games have a similar "look and feel," share a nearly identical control panel, have secret rooms with weapons, and use the same keyboard commands to operate the game. *Id.* It is virtually impossible to determine whether Apogee claims that any of these copied elements are covered by Apogee's copyright and Apogee has made no showing that either the MAP file structure (if copyrightable) or what elements of *Duke Nukem 3D* are covered by the copyright. *See Duke Nukem 3D* Copyright Registration (E.R. 750-751).

---

[11] In its interrogatory responses, quoted in Micro Star's Opening Brief at p. 14, both GTI and FormGen thought so little of this claim that they did not even mention it as part of the "coding and other materials" allegedly infringed on by the *Duke It* MAP files. Moreover, those interrogatories have never been amended.

[12] In fact, had the district court adopted this novel contention, every document created by a word processor would infringe on that word processor's "unique" file format for storing data. (E.R. 824).

[13] Apogee did not refute this damaging point made to the district court. To this Court, Apogee merely stated that "it is not necessary to assess" it since "the record contains no evidence that any MAP files.., on *Duke ft* originated as *Doom* files." First, the issue is whether the functional format of the MAP file is separately copyrighted, not whether *Duke It* MAP files originated as *Doom* files. Second, in the Moore Declaration, ¶ 8 (E.R. 414-415), Mr. Moore explains that it is impossible to tell whether a MAP file was originally created for *Doom* since a MAP file originally created for *Doom* is identical to a MAP file created for *Duke Nukem 3D.*

[This argument is, to me at least (and if I were sitting on the panel hearing the appeal, that would be important to the parties), unclear. It appears to be mixing a *tu quoque* (you too!) argument with an implication that FormGen should somehow be prevented from asserting its rights against Micro Star because the "Duke Nukem" images and sounds can also be accessed by *Doom* levels. If Micro Star is arguing waiver, that argument is, as of yet, undeveloped, and, certainly, the factual predicate for such an argument has not been laid out. If I am missing something, that hurts the party whose explanation is unclear, even though the party's explanation might have been apparent to a smarter judge. As an advocate, you must make certain that your argument is equally clear to everyone who may read your brief and have a say as to whether you win or lose.]

> Faced with two views of the evidence, the district court made a finding of fact that Apogee had not met its burden of proof that the format of the MAP files were copyrightable. Memorandum Order at 7 (E.R. 1069).
>
> **2. Apogee's Unenforceable License and Express License to Purchasers of *Duke Nukem 3D*.**
>
> As set forth in Micro Star's Opening Brief at pp. 8-10, Apogee has gratuitously included a purported "license" called LICENSE.DOC among the 40 megabytes of programs and material on the *Duke Nukem 3D* CD. The license is purported" because there is no need or opportunity for the purchaser to ever assent to the contract before using the product. Instead, there are merely vague references to LICENSE.DOC. This violates industry custom and practice. *See* Johnson-Laird Declaration, ¶¶ 20-38 (E.R. 423-428); Micro Star's Opening brief at p. 10, n. 7.

[This argument, too, is essentially undeveloped at this point, and ignores the possible distinction between a "pad contract" that purports to bind a party merely by that party's passive acquiescence—as an exculpatory "contract" on the back of an entry ticket to a spectator sport—and the situation here where reference, albeit oblique, to the restriction on commercial use of game-player created levels is triggered every time someone decides to use the "Duke Nukem 3D" software to create those levels. How do you make the underlying facts clear? Reprint in

your brief pictures of the screen (which, presumably, are in the record) to show the judges how small, or innocuous, the wording is.]

> Nowhere is the user informed that LICENSE.DOC contains any restrictions or limitations on the use of levels created with the editor, or notified that LICENSE.DOC is some sort of legally binding contract. (E.R. 437). No one purchasing the software need ever see LICENSE.DOC, much less read its contents and assent to it. (E.R. 438). The district court found that although Apogee "could have done a better job" with the license, the restrictions against commercial use were enforceable against third party Micro Star. Memorandum Order at 12 (E.R. 1074). The district court never expressly ruled that the license was enforceable against the actual creator of the MAP files, *i.e.*, the purchaser of *Duke Nukem 3D*. *Id.*

[Compare this with the district court's finding of fact:

> **"The opening screen for the build editor indicates that the build editor and associated tools may not be re-packaged and sold, and finishes by stating "Please refer to LICENSE.DOC for further information on levels created with BUILD.EXE." This LICENSE.DOC file contains several restrictions, including that there can be no commercial sales of any new levels created and that all rights are granted back to movants."**

Micro Star does not even attempt to show that this finding is clearly erroneous. This is a skirmish that Micro Star cannot win. Why fight it? The lesson here for you is that you must be alert not to toss in every possible argument with the hope that something might stick. Remember Judge Wald's admonition, which I quoted earlier, but which bears repeating here:

> **"Confident counsel should almost always go for broke and rely on their one or two best arguments, abandoning the other 9–10 wish-list entries. There is, of course, always some small risk of dropping an argument that might appeal to one or two judges, but I can assure you in the vast majority of cases that possibility is theoretical**

only, and the fewer arguments you make the more attention they will get from us in preparing and disposing of your case."

Back to Micro Star's brief:]

Similarly, the district court concluded that despite Apogee's express conduct encouraging the creation of new levels, the distribution to the public and the provision of the tools to do it, and the ineffective license, Apogee had not waived or abandoned its rights to control *commercial* distribution. Memorandum Order at 12 (E.R. 1074)

3. Apogee's Misuse Of Its Copyright Which Should Bar Their Claim of Copyright Infringement Against Micro Star.

The same misuse of its copyright that should bar Apogee's claim that *Nuke* It's packaging infringes on its copyrights, discussed in Micro Star's Opening Brief at pp. 32-3 8, should bar its other infringement claims. *See* Micro Star's Opening Brief, pp. 12-13; Benedict Decl., ¶ 14; (E.R. 401).

The misuse of Apogee's copyright extends to their attempts to overextend their copyright, since Apogee clearly knew that there were no copyrighted audiovisual elements contained on any MAP files. However, the district court failed to rule on the copyright misuse defense, even though Micro Star sought reconsideration of the injunction based on Apogee's inequitable use of the initial order granting limited injunctive relief.[14]

In sum, Apogee submitted hundreds of pages of declarations and exhibits to which Micro Star had to respond (E.R. 13-393). The district court rejected each one of Apogee's claims, which factual

---

[14] In yet another mischaracterization of the record, Apogee asserts in its Brief at p. 48 that "the Court expressly *denied* Micro Star's request for reconsideration." Yet in the transcript, the court expressly *granted* the oral motion for reconsideration, but declined to change its order after reconsideration. (E.R. 939, lines 17-18).

[This is puerile. A motion for reconsideration is granted when the court changes or modifies its decision—not when it agrees to hear counsel. This type of argument doe not win for Micro Star any points.]

findings and conclusions of law were plainly correct and should not be disturbed.[15]

[The district court granted FormGen relief in connection with Micro Star's packaging and screen savers. I do not see, therefore, how Micro Star can say that the "district court rejected each one of Apogee's claims." If Micro Star is limiting its use of the words "each one" to the claim that Micro Star's compilation of the new levels it downloaded from the internet infringed FormGen's game, it should make that clear. Even the appearance of overreaching in an argument can hurt your client's cause.]

— — —

Although I, and many other appellate judges, would read the section of each of the briefs in tandem in this type of complex case, we're going to hold off until later the reprinting FormGen's reply brief and its responses in that brief to Micro Star's statement of facts and argument. At that point, I'm going to present it without my comments, and ask that when you read it you analyze whether its responses are effective (and whether its analogies hold water) and if any of those responses should have been anticipated by Micro Star, and if so, how. Also consider whether FormGen has left any of Micro Star's arguments unrebutted, and what affect that might have on a court. Additionally, be alert to legal jargon and other things that we talked about that detracts from persuasive writing. Finally, consider whether, if you were the judge deciding the case, you would want: the statute quoted at the spot where it is referenced; excerpts from the record quoted, rather than merely paraphrased or, worse, just referenced; specific supporting language from the cited cases set out—either in a parenthetical or in a block quote. After you do all of this in connection with FormGen's reply brief, you will be well on your way to making *your* briefs, better, more persuasive, and more effective. In a very real sense, your analysis of FormGen's reply brief will be the most valuable exercise you will do in the course of reading this book: it will give you a chance to apply the winning principles in a real life situation—an exercise that will, I trust, get you in the habit of going through that analysis in every one of *your* appeals.

---

[15] Given that the district court rejected Apogee's main contention that the MAP files infringed on the *Duke Nukem 3D* copyright and rejected Apogee's Lanham Act claims *in toto,* it was indeed surprising to read in Apogee's Brief at p.16 that the district court "correctly ruled in favor of movants on virtually every point." In fact, the court termed the ruling "a major victory for Nuke It." (E.R. 937).

First, the parties' respective "summary of argument" sections.

As I mentioned earlier, the "summary of argument" is your chance to give your cause its best shot. Like most folks, appellate judges absorb and are more easily persuaded by small a portion of potent argument than they are by a long, drawn-out, circumlocutious opus. Condense your "summary of argument" the way a great chef condenses a sauce; reduce it to its essence—thick, syrupy, full of flavor.

FormGen's "summary of argument" (excluding the paragraph relating to the screen-saver and packaging-art issues):

> <u>SUMMARY OF ARGUMENT</u>
>
> The District Court incorrectly held that *Galoob* compelled a finding that the user-created MAP files included in Nuke It did not infringe Movants' protected expression. The MAP files contain detailed information uniquely structured to interact with DN3D's game engine to generate the display of protected audiovisual elements in a particular arrangement. They are sold by Micro Star and experienced by consumers as self-contained environments in which the Duke character pursues his exploits. The unique structure of the MAP files is independently subject to copyright protection.
>
> Reversal on either the misreading of *Galoob* or the file structure issue must lead to granting of a preliminary injunction against Micro Star's unauthorized sale of user-created levels. Nuke It is a purely commercial, non-transformative exploitation of DN3D's protected expression that cannot by any stretch of the imagination be deemed a "fair use." Movants will suffer irreparable harm if Micro Star is permitted to market derivative products embodying their protected expression in competition with authorized DN3D add-on products.

[Yes, this is a summary of the argument. But, as you will see, it isn't nearly as persuasive as is the argument section. This part of the brief must be powerful and pungent. I offer the following suggestion:

> **Society and our law recognize that persons who use their skills and creative energies to conceive and develop original works have the right to exploit those works as they see fit, and to prevent others from, in essence,**

stealing these creations for financial gain. *See Apple Computer Inc. v. Franklin Computer Corp.*, 714 F.2d 1240, 1254–1255 (3d Cir. 1983), *cert. denied*, 464 U.S. 1033. This is the crux of FormGen's complaint against Micro Star.

The following facts are not disputed:

- **FormGen developed and owns the copyright in the computer game "Duke Nukem 3D"**
- **"Duke Nukem 3D" is made up of the following copyrighted elements:**
  - **picture files**
  - **sound files**
  - **computer code that permits users to create new scenarios or "game levels" for the "Duke Nukem 3D" game**
- **"Duke Nukem 3D" permits those playing its game to use its computer code to construct new scenarios or game levels for the game, and to distribute or share those new game levels, so long as all this is done for a non-commercial purpose**
- **Gamers using the computer code to construct new game levels are notified every time they access that code that use of the code is subject to restrictions, and are told where in the "Duke Nukem 3D"program they can read about those restrictions**
- **Micro Star knew that gamers were not supposed to sell the new game levels that they created using the copyrighted "Duke Nukem 3D" software**
- **Nevertheless, Micro Star collected three-hundred new levels posted on the internet by "Duke Nukem 3D" gamers, did not pay—or even receive permission from—the gamers for those levels, put those levels on a CD, and sold the CD, all without receiving a**

license to do so from FormGen

- The Micro Star CD competes directly with game-level CDs sold by, or under a license issued by, FormGen or one of its related companies

- The levels loaded on the Micro Star CD works by reaching into the "Duke Nukem 3D" game and taking the copyrighted "Duke Nukem 3D" image and sound files. This lets a person using the Micro Star CD play the copyrighted "Duke Nukem 3D" game—manipulating the "Duke Nukem 3D" characters, backgrounds, and sounds

- No one would buy the Micro Star CD if they could not play the game using FormGen's copyrighted characters, scenes, and sounds

- Accordingly, Micro Star is profiting directly from its taking, for its own commercial benefit, the copyrighted characters, scenes, and sounds of FormGen's copyrighted "Duke Nukem 3D" game.

All this is infringement of the most elemental sort. The district court's conclusion to the contrary was based on its erroneous reading of this court's decision in *Galoob*, which held that a device that did not use any of the protected images or sounds of a computer game, but merely altered, temporarily, they way those images or sounds appeared, neither infringed nor caused the infringement of any of the game's protected elements—anymore than would playing a 33 rpm record at 45 rpm infringe the record company's copyright by altering the way the music on that record sounded. Indeed, as we will show, *Galoob* itself demonstrates that Micro Star has infringed FormGen's copyright.

By building the argument sequentially, and by breaking it into irrefutable steps that ineluctably lead to our desired conclusion, I have made the "summary of argument" a powerful tool to get the appellate judges leaning our way. The inexorable force of the argument is helped by using bullets to separate and highlight the

sequential steps. This is the same technique that I demonstrated with the simple automobile accident hypothetical discussed earlier. Try to use this format as a template—do this or something similar in every one of your briefs.]

Micro Star's "summary of argument" (excluding the paragraphs relating to the screen-saver and packaging-art issues):

SUMMARY OF ARGUMENT

The district court made findings of fact based on an extensive record, albeit an extensive record obscured by Apogee's cleverly worded and evasive declarations and magical demonstrative evidence.[1] Those findings of fact, *i.e.*, that the MAP files do not contain any protected expression *of Duke Nukem 3D,* and that Apogee did not sustain its burden of proving that the file format of the MAP files was more than a functional element *of Duke Nukem 3D* excluded from copyright protection by 17 U.S.C. § 102, are only reversible if clearly erroneous. Fed. R. Civ. P. 52(a); *Anderson v. City of Bessemer City, N.C.*, 470 U.S. 564, 573, 105 S.Ct. 1504, 84 L.Ed.2d 518 (1985). As disclosed by the record before the district court, there were clearly two permissible views of the evidence on these issues; the factfinder's choice between them cannot be clearly erroneous. *Id*

---

[1] Micro Star has already discussed many of the instances of evasive and misleading declarations and discovery responses. However, the "demonstrative" video for the district court went beyond evasion. For example, in an attempt to show that the file LICENSE.DOC was not hidden, Apogee surreptitiously typed in a computer command to cause the computer to seemingly "automatically" display the LICENSE.DOC at the conclusion of a level. (E.R. 796-797).

[This is a very serious charge. I do not have the record, so I cannot check the reference. But if the district court made a finding that FormGen tried to mislead it, the argument around that finding should not be relegated to a footnote. If the district court did not make any finding one way or another, but Micro Star believes that FormGen misrepresented what a consumer would see when either playing the game or invoking the level-creating software, it should showcase every bit of record evidence that supports that belief. The mere reference to "(E.R. 796–797)" is not enough—for all the reasons I have already discussed. Moreover, as we have seen, the district court made a specific finding about the "license" and the degree to which gamers would have reason to know about it. As I've also mentioned, Micro Star has not shown how the district court's finding concerning the license is clearly erroneous.]

[With the exception of the *ad hominem* attack on FormGen (Apogee), this is good—so far. The strongest point that Micro Star has is the district court's findings of fact. But it does not go far enough, and undercuts this powerful opening salvo in its "summary of argument" by the very next sentence—the start of the next paragraph!]

> Even without the deference accorded to the district court's findings of fact, settled copyright law shows that injunctive relief is unwarranted, since Apogee has not shown originality of the protected expression and copying of that expression by Micro Star. *Feist Publications, mc, v. Rural Telephone Service Co.*, 499 U.S. 340, 361, 111 S.Ct. 1282, 1296, 113 L.Ed.2d 358 (1991). Without showing both elements, Apogee has not established a likelihood of success on the merits since Apogee bears the burden of proof on the elements. *Brown Bag Software v. Symantec Corp.*, 960 F.2d 1465, 1472 (9th Cir.), *cert. denied,* 113 S.Ct. 198 (1992).

[The old, and suicidal "but even if" that we discussed at length in *The "How-To-Win" Trial Manual* and earlier here. Why not phrase it "Moreover, Apogee [or FormGen] has not come close to sustaining its burden of proof of showing ... " Use of "moreover" or "additionally" or some similar word allows you to make consistent arguments with having them *appear* to be inconsistent. When you argue inconsistent positions you are, tacitly at least, conceding weakness. Don't do it.]

> Despite Apogee's understandable efforts to distance itself from this Court's holding *Galoob* and *Sega Industries, Ltd. v. Accolade, Inc.*, 977 F.2d 1510 (9th Cir. 1992), both cases are dispositive of Apogee's appeal. The MAP files are not derivative works, because, as the district court found, the MAP files do not "incorporate a portion of the copyrighted work in some form." *Accord, Galoob,* 964 F.2d at 968. Similarly, even if this Court was willing to stretch the definition of a derivative work further than any court has yet gone, the MAP files are still protected by the fair use doctrine pursuant to *Galoob* and *Sega.*

[Again, the suicidal "even if." This is the way it should be phrased: "Moreover, Micro Star's compilation is well within the protection of 'fair use' ... " Additionally, try not to challenge the court, as in: "even if this Court was willing to stretch the

definition of a derivative work further than any court has yet gone." Judges, like all folks, dislike criticism; this sentence says, essentially: "Even if you are stupid enough to make a decision so absurd that no other court has come even close ..." This is not the way to win over someone you need to persuade.]

> Even if Apogee otherwise had a viable claim of infringement, the only objective evidence before the district court is that Apogee, by urging purchasers to create new levels and screen shots, providing the tools to do so, and urging them to distribute the creations throughout the world, is now precluded from asserting that Micro Star's use of those third party-created materials is an infringement, through an implied license, or in the alternative, waiver or abandonment of those rights. Additionally, Apogee's unclean hands and inequitable conduct should prevent any equitable relief.

[Another, "but even if" argument. If you are going to make this argument, phrase it this way: "Additionally, FormGen cannot complain that Micro Star has done what it is has encouraged; namely, putting new levels of its game on the market to do two things: 1) increase the market for FormGen's game; and 2) keep gamers playing "Duke Nukem 3D" longer than they would because of the new challenges posed by the new levels. FormGen encouraged its gamers to post their new levels on the internet, it cannot now complain that Micro Star has made it easy for purchasers of "Duke Nukem 3D" to have easy access to those levels. In a sense, FormGen is telling this court that FormGen wants those playing "Duke Nukem 3D" to be able to play new levels created by "Duke Nukem 3D" gamers, but objects to Micro Star making that easy—and being compensated for that effort. This is like telling someone that it is 'OK to go swimming, but don't go near the water.'"]

Now let's look at each party's formal "argument" section (I say "formal" because, as we have seen, each party argued in their "statement of the case" and in their "statement of facts." First, FormGen's "Argument":

ARGUMENT

I. STANDARDS GOVERNING GRANTING AND REVIEW OF A PRELIMINARY INJUNCTION

[Do not use all uppercase caps; they are very hard to read. You will get the same emphasis by capitalizing the first letter of each word.]

On a claim for copyright infringement, preliminary injunctive relief is warranted upon a demonstration of *either* (1) a combination of likelihood of success on the merits and the possibility of irreparable injury *or* (2) serious questions going to the merits and a balance of hardships tipping sharply in movant's favor. *See Triad Sys. Corp. v. Southeastern Express Co., 64* F.3d 1330 (9th Cir. *1995), cert. denied,* 116 S. Ct. 1015 (1996). Likelihood of success is by far the most important factor. "In a copyright infringement claim, a showing of a reasonable likelihood of success on the merits raises a presumption of irreparable harm." *Johnson Controls, Inc. v. Phoenix Control Sys., Inc.,* 886 F.2d 1173, 1174 (9th Cir. 1989). On appeal, a district court's decision to grant or deny a preliminary injunction is generally reviewable for abuse of discretion, but its legal rulings are reviewed *de novo. Employers Ins, of Wausau v. Albert D. Seeno Constr. Co., 945* F.2d 284, *285* (9th Cir. 1991).

[This is good and clear. The only thing that I would do differently would be to put a colon after the word "*either*" and break out the (1) and (2) in separate mini-paragraphs, as in the following:

***either* :**

(1) a combination of likelihood of success on the merits and the possibility of irreparable injury *or*

(2) serious questions going to the merits and a balance of hardships tipping sharply in movant's favor.

***See Triad Sys. Corp. v. Southeastern Express Co., 64* F.3d 1330 (9th Cir. *1995), cert. denied,* 116 S. Ct. 1015 (1996).]**

To establish copyright infringement, a plaintiff must prove (1) ownership of a valid copyright and (2) that defendant copied a substantial portion of protected elements from the copyright work. *See, e.g., Feist Publications, Inc. v. Rural Tel. Serv. Co.*, 499 U.S. 340, 361 (1991); *Smith v. Jackson,* 84 F.3d 1213, 1218 (9th Cir. 1996). Movants did so here.

II. THE DISTRICT COURT ERRED IN DENYING A PRELIMINARY INJUNCTION BARRING THE REPRODUCTION AND DISTRIBUTION BY SALE OF USER-CREATED MAP FILES

The District Court correctly ruled in favor of Movants on virtually every issue in the case. It declined to extend the preliminary injunction granted to cover the sale of user-created levels *solely* because of its erroneous preliminary finding that those levels, embodied in MAP files, did not contain DN3D's expression in protectable form. Had it not made this error, the District Court would have properly enjoined the sale of all Micro Star products containing additional levels of play for DN3D.

A. The Visual Display of the Protected Expression of DN3D Resulting from the Use of Nuke It Constitutes an Infringement of the Copyright in DN3D

What should be the controlling legal principle was never contested below: Audiovisual elements of computer games and other computer programs are protected under the Copyright Act. *See, e.g., M. Kramer Mfg. Co. v. Andrews,* 783 F.2d 421, *435* (4th Cir. 1986); *Atari, Inc. v. North Am. Philips Consumer Elecs. Corp.*, 672 F.2d 607, 617 (7th Cir.), *cert. denied,* 459 U.S. 880 (1982); *Stern Elecs. Inc. v. Kaufman,* 669 F.2d 852, 856 (2d Cir. 1982); *Sega Enters. v. Maphia, 857* F. Supp. 679, 686 (N. D. Cal. 1994); *Broderbund Software, Inc. v. Unison World, Inc.*, 648 F. Supp. 1127, 1132-33 (N.D. Cal. 1986). Particular fanciful characters -- such as Duke himself and his various alien enemies -- are independently copyrightable, as are fanciful props such as Duke's Medkits, armor, and other gear. *See, e.g., Atari,* 672 F.2d at 617-18; *Walt Disney Prods. v. Air Pirates,* 581 F.2d 751. 754 (9th Cir. 1978), *cert. denied,* 439 U.S. 1132 (1979).

[This is good, but would even better if: First, the writer did not string cite. String cites clutter a brief, and should only be used

where you need to show something besides that there is case authority for your proposition. Thus, for example, if you are seeking review by the United States Supreme Court and are arguing that there is a split among the circuits that needs to be resolved, you should list all the cases on one side of the issue, and all cases on the other side of the issue. Here, there is no dispute about this aspect of the controlling law; and a string cite is not needed to counterbalance one or two "islands in the law" cited by an opponent.

***Strategy*:**

☞ **Cite a decision from your jurisdiction (here, the Ninth Circuit) or, if there is none, cite a treatise and a decision from a jurisdiction that your jurisdiction respects.**

Second, the writer should use parentheticals so we can see at a glance that the cases support *directly* (and not by mere inference) the point for which they are cited.]

Where a product sold without license generates an audiovisual display substantially similar to the copyrighted work, that product constitutes an infringement, regardless of whether underlying computer code has been copied. *See Atari,* 672 F.2d at 617-18. Expression generated by a Read Only Memory ("ROM") computer device, such as a CD-ROM, is sufficiently "fixed" to constitute a copy of protected expression. *M. Kramer Mfg. Co.*, 783 F.2d at 440-42. Thus, the starting point for analysis is that Micro Star's appropriation of DN3D's protected audiovisual expression on its competing CD-ROM product is an infringement.

Section 106(2) of the Copyright Act grants to authors the exclusive right to prepare derivative works based on their copyrighted work. Where the author grants a limited license to another party to prepare a derivative work *(e.g.*, a film version of a novel), the original author's rights in the underlying material are unaffected. *See* 17 U.S.C. § 103(b). Where the licensee's use of the material exceeds the scope of the license, or a third party appropriates material from the derivative work protected by the underlying copyright, the original copyright owner may sue for infringement. *See Gilliam v. American Broadcasting Cos.*, 538 F.2d 14, 20 (2d Cir. 1976). Moreover, rights under the Act are severable; waiver of one does not affect any other. *See Columbia Pictures Indus., Inc. v. Redd Horne, Inc.*, 749 F.2d 154, 158 (3d Cir. 1984).

[The statutes should be quoted here! Also, the last sentence seems to be conceding "waiver" here—at least on one or some matters. Don't throw in boiler plate merely because you have it in your word-processing file. The point referenced in the last sentence is not further developed.]

Thus, Movants are entitled to enforce their § 106(1) and (3) rights to control reproduction and distribution by sale of audiovisual expression contained in the underlying game, whether elements were copied directly from the product or taken from derivative works -- such as user-created levels -- containing such elements. Lifting protected expression from third party sources and reproducing it for commercial purposes without permission infringes the underlying copyright: "Copying a copy of copyrighted materials is a cognizable countervention **[*sic* in FormGen's brief; *Kepner-Tregoe* spells it correctly: "contravention"]** of the copyright code." *Kepner-Tregoe, Inc. v. Leadership Software, Inc.*, 12 F.3d 527, 533 (5th Cir.), *cert. denied.* 115 S. Ct. 82 (1994). *See also 1 Melville B.Nimmer & David Nimmer, Nimmer on Copyright* § 3.05, at 3-34.2-34.3 (1996) ("[I]f the material copied was derived from a copyrighted underlying work, this will constitute an infringement of such work regardless of whether the defendant copied directly from the underlying work, or indirectly via the derivative work."). This is precisely what Micro Star has done here, since the user-created levels are made up entirely of DN3D's protected characters and other audiovisual expression. *See* Blum Reply Decl. ¶¶ 8-12 (and Exhs. 1, 3, 5, 7, and 9) (E.R. 586, 595-600) (showing DN3D characters found in Nuke It play).

[This is good, powerful, and goes to the heart of FormGen's argument that Micro Star infringed its copyright.]

B. *Galoob*, Decided on Very Different Facts, Does Not Eviscerate the Copyright Protection for Computer Games

[In my view, this phrasing is too defensive. A very good argument can be made that *Galoob* supports, rather than undercuts, FormGen's position. We'll develop that after we see how

FormGen handles this case, upon which the district relied in refusing to stop Micro Star from selling its CD.]

Facing undisputed evidence that Nuke It, used as directed, displayed protected expression of DN3D, Micro Star labelled the contents of Nuke It as "mere data," basing its argument on an analogy to the very different product involved in *Galoob.* The District Court accepted this argument and, thus, denied an injunction based on the visual display of DN3D's protected expression reproduced with the Nuke It MAP files. This was clear legal error, because the general protection for audiovisual works should govern and *Galoob* is entirely inapposite.

[In my view, this is a weak opening salvo. Again, I'll outline a suggested approach later. In the meantime, until we get there, and as you read FormGen's arguments, think about how you would do it. Then compare your sequence of points with my suggestions. This exercise will help you get into the habit of linking your arguments into a sturdy, sequential chain.]

It is not disputed that Nuke It generates an audiovisual presentation including the protected expression of DN3D. By cutting and pasting elements of DN3D through the Build Editor, users have created derivative works comprised substantially of the sights and sounds of DN3D. These derivative works are fixed in a data structure created by Apogee, stored in the MAP files. Indeed, the 29 levels of play that come with DN3D are composed of data organized in the same structure. (E.R. 56-57.) When any level of DN3D is played -- be it an original level with the game, a level downloaded by a player from the Internet, or a level reproduced on Nuke It -- DN3D reads the stored data and the protected expression of DN3D is displayed as preordained by the structured data. (E.R. 587-93.) As Micro Star puts it (Br. 12), the "pictures are generated by the MAP files contained in the Nuke It CD when used in conjunction with [DN3D]."

Simply put, Nuke It consists of 300 permanent, self-contained scenarios that were created and are used for only one purpose -- to produce additional game play of DN3D. The consumer who uses Nuke It in accordance with its instructions will cause the display of

DN3D protected expression -- just as the screen shots shown on Micro Star's infringing packaging promise.[1]

Galoob involved a very different product. In *Galoob,* the defendant. Lewis Galoob Toys. Inc., distributed a device called Game Genie, designed for use with the video game system and cartridges offered by Nintendo of America, Inc. Game Genie did not contain derivative works based on Nintendo's protected expression. It was merely a tool inserted into the Nintendo machine that allowed players to alter a small number of variables, such as the number of "lives" assigned to a character, and otherwise to vary the visual display that Nintendo projected onto the home user's television screen. The changes in Nintendo's audiovisual display were entirely ephemeral: They existed only so long as that particular round of play continued and vanished as soon as the game was reset, power was turned off, or the Game Genie was removed. No copy of a particular scenario or storyline was ever made using the Game Genie, and the Game Genie could not change the plot, theme, or characters of any game. *See Lewis Galoob Toys, Inc. v. Nintendo of Am., Inc.,* 780 F. Supp. 1283, 1287-89 (N.D. Cal. 1991), *aff'd,* 964 F.2d 965 (9th Cir. 1992), *cert. denied,* 507 U.S. *985* (1993).

On these facts, Nintendo never even alleged that the sale of Game Genie directly infringed Nintendo's copyright, only that it *contributed* to infringement by home users. As a result, the district judge there understandably focused entirely on the home user and analogized the changes wrought by the Game Genie to private non-commercial alteration of works for home enjoyment. exempt from copyright enforcement:

---

1 Micro Star's counsel repeatedly argued below that the screen shots on Nuke It's box were "taken from the MAP files" (E.R. 840, 843, 847) -- showing that Micro Star understands full well that the user-created levels do "contain" DN3D's protected expression in a very meaningful sense. After counsel stated for the third time within a few minutes that the screen shots were "taken" from the MAP files, the District Court asked: "How do you get them from the MAP files?" (E.R. 847.) Counsel was unable to explain the clear contradiction in Micro Star's positions, but offered to submit a supplemental expert declaration. (E.R. 848.) Such a declaration has never been submitted. Counsel's statements were no mere slip: On appeal, Micro Star describes the screen shots as "snapshots of the scenes from the Nuke It files." Micro Star Br. 3.

> The Game Genie is a tool by which the consumer may temporarily modify the way in which to play a video game, legally obtained at market price. Any modification is' for the consumer's own enjoyment in the privacy of the home. Such a process is analogous in purpose, if not in technology, to skipping portions of a book, learning to speed read, fast-forwarding a video tape one has purchased in order to skip portions one chooses not to see, or using slow motion for the opposite reasons. None of those practices permanently modifies or alters the original work, none produces a separate work which can then be transferred in any way, none replaces the original work, and none deprives the copyright holder of current or expected revenue.

780 F. Supp. at 1291.

In affirming, this Court found that Game Genie "merely enhances the audiovisual displays" in a computer game in the manner of a special lens or a kaleidoscope and that the "altered displays do not incorporate a portion of a copyrighted work in some concrete or permanent form." 964 F.2d at 968-69. The Court stressed the private, non-commercial nature of the alterations created by Game Genie and emphasized the district court's finding of a lack of any economic harm to Nintendo. The Court found significant, both in its derivative work and fair use analysis, that Nintendo had presented no evidence of a concrete plan to issue competing derivative products whose sales might be injured by those of Game Genie. *See id.* at 969-71.

The two key issues in *Galoob* -- the lack of any fixed output and the lack of any commercial harm -- dictate the opposite result here.

[This is better—it takes the affirmative of the position. Rather than arguing that *Galoob* is, as we lawyers like to say, "inapposite," FormGen here is using *Galoob* as a sword. As I point out in *The "How-To-Win" Trial Manual*, you must make the so-called "bad facts" *work* for you. The same principle applies on the appellate level; don't just "distinguish" cases that seem adverse to you—make them work for you! As you read along, try to think how you would do it here. Later, I'll show you how I would do it.]

In contrast to Game Genie. Nuke It is a CD-ROM containing hundreds of fixed MAP files, each one a separate, self-contained scenario within which the Duke character carries out his exploits -- in essence a new adventure with its own narrative. These tangible files were created by cutting and pasting audiovisual elements from DN3D, saved by their user-creators, uploaded onto the Internet, and downloaded by Micro Star for inclusion in Nuke It.

Contrary to the court's holding below, the process by which the Nuke It disk and the DN3D game interact to display the protected audiovisual elements on the computer screen distinguishes this case from *Galoob.* There is no factual dispute on this process: Micro Star is correct in stating that DN3D reads the data stored in the MAP files to display characters and other specific pieces of art of DN3D. Those characters and that artwork exist in a unique image library created by Apogee's designers. The MAP file, however, is a crucial part of the process by which the level is replicated on the user's screen. The MAP file contains hundreds of fixed, specific instructions that the computer reads to assemble the audiovisual elements in a particular sequence to recreate the level as designed by its creator. (E.R. 588-93.) These instructions embody the narrative and specific juxtapositions of images that make up a particular level. Indeed, the specific *combination* of elements comprising each level, embodied in the MAP file, is protected expression separate and apart from each individual piece of protected art. Since important components of the ultimate screen display are included in *both* Nuke It and DN3D, Nuke It does "contain or produce [DN3D's] output in some concrete or permanent form." See *Galoob*, 964 F.2d at 969.

Micro Star has stressed that Nuke It cannot create audiovisual displays by itself but must interact with the DN3D program. The issue, however, is the extent to which Nuke It infringes the protected expression of DN3D, and users cannot obtain access to any of the 300 user created levels on Nuke It simply by using the original DN3D game alone; they need the MAP files contained on the Nuke It disk. Remove those MAP files from the computer and all 300 user-created levels will be gone from the game play. That is because the levels themselves -- including each one's layout, narrative, and specific juxtaposition of elements -- are contained permanently in the MAP file. Put another way, the derivative work, or level, created by the user is fixed in the MAP file, whether that MAP file exists in that user's PC, on the Internet, or on the Nuke It disk.[2]

The key distinction between Nuke It and the Game Genie is confirmed by the way the respective products are marketed and used. The Game Genie was not offered as a product containing new stories or scenarios for Nintendo's games, but rather as a tool that players could use to alter temporarily certain character attributes. In contrast, Nuke It is advertised as containing more than 300 new scenarios for DN3D, and Micro Star's own attorney has stated: "The screen shots accurately described the levels that consumers would find *"on the Duke Nukem 3D" CD."* Micro Star Emergency Stay Application at 5 (emphasis added).

Consumers buying the Nuke It CD will take it home, insert it in their computers (already loaded with DN3D), and have access to the 300 levels fixed on this product. From the consumer's point of view, it would not matter whether the code or data to draw each piece of artwork were contained on the new disk or whether, as is the case, the disk contains commands that cause the creative artwork to be displayed and positioned. Since infringement would be clear in the former situation, it makes no sense to hold that the exact same result achieved in the latter, more efficient way robs the expression underlying the derivative work of protection from unauthorized commercial exploitation. Either way, the interaction between expression contained in the disk and the game engine is a far cry from the Game Genie. Notably, once play on a particular level is completed, that level remains fixed in the MAP file and does not evaporate, as does game play altered by the Game Genie.

The other crucial factor distinguishing *Galoob* is the substantial and unrebutted evidence of economic harm in this case. It is not disputed that Movants are distributing their own professionally produced set of new levels for DN3D, with which Nuke It and its sequel will attempt to compete during the current holiday sales

---

[2] It is not disputed that many of the levels on Nuke It include substantial segments of one or more of the original 29 levels in the DN3D game, sometimes embodying the whole level with very minor changes. Thus, much of the protected design and narrative expression contained directly on the Nuke It disk is original expression of Movants covered by the DN3D copyright. To call this expression "mere data" because it is stored in digital form is tantamount to claiming that the digital storing of music on an audio CD is not subject to copyright protection.

season. Rubin Reply Decl. ¶ 10 (E.R. *562).* In addition, Wizardworks, another GTI subsidiary, has already produced an authorized collection of user-created DN3D levels, as to which Movants take responsibility for quality control. *Id.* ¶ 3 (E.R. 558-59).

Thus, unlike the defendant in *Galoob,* Micro Star is interfering with the statutorily protected exploitation of Movants' copyrighted work. Such economic impact was key to the *Galoob* Court in distinguishing *Midway Mfg. Co. v. Artic Int'l, Inc.*, 704 F.2d 1009 (7th Cir.), *cert. denied,* 464 U.S. 823 (1983), in which the marketing of a computer chip that could be inserted in arcade video games to alter play was held to create an infringing derivative work. This Court observed that the chip in *Midway* "substantially copied and replaced" the chip included in the original game and that purchasers of the chip "benefitted economically by offering the altered game for use by the general public." *See* 964 F.2d at 969. These distinctions weigh heavily in favor of Movants here.[3]

In sum, Micro Star's argument that Nuke It does not "contain" DN3D's protected expression is at sharp variance with the reality of how the product is marketed and played. The District Court erred in

---

[3] In analyzing *Galoob,* commentators have stressed the interrelated factors of non-commercial home use and lack of competitive injury as being key to the Court's finding of no fixation. *See, e.g.,* Carla Passero, *Comment, Copyright Implications of Collage Works* 11 SANTA CLARA COMPUTER & HIGH TECH. L.J. 319, 326 (July *1995);* Martin R. Glick and M. Patricia Mayer, *Galoob v. Nintendo: When is a Modified Computer Program an Infringing Derivative Work?* 8 COMPUTER LAW 1, *5* (September 1991).

Other cases similarly suggest that where commercial uses are involved, fixation may more readily be found. In *MM Sys. Corp. v. Peak Computer Inc.*, 991 F.2d 511, 517-19 (9th Cir. 1993), *cert. denied, 510* U.S. 1033 (1994), the Court held that a competitor's loading of software into a computer's random access memory ("RAM") involved the creation of a sufficiently fixed copy to constitute copyright infringement, even though the copy may exist Only for a short time. This holding implicitly rejects a broad reading of *Galoob's* fixation analysis. Indeed, another court reaching the same conclusion distinguished *Galoob* as holding that "non-commercial private enjoyment did not constitute a derivative work for purposes of copyright law." *Advanced Computer Servs. v. MM Sys. Corp.*, 845 F. Supp. 356, 364 n.9 (E.D. Va. 1994). "Galoob focuses on the doctrine of fair use and does not hold that a RAM copy is insufficiently fixed to constitute a copy under the Act." *Id.*

[In my view, much of this material should have been incorporated into the main body of the text, especially the first paragraph of this footnote, explaining how the commentaries reflecting on the *Galoob* decision have, in essence, made the decision work for FormGen.]

its overly broad interpretation of and reliance on *Galoob.* In view of the District Court's other rulings in favor of Movants, reversal on this legal issue leads inexorably to the conclusion that a broader injunction --barring the sale of *any* user-created levels without Movants' permission --should be entered pending trial.

[This is what FormGen could have done with the *Galoob* decision:

***Galoob* makes it clear that Micro Star has infringed FormGen's copyright by taking FormGen's "Duke Nukem 3D" protected images, sounds, and computer code, and using these elements for its commercial gain. As *Galoob* recognized, a "derivative work" is defined by the copyright act as being "based upon one or more preexisting works." 17 U.S.C. § 101, quoted in *Galoob*, 964 F.2d 965, 967. Micro Star so much as admits that its CD compilation is based on "Duke Nukem 3D." Thus, Micro Star's lawyer admitted to the district court that the screen shots on its CD box were a representation of what someone purchasing the CD would get by using the CD. (E.R. 840, 843, 847) Indeed, in its brief on this appeal, Micro Star again admits that the screen shots pictured on its packaging are "snapshots of the scenes from the" files on the Nuke It CD. (Micro Star Br. 3.)**

Additionally, and significantly, 17 U.S.C. § 101 gives the following examples of what the statute considers, without limitation, to be a "derivative work":

> **A "derivative work" is a work based upon one or more preexisting works, such as a translation, *musical arrangement*, dramatization, fictionalization, motion picture version, sound recording, *art reproduction*, abridgment, condensation, *or any other form in which a work may be recast, transformed, or adapted.***

17 U.S.C. § 101, quoted in *Galoob*, 964 F.2d at 967. (Emphasis added.) Micro Star's CD is akin to a "musical arrangement"; rather than taking music composed by someone and recasting it, Micro Star's CD takes protected sounds and images of the "Duke Nukem 3D" game and recasts them into

varying arrangements of action and scene or "levels" as these arrangements are referred to the computer gaming industry. As such, it is like taking someone's art and reproducing it for one;s own commercial benefit. Under 17 U.S.C. § 101 the reproduction and arrangement would be a "derivative work," and the three-hundred arrangements of the "Duke Nukem 3D" play on Micro Star's CD are, similarly "derivative works." That this is true is demonstrated by the statute's generic description of the "derivative work": "or any other form in which a work may be recast, transformed, or adapted." There can be no dispute but that Micro Star's CD-loaded arrangements or levels have done all three. They have:

> **1) "recast" the "Duke Nukem 3D" action by taking the copyrighted images and sounds;**
>
> **2) "transformed" the "Duke Nukem 3D" action by taking the copyrighted images and sounds; and**
>
> **3) "adapted" the "Duke Nukem 3D" action by taking the copyrighted images and sounds.**

There can thus be no dispute but that the levels or arrangements on the Micro Star CD are "derivative works."

Galoob **itself recognizes that what the Micro Star CD does infringes the copyrighted "Duke Nukem 3D" game, its images and sounds. The code on the CD's various levels or arrangements reach in and recast, transform and adapt those "Duke Nukem 3D" sounds and images, and each level does it permanently—the combination of the code on each of the levels in combination with the "Duke Nukem 3D" game software will produce the** ***same sequence of action and sounds against the same background and effects*** ***<u>each time</u>*****. Under** ***Galoob*****, this is infringement: the CD thus, to use the phrasing of** ***Galoob*****, "incorporate[s] a protected work [the "Duke Nukem 3D" images and sounds] in some concrete or permanent form." 964 F.2d at 969. Indeed, Micro Star does not, and cannot, not dispute but that many of the levels on its CD**

include substantial segments of one or more of the original twenty-nine levels in the "Duke Nukem 3D" game, sometimes embodying the whole level with only very minor changes.

This case is on all fours with *Mirage Editions, Inc. v. Albuquerque A.R.T. Co.*, 856 F.2d 1341 (9th Cir. 1988), *cert. denied*, 489 U.S. 1018, cited and relied on by *Galoob*, 964 F.2d at 968. In *Mirage Editions*, this circuit held: "[b]y borrowing and mounting the preexisting, copyrighted individual art images without the consent of the copyright proprietors ... [Albuquerque A.R.T.] has prepared a derivative work and infringed the subject copyrights." *Mirage*, 856 F.2d at 1343. *Galoob*'s analysis of *Mirage Editions* underscores its significance here:

> **The ceramic tiles physically incorporated the copyrighted works in a form that could be sold. Perhaps more importantly, sales of the tiles supplanted purchasers' demand for the underlying works. Our holding in Mirage Editions would have been much different if Albuquerque A.R.T. had distributed lenses that merely enabled users to view several artworks simultaneously.**

***Galoob*, 964 F.2d at 968. The code on the Micro Star CD physically takes and incorporates the "Duke Nukem 3D" copyrighted works so Micro Star can sell its CDs; without this incorporation the Micro Star CDs would be worth nothing more than their value as a coaster.**

Dealing with *Galoob* along the lines that I suggest can turn that case, relied upon by the district court to deny FormGen the relief it wanted, into FormGen's sword. You must do that with every adverse case that is cited by either a trial court or an opponent; as you will do on the trial level, make the "bad" facts or cases work *for you!*]

C. The Distinctive Structure of DN3D MAP Files Constitutes Separately Protectable Expression

The District Court erred in declining to accept a separate and alternative ground that independently supports a broader injunction: that the MAP file structure created by Apogee itself embodies substantial protected expression improperly copied and distributed for commercial gain by Micro Star. *See NIMMER* § 2.18[H][3][b], at 2-204.20-2.204.21 (1996) (audiovisual work is copyrightable separately from computer program).

Copyright protection extends both to "literal" aspects of computer programs (the specific, verbatim commands embodying protected original expression) and their "non-literal" aspects *(e.g.,* distinctive structure). *See Johnson Controls, Inc. v. Phoenix Control Sys., Inc.*, 886 F.2d 1173, 1175 (9th Cir. 1989). Among the non-literal elements that may be protected is the unique or distinctive structure of data files. *See CMAX/Cleveland, Inc. v. UCR, Inc.*, 804 F. Supp. 337, 354 (M.D. Ga. 1992). The sequence of field definitions and other variables defining a file structure may be protected where they are not dictated by mere functionality or compatibility requirement with other systems but are selected creatively "from a myriad of possible options and alternatives" and therefore reflect the computer programmer's art. *Id.* at 355.

[I haven't the foggiest idea of what this last sentence says. Admittedly, federal judges have more familiarity with the arcane terminology of computer programming—especially those whose jurisdiction encompasses Silicon Valley. Nevertheless, never write a sentence in your brief that non-specialists will not understand.]

The record contains detailed and entirely unrefuted evidence submitted by Allen H. Blum III, Producer for DN3D, describing the protected expression reflected in the DN3D MAP file structure.

[This goes to the heart of this aspect of the argument. But is the argument as forceful and clear as it could be? Let's see if the brief demonstrates that the MAP files are "protected expression."]

In particular, each MAP file is comprised of four main sections, describing (a) the position within the level at which game play begins; (b) the "sectors" (broad physical game play areas) in the level; (c) the "walls" (other physical structures and boundaries within the level); and (d) the "sprites" (characters, monsters, and other objects) in the level. Blum Reply Decl. ¶91 20-24 (E.R. 588-89).

[This is beginning to edge into a fairly technical area. Let me suggest that when you face the problem of dealing with technical terms, that you *invert the sequence*: use the common words first, so the reader will grasp initially what you're talking about, and then use the technical term:

> ***Example:*** **Each MAP files is comprised of four main parts, each of which helps to create the display that the gamer sees on the computer screen. One part of the MAP file picks the level of play. Another part of the MAP file sets up and electronically paints the area—called a "sector"—where the game will be played at the specified level. A third part paints electronically the physical structures—called "walls"— within the "sector." Finally, there are the various creatures or objects whose movements and actions either the gamer or the computer directs. These creatures are called "sprites."**

***Strategy*:**

> **☞ When you have a technical term that has to be defined, *invert the definitional sequence*: use the common words of definition first, then the technical word. Another example: In the movie, Mary is someone with whom Jane, the main character, can talk to and express her innermost thoughts. Mary is used by the screenwriter to be a reflector for Jane's thoughts and is known in the movie business as the "reflection."]**

Each of these four main sections in turn contains a number of specific pieces of information, known as "parameters," that determine the selection, placement, and characteristics of the various elements contained in the level. *Id.* ¶91 25-3 1 (E.R. 589-92). For example, the "sprite" section contains 23 different parameters determining such variables as the "visual and functional characteristics of the sprite," the "visual angle that the sprite is facing," and the "characteristics of special visual effects of the sprite." *Id.* 91 30 (E.R. 591-92). This complex series of parameters included in the MAP files, arranged in a particular sequence, determines the placement and characteristics of sprites and other audiovisual elements and the overall look and feel of a particular level. Blum Reply Decl. ¶9118-35 & Exhs. 12, 13 (E.R. 588-93). As Mr. Blum stated:

[*Exercise:* re-write the above paragraph and make it clear by inverting the definitional sequence, and by using simple, non-technical words wherever possible:

____

____

(continue on your own paper)]

Each of the parameters that define and describe the DN3D elements that appear in each level were defined by the DN3D programmers. These parameters are not determined by any computer hardware requirements or software industry standards, and involve a substantial exercise of judgment and creativity. DN3D will operate correctly only with map files that conform to the unique DN3D map file structure. *Id.* at 91 33 (E.R. 592). Micro Star's own expert admitted that the MAP files "must comply with the structure of a MAP file predetermined by the [sic] Duke Nukem." Johnson-Laird Decl. ¶17 (E.R. 422).

Thus, on the undisputed law and facts, Micro Star violates DN3D's copyright by reproducing and distributing by sale MAP files embodying the unique file structure created by Apogee's designers. The District Court failed to address this argument in any detail, simply stating that "the Court is not convinced that Movants have shown that the data sequence in the Nuke ft MAP files is subject to copyright protection." (E.R. 1069.) Given the undisputed facts in this issue, the Court's determination was an error of law. Based on the present record, Movants have demonstrated a substantial likelihood of success at trial on this additional ground of copyright infringement warranting the issuance of a broader injunction -- barring the sale of any user-created levels without Movants' permission -- pending trial.

[Nice summation paragraph.]

D. The Reproduction and Distribution for Sale of User-Created Levels is Not a Fair Use of Movants' Protected Expression

Recognition that the sale of MAP files containing user-created levels infringes DN3D's copyright requires the granting of a preliminary injunction against such sale unless Nuke It constitutes a "fair use" under § 107 of the Copyright Act. Micro Star's failure to satisfy that affirmative defense follows a *fortiori* from the District Court's ruling that use of the screen shots alone was not a fair use.

Section 107 of the Copyright Act codifies the four non-exclusive factors that a court is to consider when making its fair use assessment --(1) the purpose and character of the use; (2) the nature of the copyrighted work; (3) the amount and substantiality of expression taken; and (4) the harm to the copyright owner's rights. *See Triad Svs. Corp. v. Southeastern Express Co.*, 64 F.3d 1330, 1336 (9th Cir. 1995), *cert. denied,* 116 S. Ct. 1015 (1996). Here, each factor weighs heavily against a finding of fair use.

[As you will see in a few paragraphs, FormGen's discussion of the fourth factor is the most powerful. This, then, is where this section should start.

***Strategy*:**

☞ When you must discuss several factors of a multi-part test, start with your strongest point first.]

Under the first factor, the purpose and character of the use of DN3D in Nuke It, Micro Star concedes (Br. 11 n.9) that the product involved no creativity. Micro Star merely compiled levels otherwise available for non-commercial use on the Internet and did not create even one of the files. This compilation, even if it arguably simplifies access to user levels, is not a transformative use. *See Princeton Univ. Press v. Michigan Document Servs., Inc.*, 1996 WL 648261, *67 (6th Cir. Nov. 8, 1996) *(en banc)* (photocopying of academic material for ease of use not transformative); *American Geophysical Union v. Texaco, Inc.*, 60 F.3d 913, 923 (2d Cir. 1994) (same), *cert. denied,* 116 S. Ct. 592 *(1995).* Accordingly, the obvious commercial character of Nuke It "loom[s] large," *Campbell v. Acuff-Rose Music, Inc.*, 510 U.S. *569*, 580 (1994).

Micro Star's purely commercial use bears no relationship to the examples of fair use purposes set forth in the preamble to § 107: criticism, comment, news reporting, teaching, scholarship, and research. While this list is not exhaustive, integral to any finding of fair use is the conclusion that the "public interest in the free flow of information outweighs the copyright holder's interest in exclusive control over the work." *Hustler Magazine, Inc. v. Moral Majority, Inc.*, 796 F.2d 1148, 1151-52 (9th Cir. 1986). Such public interest is in no way served by Micro Star's non-transformative commercial exploitation of Movants' protected expression.

The second factor, the nature of the copyrighted work, also cuts against Micro Star. As noted in *Galoob,* "the creative nature of audiovisual displays weighs against a finding of fair use." 964 F.2d at 972. Because DN3D is a purely fictional, artistic work, the public interest in the free flow of information is not served by Micro Star's misappropriation.

The third factor -- the amount of expression taken -- is easily applied: Nuke It qualitatively and quantitatively uses the protected expression of DN3D. User-created levels are simply cut and paste jobs that include exact copies of the distinctive characters and artwork of DN3D and that are stored in a distinctive data structure. To defeat fair use, it need not be shown that Nuke It uses all or substantially all of the expression in DN3D, so long as the expression taken was qualitatively important. *See Hi-Tech Video Prods., Inc. v. Capital Cities/ABC, Inc.*, 804 F. Supp. 950, 956 (W.D. Mich. 1992) (use of 38 seconds out of 18-minute video weighs against finding a fair use where material taken amounted to "at least an important ingredient, if not the heart, of a copyrighted work") (citation omitted), *rev 'd on other grounds, 58* F.3d 1092 (6th Cir. 1995). *Campbell* reiterated the rule that -- in evaluating the fourth factor --a court must weigh not only harm to the original product but also harm to the market for derivative works. 510 U.S. at 590. The District Court here, observing that it was critical to this Court's holding in *Galoob* that Nintendo had no plans to put out something like Game Genie (E.R. 1071), concluded that the fourth factor weighed against Micro Star because FormGen has plans to put out new add-on products for DN3D. "As such, the Court finds that Nuke It does affect the value of Movants' copyrighted work." *Id.* Moreover, Apogee has licensed Wizardworks to distribute an authorized user-created level pack. Rubin Reply Decl. ¶ 3 (E.R. 558-59). Simply put, Micro Star is invading the market for authorized DN3D products at the height of the holiday season. No greater harm to the market for derivative works of copyrighted expression could be stated.

In *Princeton Univ. Press,* the Sixth Circuit recently reaffirmed that the fourth factor alone can defeat a fair use claim where a derivative product -- in that case, unlicensed "coursepacks" compiling excerpts of protected academic works for classroom use -- occupies a market niche in which the copyright owner is competing. Since a market existed in which publishers collected licensing fees from other sellers of coursepacks, issuance of competing unauthorized coursepacks was not a fair use. 1996 WL 648261, at *5. Thus, Micro Star's suggestion that the wholesale downloading, copying, and commercial distribution of DN3D MAP files in competition with licensed products could constitute a "fair use" borders on the frivolous.

[This discussion and especially this last paragraph is first-rate. It is powerful and persuasive.]

E. The Other Factors Governing the Granting of an Injunction Strongly Favor Movants

A finding of likelihood of success on the merits entitles Movants to a presumption of irreparable harm. *See Johnson Controls, Inc. v. Phoenix Control Sys., Inc.*, 886 F.2d 1173, 1174 (9th Cir. 1989). Even without the presumption, the irreparable harm here is classic and indisputable: Micro Star is marketing without license *(i.e.,* without paying royalties) an infringing product in direct competition with Movants and is launching a new similar product (Nuke It 1000) on the eve of the crucial holiday season. Nuke It will directly impact upon sales of a licensed professionally produced DN3D level pack and an authorized collection of user-created levels, marketed by FormGen and Wizardworks, respectively. Rubin Reply Decl. ¶¶ 9-13 (E.R. *561-63).*

Moreover, the harm to Movants' goodwill flowing from dissemination of the amateur-quality levels contained in Nuke It will be hard to remedy and impossible to quantify fully. The harm embraces not just lost sales on authorized level pack products but also injury to the reputation and commercial viability of the DN3D franchise as a whole. Such injury through a loss of quality control has been widely recognized as irreparable harm. *See, e.g., King v. Innovation Books,* 976 F.2d 824, 832 (2d Cir. 1992); *Polo Fashions, Inc. v. Craftex, Inc.*, 816 F.2d 145, 147 (4th Cir. 1987); *Sega Enters., Ltd. v. Maphia,* 857 F. Supp. 679, 683-84 (N.D. Cal. 1994). "[I]f an infringer's product is of poor quality, or simply not worth the price, a more lasting but not readily measurable injury may be inflicted on the plaintiffs reputation in the market." *Omega Importing Corp. v. Petri-Kine Camera Co.*, 451 F.2d 1190, 1195 (2d Cir. 1971).

The relative standing of the parties also underscores the dramatic balance of hardships. Movants have expended substantial effort and creativity in developing, publishing, and marketing DN3D and in building it into the most exciting and lucrative computer game franchise of the year. Micro Star, in contrast, has created nothing. It has simply downloaded levels created by others, put them on a disk, and placed its knock-off product in software stores where it could be sold next to DN3D'[4] and benefit (without paying royalties) from the association with that successful product.

Micro Star may argue that an injunction barring its sale of user-created levels will harm it by depriving it of the opportunity to exploit the present demand for DN3D with its knock-off product. But as between Micro Star and Movants, it is clearly the latter who have the greater legal and equitable claim -- indeed, the exclusive rights -- to exploit the Duke Nukem franchise while it remains so valuable, in the same way that the copyright owner of a Grisham novel, a "Star Wars" film, or a Springsteen song will seek to garner revenues from authorized derivative and ancillary products. So clear is this balance of equities that an injunction pending trial is warranted even if Movants establish only serious issues on the merits and not a likelihood of success on their appeal. In any event, a bond in the amount of $500,000 has already been posted by Movants for Micro Star's protection in the unlikely event that Movants do not prevail at trial. (S.E.R. 1246-51.)

---

[4] Indeed, uncontroverted evidence was presented at the hearing below that Nuke It is still being sold by Software, Etc. as a "Duke Nukem 3D Add-on." (E.R. 754-59.)

Finally, the public interest strongly favors an injunction here. The rationale for protecting copyrighted works is to encourage creativity, from which the public benefits:

> Since Congress has elected to grant certain exclusive rights to the owner of a copyright in a protected work, it is virtually axiomatic that the public interest can only be served by upholding copyright protections and, correspondingly, preventing the misappropriation of the skill, creative energies, and resources which are invested in the protected work.

Apple Computer Inc. v. Franklin Computer Corp., 714 F.2d 1240, 1254-55 (3d Cir. 1983) (citation omitted), *cert. denied,* 464 U.S. 1033 (1984).

[This quotation is powerful and should go at the beginning of the argument section; it sets the policy (justice among the parties and for society) tone.]

Failing to protect the expression contained in the user-created levels would have significant consequences. Movants included the Build Editor to permit consumers to enjoy, on a non-commercial basis, additional levels of play created by themselves and other users. If Micro Star were to prevail, a game creator would lose the valuable right to control commercial exploitation through the release of authorized add-on games. This result would likely lead to the elimination of the "Build Editor" type of feature -- to the detriment of the consumer. Neither the facts nor the rationale of *Galoob* suggests that the distribution of hundreds of selfcontained scenarios for DN3D -- however the images are generated --should be subject to unlimited commercial exploitation by anyone with access to the Internet. A preliminary injunction barring the sale of user-created levels is therefore warranted.[5]

---

[5] Micro Star's own characterizations of this case refute its invocation of the purported doctrine of "copyright misuse'. Micro Star told the District Court that Movants "have a good faith argument regarding copyright law" (Micro Star Br. in Opposition to Preliminary Injunction Motion, S.E.R. 1115-30) and in this Court (Br. 20) concedes that the copyright issues present at least a "close question." The assertion that Movants acted with "actual malice" by writing a demand letter before they had formally effected copyright registration (Br. 38) is frivolous; the registration was not necessary to create copyright protection, and by filing the application

(continued)

[Material Relating to the Other Issues Omitted]

* * *

CONCLUSION

For the foregoing reasons, Movants respectfully request the Court to affirm the injunctive relief granted by the District Court, reverse the District Court's erroneous legal ruling that the user-created levels do not contain protected expression, and remand the case for entry of a broader preliminary injunction (1) barring Micro Star from marketing and selling unauthorized products containing user-created levels or other protected expression of DN3D; and (2) ordering an immediate recall of any such products that have entered the distribution channel during pendency of this appeal.

— — —

Now we'll look at Micro Star's Argument:

(continued)
Movants gained the right to sue. *See, e.g., Dielsi v. Falk*, 916 F. Supp. 985, 994 & n.6 (C.D. Cal. 1996); *Wilson v. Mr. Tee's*, 855 F. Supp. 679, 682 (D.N.J. 1994). Micro Star's hearsay allegations of supposed threats to retailers (unsupported by any testimony in the court below) would, if they even existed, concern statements privileged in the presence of a good faith intellectual property claim. *See Kaplan v. Helenhart Novelty Corn.*, 182 F.2d 311, 313-14 (2d Cir. 1950).

Moreover, Micro Star's repeated references (Br. 4 n.2, 13, 38) to the supposed lack of a valid copyright registration is misleading at best. Micro Star somehow forgets that it commenced this pre-emptive suit, putting in issue Movants' claims. Before asserting their compulsory counterclaims on August 9, 1996, Movants applied to register with the Copyright Office on an expedited basis, and Apogee now holds copyright certificates effective as of August 8. Remarkably, Micro Star continues to rely upon the Sekela Declaration asserting that no registration was found on file (Br. 13), although Micro Star knew (and knows) that the dated certificates were already in the record of the case (Kirby Decl. dated August 24, 1996, ¶ 13, S.E.R. 1120), and are now on file in the Copyright Office. *See* Kirby Reply Declaration; Supplemental Sekela Declaration (E.R. 721-23, 748-49).

ARGUMENT

I.
STANDARDS OF REVIEW

A district court's decision to deny an injunction is subject to very limited review. *Apple Computer, Inc. v. Formula International, Inc.*, 725 F.2d 521, 523 (9th Cir. 1984). The denial of an injunction will only be reversed where the district court abused its discretion, based the injunction on an erroneous legal standard, or on clearly erroneous findings of fact. *Miller v. California Pacific Medical Center,* 19 F.3d 449 *455* (9th Cir. 1994)(en banc).

> A district judge may abuse his discretion in any of three ways: (1) he may apply incorrect substantive law or an incorrect preliminary injunction standard; (2) he may rest his decision to grant or deny a preliminary injunction on a clearly erroneous finding of fact...; or (3) he may apply an acceptable preliminary injunction standard in a manner that results in an abuse of discretion.

Zepeda v. United States I.N.S., 753 F.2d 719, 724 (9th Cir. 1983).

[This is good. Clear, concise, and unassailable because it is a direct quote.]

> In reviewing the district judge's application of a preliminary injunction test to the substantive legal area, the court of appeals cannot reverse the order simply because it would have decided the case differently. *Id.* Apogee may not like the factual findings and ultimate decision on the issues raised in its cross-appeal, but on these facts, there has been no "clear error in judgment" in determining that the *Nuke It* CD did not infringe on any *Duke Nukem 3D* copyright.

II.
APOGEE CANNOT SHOW BOTH ORIGINALITY AND COPYING OF PROTECTED ELEMENTS OF *DUKE NUKEM 3D* IN ORDER TO ESTABLISH A LIKELIHOOD OF SUCCESS ON THE MERITS

[All uppercase caps *and* underlining makes this very difficult to read.]

To prevail on a claim of copyright infringement, the plaintiff must show (1) ownership of a valid copyright and (2) copying by Micro Star of protected components of the copyrighted material. *Feist,* 499 U.S. at 361, 111 S.Ct. at 1296.[1] The district court held that neither prong was met and those findings of fact cannot be disturbed unless clearly erroneous. Moreover, even without such a deferential standard of review, Apogee has not shown either copying or that the format of the MAP files is either original or non-functional. Apogee's attempt to create new law has already been explicitly rejected in *Galoob.* Micro Star has successfully rebutted the presumption of originality normally arising from a valid Certificate of Registration. *See Brown Bag Software,* 960 F.2d at 1474-1475.

[This is a typical way lawyers present their arguments. But, so far this is just rhetoric, without showing support in the record and specific case law (rather than generic statements about copyright law). To most judges, this will be seen as merely introductory—to paraphrase that commercial for the hamburger chain that was popular a decade or so ago: there is no "beef" yet!]

A. The District Court's Finding of Fact That There was No Copying Establishes That There Is No Likelihood Of Success.

Copying is a factual issue. *Gates Rubber Co. v. Bando Chemical Industries, Ltd.*, 9 F.3d 823, 831 (10th Cir. 1993); *Sid & Marty Krofft Television Productions, Inc. v. McDonalds Corp.*, 562 F.2d 1157, 1164 (9th Cir. 1977). The district court made findings

---

[1] This is obviously the correct law regarding the underlying issues, and therefore is not an abuse of discretion.

[This footnote does not make sense.]

of fact that (1) the MAP files did not contain any protected elements of *Duke Nukem 3D, i.e.*, no copying, and (2) that Apogee did not carry its burden of proving that the file format of the MAP files was protectible expression, *i.e.*, either not original or not protectible. These findings of fact by the district court should end the inquiry into the district court's denial of injunctive relief, since without copying of protected elements of *Duke Nukem 3D,* Apogee cannot show a likelihood of success on its infringement.

[This focuses on the standard of review, and is good. The underlying assumption of this part of the argument—that the party seeking a preliminary injunction must demonstrate, among other things, a likelihood of success—should be stated specifically, however, perhaps in this sequence:

> **A party seeking a preliminary injunction must establish both: 1) that it will suffer irreparable harm unless the injunction is granted, and 2) that it is likely to succeed on the merits so that unless a preliminary injunction is granted, the ultimate success on the merits would be largely meaningless. [citation] Of course, if the party seeking a preliminary injunction cannot show that it will ultimately succeed on the merits, granting of a preliminary injunction will harm the party enjoined. [citation, with parenthetical] Here, given the district court's findings of fact, which, as we will demonstrate, are not—by any stretch of the imagination— "clearly erroneous," FormGen will not succeed on the merits, and, therefore, the district court did not abuse its discretion in refusing to grant the preliminary injunction. *See* [citation and parenthetical].**

[You have to be alert that all the bases are touched: you can't run from first to third unless you touch second along the way. Here, Micro Star forgot to touch second base. Although that would not be fatal when the underlying assumption is well-known and has been mentioned by the trial court as well as by the parties in other parts of the brief, and the "likelihood of success" criterion is well-known to every judge, there will be other times when the underlying assumption is not so well known, and omission of a clear statement, with supporting authority, could be fatal—just as

failure to touch second base would be fatal if that invalidated the winning run.]

> Apogee avoided any discussion of the standard of review of these factual findings, with good reason. Fed. R. Civ. P. 52(a) states that findings of fact "shall not be set aside unless clearly erroneous ... "; *Anderson,* 470 U.S. at 573, 105 S.Ct. at 1511.
>
> > If the district court's account of the evidence is plausible, the court of appeals may not reverse it even though it would have weighed the evidence differently. Where there are two permissible views of the evidence, the factfinder's choice between them cannot be clearly erroneous. [citations omitted] This is so even when the district court's findings do not rest on credibility determinations, but are based on physical or documentary evidence or inferences from other facts.
>
> *Id.* Both findings are supported by evidence in the record and inferences reasonably drawn from evidence in the record. Moreover, even Apogee now apparently concedes that the MAP files do not contain any copyright-protected elements of *Duke Nukem 3D.* Thus, the district court's first finding of fact cannot be disputed. Since the *Nuke It* data files have not copied any protected audiovisual elements from *Duke Nukem 3D,* there is no likelihood of success on the infringement claim.

[The key and Achilles Heel to the above paragraph is, as phrased by Micro Star: that "the *Nuke It* data files have not copied any protected audiovisual elements from *Duke Nukem 3D*." It is the key because Micro Star is arguing that under *Galoob*, transitory use—as opposed to physical copying—is not infringement. It makes Micro Star vulnerable because under FormGen's theory Micro Star is appropriating, and profiting from, FormGen's protected expressive creations—the "*Duke Nukem 3D*" sights and sounds. Thus, according to FormGen, Micro Star is similar to the infringer in *Mirage Editions*, where the images were taken for the infringer's profit. Here, the district court's finding that the sights and sounds come from the "*Duke Nukem 3D*" game when a player uses the Micro Star CD supports, in my view, FormGen, not Micro Star. This is a major weakness in Micro Star's position,

and, in order to win, Micro Star is going to have to hit the transitory nature of the images and sounds, and tie that to the *Galoob* holding. We'll see if Micro Star does that.]

> B. The District Court's Finding Of Fact That Apogee Failed To Show That The File Format Of The MAP Files Is Subject To Copyright Protection Is Dispositive Of Apogee's Likelihood Of Success On That Claim.

[This goes to the district court's alternative ruling, summed in its enigmatic sentence: "As to the Nuke It [Micro Star] CD-ROM itself, and the programming it contains, the court is not convinced that the movants have shown that the data sequence in the Nuke It MAP files is subject to copyright protection."]

> The district court found that Apogee had not carried its burden of proving that the actual file format of the MAP files was subject to copyright protection. Whether a particular element of a computer program is subject to copyright protection is a finding of fact subject to a clearly erroneous standard of review. *Johnson Controls, Inc. v. Phoenix Controls Systems, Inc.*, 886 F.2d 1173, 1175-1176 (9th Cir. 1989).

[This is a bit misleading. On first reading, it seems to say that the *legal* question of whether an element is subject to copyright protection is decided under the "clearly erroneous" deferential standard. That of course, is not true. Legal questions are decided by an appellate court *de novo.* What *Johnson Controls* says, is that although the question of what constitutes a copyrightable element is a question of law, it is an issue of fact whether a particular element is that *type* of element. *See Johnson Controls*, 886 F.2d at 1175 ("Whether the non-literal components of a program, including the structure, sequence and organization and user interface, are protected depends on whether, on the particular facts of each case, the component in question qualifies as an expression of an idea, or an idea itself.") This distinction is something that every judge (or at least most judges) will know instinctively—without having to even look at the cases. Putting out the spin that blurs this distinction will, even if it is done inadvertently, hurt your credibility. In writing your briefs, be alert to this potential problem.]

Micro Star presented evidence showing that the MAP files were merely data in a form readable by *Duke Nukem 3D.* Micro Star established that add-on levels originally created for *Doom* could be played by *Duke Nukem 3D.* Micro Star showed that the structure of the MAP file is merely the order of the elements referencing various images in the *Duke Nukem 3D* file libraries. Additionally, Micro Star argued successfully that the data file's format was no more copyrightable than the data file created when a lawyer (or a judge) used a word processor to create a brief, or the rules of grammar underlying the English language.[2] Both logic and Micro Star's evidence and testimony, as well as the inferences reasonably drawn from those facts and the weight accorded the differing expert declarations (to the extent that Mr. Blum, Apogee's programmer, can be termed an "expert"), show that at the very least there were two permissible views of the evidence from which the district court could choose. The district court's choice cannot be clearly erroneous.[3] *Anderson,* 470 U.S. at 573.

1. Apogee Failed to Demonstrate That the .Map File Format Is Protected by Copyright

When a computer program's structure may be protected from non-literal copying is a complex subject treated at length in many important opinions. See e.g. *Computer Associates International, Inc. v. Altai, Inc.*, 982 F.2d 693, 703-715 (2nd Cir. 1992); *Gates Rubber,* 9 F.3d at 846. A computer program's structure cannot be protected by copyright when the part of the program alleged to be

---

[2] For example, when a lawyer creates a brief on a specific word processor, the brief is unreadable unless viewed with that word processor because it is stored in a particular file format readable by that word processor. In order to have compatibility with another word processor, the same data file format must be used. This concept was implicitly and explicitly recognized in the "spell checker" analogy in *Galoob,* 964 F.2d at 969. Moreover, "an author cannot acquire patent-like protection by putting an idea, process, method of operation in an unintelligible format and asserting copyright infringement against those who try to understand that idea, process or method of operation. *Atari Games Corp. v. Nintendo of America, Inc.*, 975 F.2d 832, 842 (Fed. Cir. 1992).

[3] The Supreme Court also stated that "when a trial judge's finding is based on his decision to credit testimony of one of two or more witnesses, each of whom has told coherent and facially plausible story that is not contradicted by extrinsic evidence, that finding, if not internally inconsistent, can virtually never be clear error." *Anderson,* 470 U.S. at 575. Thus, the district court's decision to credit Mr. Johnson-Laird's testimony (and the inferences drawn therefrom and from the record) over Mr. Blum's cannot be clearly erroneous.

protected constitutes a "process" or "method of operation"; when the structure involved was dictated by the nature of the program; or when the programming was created as a result of the compatibility requirements of the other programs with which the software was designed to operate. All of these exceptions apply here.

(a). *A Data File Format Is A "Method of Operation" And Is Consequently Ineligible for Copyright Protection*

In order to determine whether one piece of software infringes on the copyright of another, it is necessary to eliminate from consideration those elements of the allegedly infringed program that are not protected by copyright. 3 M. Nimmer, *Nimmer on Copyright,* (1996) §13.03(f), 13-117 (*"Nimmer"*). This is accomplished by filtering out various elements of the allegedly infringed program which would not be protected as a result of well established copyright doctrines. *Sega,* 977 F.2d. at 1525; *Gates Rubber*, 9 F.3d at 834. In order to perform this analysis, one must first examine what is claimed to be protected expression in the allegedly infringed software program.

Here, Apogee claims the .MAP file format is unique because in order to create levels under the *Duke Nukem 3D* program the data file used by the program must provide information about four types of "elements". Each of these elements are [*SIC*] defined by a number of variables, which must be set forth in a specific order. Many elements can be placed in a level, and each one must be accompanied by the specific variables (or parameters) which define the object. Thus, the .MAP file must be organized in a specific format so that the *Duke Nukem 3D* program knows which elements are included in the level and what the parameters are for each element selected. If the data is not inserted in the proper format or at a proper location in the file, the program will not be able to read the file correctly.

It is clear that the structure of a .MAP file is determined by the complex variables that the program must read in order to generate a new level. But where the content of an allegedly protected work is dictated by the function of the work, copyright protection will rarely be found. This is the lesson of the seminal case, *Baker v. Selden* 101 U.S. 99, 103 (1879), where the Court held

> "And where the art [a work] teaches cannot be used without employing the methods and diagrams used to illustrate the [work], or such as are similar to them, such methods and diagrams are to be considered as necessary incidents to the art, and given therewith to the public."

See also, 17 U.S.C. § 102(b). Here, the "art" involved is the creation of complex levels through use of *Duke Nukem 3D*. A "necessary incident" to the art is the use of the .MAP file format, since that is the only way the "art" can be generated. Under *Baker* such necessary incidents are in the public domain.

[Micro Star appears to be citing *Baker* for the proposition that the file format that permits the extraction and use of the "Duke Nukem 3D" images and sounds is a "method of operation." But all *Baker* holds is that one cannot get patent-like protection for a process by writing a description of that process, as looking at the excerpt from *Baker* that Micro Star quotes (which I have underlined) in its context:

> **"The copyright of a book on perspective, no matter how many drawings and illustrations it may contain, gives no exclusive right to the modes of drawing described, though they may never have been known or used before. By publishing the book, without getting a patent for the art, the latter is given to the public. . . . The very object of publishing a book on science or the useful arts is to communicate to the world the useful knowledge which it contains. But this object would be frustrated if the knowledge could not be used without incurring the guilt of piracy of the book. <u>And where the art it teaches cannot be used without employing the methods and diagrams used to illustrate the book, or such as are similar to them, such methods and diagrams are to be considered as necessary incidents to the art, and given therewith to the public</u>; not given for the purpose of publication in other works explanatory of the art, but for the purpose of practical application."**

101 U.S. at 103. 17 U.S.C. § 102(b) says the same thing:

> **"In no case does copyright protection for an original work of authorship extend to any idea, procedure, process, system, method of operation, concept, principle, or discovery, regardless of the form in which it is described, explained, illustrated, or embodied in such work."**

FormGen's main contention is that Micro Star is glomming on to, and therefore infringing, its protected "Duke Nukem 3D" sounds, images, and code. That the "device" used to make the copyrighted images and sounds visible and audible may not be protectable *via* the copyright law (and FormGen disputes that), does not negate the copyright protection in those images and sounds, any more than a record player whose patent protection might have expired strips copyright protection from every vinyl record that uses that device—now in the public domain because its patent protection has expired.]

> If the format of a .MAP file constitutes or is a critical part of a "procedure", process", or "method of operation" it is not protected. It is difficult to see how any other conclusion could be reached here. The form of a .MAP file was established solely because of its function. It is a critical component in the process of transforming a string of data parameters into a playable level. It is an integral part of the process which instructs the computer to perform the operating functions of the program, *Apple Computer, Inc. v. Franklin Computer Corp.* 714, F.2d 1240, 1251(9th Cir. 1983) and thus, is consequently unprotectible. *See also Lotus Development Corporation v. Borland International, Inc.*, 49 F.3d 807, 8 15-816 (1st Cir. 1995) *aff'd by an equally divided court* 116 S.Ct. 804 (1996) (where program could not operate without use of allegedly protected menu system, menu system was unprotectible).[4]

[Micro Star seems to be relying on a false syllogism: *Some* computer-command sequences may not be copyrightable (for which it cites *Lotus Development*); therefore *all* computer-command sequences are not subject to copyright protection. If Micro Star is to win on this aspect of the district court's ruling, it

---

[4] It is immaterial that Apogee could have structured the MAP file format in a different way. As the First Circuit noted in *Lotus,* the initial inquiry is not whether the computer program "incorporates any expression", the initial inquiry is whether the material in question "is a 'method of operation'". 49 F.3d at 816.

will have to show that the district court's analysis—which appears to me, at least, to be a mixed question of law and fact—has support in the record. So far, Micro Star has not done that. You decide whether it ever does.]

It is ironic that the Supreme Court case decided a century before the existence of personal computers definitively shows that file formats cannot be copyrighted. The plaintiff in *Baker v. Selden* held a copyright on a book explaining a bookkeeping system. The Supreme Court held that authorship of a book about bookkeeping did not give the author a monopoly on all ledger systems which used bookkeeping methods similar to those described in the work. 101 U.S. at 103. A system which organizes data for subsequent manipulation is simply not copyrightable.

(b) *Similarities In Computer Files Necessitated By Compatibility Can Not Be A Basis For Infringement*

Under traditional copyright doctrine, the scenes a faire doctrine denies copyright protection to standard elements one would expect to find in a work on a particular subject. *Landsberg v. Scrabble Crossword Game Players, Inc.*, 736 F.2d 485, 488-489 (9th Cir. 1984). Analogously, similarities in computer files which arise as a result of external considerations such as programming conventions or technical specifications can also not be infringements. Such elements are standard in this specific milieu. *Nimmer* at §13.3(F)(3), p. 13-130. Thus numerous courts have recognized that the scenes a faire doctrine as applied to computer programs permits similarities which arise as a result of the **compatibility requirements** of the programs with which a particular piece of software is designed to operate. *Sega,* 977 F.2d at 1525-1527; *Altai,* 982 F.3d at 709; *Gates Rubber,* 9 F.3d at 838.

Compatibility, of course, is the precise reason why *Nuke It* contains .MAP files. Only by using these files can the software distributed by Micro Star be compatible with *Duke Nukem 3D.* Creating or distributing files which are compatible with the software program created by another entity is simply not a copyright violation and has never been found to be one.

The most analogous case concerns compatibility of macro formats as opposed to file formats. In *Lotus,* Lotus contended the defendant's program infringed because its "key reader" could translate macros written for Lotus' "1-2-3" program into macros readable by the defendant's competing spreadsheet. The First Circuit found nothing wrong with a computer program that transformed a macro written in one format into another, particularly since the macro was "clearly the user's own work product"--an observation which also applies here. See, *also Nimmer* at § 13.03 [f][3] [e], p. 13-139-13-140; *Engineering Dynamics, Inc. v. Structural Software, Inc.*, 46 F.3d 408, 410 (5th Cir. 1995) (expressly holding that earlier finding of infringement should not be interpreted as a finding that software that reads and translates different file formats is a violation of the Copyright Act.) Surely, if there is nothing wrong with translating a macro written in a specific format into a competing product's format, there can be no impropriety in creating or distributing data files that have always been intended to be read by a specific computer program, albeit a program created by another company.

The case Apogee relies upon, *CMAX/Cleveland, Inc. v. USR, Inc.*, 804 F. Supp. 337 (N.D. Ga. 1992) does not hold to the contrary. CMAX was concerned with a computer program, not a computer format. In *CMAX* the defendants had essentially copied the plaintiffs inventory control program making only fig leaf changes to the system. They did not just create data files that could be run with the plaintiffs program, they duplicated the plaintiffs program so that their old data files could be used by the "new program". This would be analogous to Micro Star attempting to write a *Duke Nukem 3D* replacement program that was facially different but could run .MAP files. Moreover, the court implicitly approved the use of third party conversion programs which translated data files from one file format to another. 804 F.Supp. at 350, 354. Permitting use of these programs is at odds with Apogee's position that the software designer should have control over the creation and distribution of all files which use its program's data file format.

(c). *Granting Apogee A Monopoly In The .MAP Format Would Be Contrary To The Goals Of The Copyright Act*

Apogee does not discuss the enormous consequences of the ruling it seeks, which would affect every computer user (including virtually every business) in the United States. This is because a ruling that the author of software has the right to control the creation and distribution of all files which use its data file format would affect every user of every piece of commercial software, including users of word processors, computer spreadsheets and database applications.

[This seems to me going for a "bridge too far." It is on the right track. Policy arguments affect a judge's analysis when they are consistent with 1) the judge's views about how the competing interests in society should be balanced; *and* 2) they are consistent with recognized and accepted principles in the field under review. The *sine qua non* of both patent law and copyright law is to spur development and growth by protecting creative enterprise. The interest in limiting a predatory overreaching by the copyright or patent owner is secondary.

An effective policy argument in this area must resonate with the goals in the field under review. Micro Star's "sky is falling" argument, reflected in the paragraph immediately preceding this comment, almost splashes cold water in face of the copyright law's goals. Yes, authors of copyrighted material *are* entitled, to use Micro Star's words, "the right to control the creation and distribution" of their protected work. Thus, Micro Star's paragraph really misstates the argument, which is that in their view the "Duke Nukem 3D" .MAP files are not protectable. But, in order to succeed on this issue, Micro Star has to show why. So far, it has not done so. All we have is rhetoric.

What would be an argument that is *consistent* with the underlying policy of the copyright law? Micro Star has merely facilitated gamers doing what FormGen wanted them to do: download from the internet added levels for the "Duke Nukem 3D" game, and Micro Star is entitled to recoup its costs and to have a fair profit. Indeed, the FormGen/Micro Star situation is similar to that of a publisher who has made its free community-newspaper available in street-corner newspaper boxes complaining because an entrepreneur has taken those free newspapers, and, for a price, distributed them to the homes of readers who were willing to pay for that convenience. Or, changing the facts slightly, an entrepreneur buys books at the customer's request and, saving the customer the bother of having to make a trip to the store, delivers those books to the customer at his or her home, again

taking a cut to recoup costs and make a profit. The distributor's service benefits both the consumer and the publisher. Indeed, the latter scenario is pretty much what Jeff Bezos has done with Amazon.com.]

> Under Apogee's theory, the designer of commercial software would have a monopoly on all files that could be used with its product.

[No. Only those files that infringe. This one sentence shows how circular Micro Star's reasoning is. The copyright law gives to the creator a limited time during which to exploit the creation—a monopoly. The real question is two-fold: whether there is a copyrightable creation; and, if there is 2) whether other work infringes. So far, all Micro Star is giving us is rhetoric.]

> The ruling requested by Apogee would also have an enormous effect on many businesses which specialize in modifying and customizing commercial software. These types of companies do not only make "add on" products for commercial games but provide useful innovations for all types of commercial software. In the legal market, for example, software companies have customized popular word processing software so that they can more easily compile complex commercial contracts, or generate tables of authorities. Such businesses would be ruined overnight if this Court ruled that unauthorized creation or modification of files with proprietary formats constituted copyright infringement.

[Again, this puts the cart before the horse. This argument has the seeds of being a good one. But what must be done? Set out the so-called "horribles" (the horrible stuff that will flow from a ruling adverse to your client) — supported by case authority if possible — that shows that the concern about which the *rhetoric* shouts is a concern that the real world mirrors. In short, *give examples*, and *show how those examples* are similar to the dispute over the computer code here. In a sense, you will be writing a modified Brandeis Brief—lifting the cover from the arcane world where all this is playing out. Just as the Supreme Court might not have decided *Brown v. Board of Education* the way it did without all the empirical data referenced in the briefs seeking to set aside the "separate but equal" precedent, you want to give to your appellate court the data that shows that your chicken-little shouts

of gloom (and, in this case, apparently *Doom*) are founded in reality—specifics! You must do this in every case!]

Such a ruling would not necessarily be bounded by file formats. Under Apogee's theory, any software product that permits the creation of a file format should have the ability to control all file formats created as a result of its product. This logic would mean that the developers of operating systems--the software that permits computer hardware to interact with computer software--would ultimately control all files created on a computer system. After all, without the operating system, software products such as *Duke Nukem 3D* or standard word processors and spreadsheets could not operate at all.

The goal of the copyright laws is not to create a monopoly of information in the hands of a few. The Copyright Act cannot be used in a way which would cause this result. Granting Apogee and other software companies a monopoly on the file format used by their software would hinder the development of creative expression, not further it.

2. Micro Star Has Rebutted Any Presumption Of Originality Arising From The Certificate Of Registration.

Only the original elements of a copyrighted work are protected by the copyright. 17 U.S.C. § 102(a).

[Statutes should be quoted in the text: 17 U.S.C. § 102(a), provides:

> **Copyright protection subsists, in accordance with this title, in original works of authorship fixed in any tangible medium of expression, now known or later developed, from which they can be perceived, reproduced, or otherwise communicated, either directly or with the aid of a machine or device. Works of authorship include the following categories:**

(1) literary works;
(2) musical works, including any accompanying words;
(3) dramatic works, including any accompanying music;
(4) pantomimes and choreographic works;
(5) pictorial, graphic, and sculptural works;
(6) motion pictures and other audiovisual works;
(7) sound recordings; and
(8) architectural works.

Don't make the judges who will deciding your case have to go to the books to see what the statute says.]

"Originality" requires that the work be independently created by the author. *Feist,* 499 U.S. at 361. Thus, a court must filter out all unoriginal elements of a program. *Gates Rubber,* 9 F.3d at 837. Although it is clear that Apogee is entitled to a presumption of originality arising from a valid Certificate of Registration of Copyright, that presumption can be rebutted by a showing that various elements have been used in other programs prior to the registration of *Duke Nukem 3D. Brown Bag,* 960 F.2d at 1474.

The presumption of originality has been rebutted by Micro Star. Substantial portions of *Duke Nukem 3D* were directly copied from *Doom,* including the look and feel of the games, the structure and sequence of the game play, an almost identical copy of *Doom's* control panel, many similar weapons, substantially similar characteristics of play, numerous identical or virtually identical visual elements and the identical keyboard keystrokes to play the game. *See* Moore Declaration (E.R. 409).[5]

[Micro Star should set out a table, that shows the similarities, and then marshall case law to back up its claim that either part or all of "Duke Nukem 3D" is not entitled to copyright protection; every stone in the mosaic must be there is you want the court to accept your argument.]

---

5 It is ironic that Apogee claims that a clearly functional and minor aspect of the *Duke Nukem 3D* game such as the MAP file format is subject to copyright, when the entire *Duke Nukem 3D* game is itself substantially a copy *of Doom* with a few different monsters thrown in along with "Duke Nukem's" ability to jump up and down.

> Whether functional or lacking originality, the district court therefore had ample evidence from which it could reasonably infer that the MAP file format was not "original" for the purpose of injunctive relief. *Brown Bag,* 960 F.2d at 1475. Finally, as factual findings, those determinations cannot be deemed "clearly erroneous.

[Micro Star has not demonstrated this. We have not seen anything in this brief that gives us a basis to conclude that the district court had any evidence from which it conclude that the .MAP file format was not sufficiently original to be entitled to copyright protection. Interestingly, as we have seen, FormGen has not demonstrated that the .MAP file format *is* original; it too relies mostly on rhetoric. But, FormGen has one thing going for it that Micro Star does not have, even though FormGen is the appellant: the presumption of originality. Micro Star has not demonstrated how it rebutted that presumption. When you write your briefs, be alert to the trap of rhetoric. You need facts—fact stacked upon fact stacked upon fact until you have built your case. Stated another way, cases are made (or lost) on the facts (or lack of facts).]

III.

EVEN IF THE DISTRICT COURT'S DISPOSITIVE FINDINGS OF FACT COULD BE DISREGARDED, *NUKE IT* DOES NOT INFRINGE BECAUSE IT IS NOT A DERIVATIVE WORK.

[Again, do not use all uppercase caps. Underlining to this extent also does not help. We know that it is a caption.]

> Even if this Court were as free to disregard the district court's findings of fact as is Apogee,

[Oh my ... avoid snide remarks. Your client may think it clever; the judges will see a lack of professionalism.]

> the result would still be the same since *Nuke It* is not a derivative work, and therefore does not violate any *Duke Nukem 3D* copyright. Fundamentally, "a derivative work must incorporate a protected work in some concrete or permanent form." *Galoob,* 964 F.2d at 967. As discussed above, Apogee concedes that no portion of *Duke*

Nukem 3D is incorporated into any MAP file in some permanent form. To avoid the clearly erroneous standard, Apogee has created a convoluted argument that the audiovisual display generated by *Duke Nukem 3D* when using a *Nuke It* MAP file is incorporated into the MAP file on the *Nuke It* CD. Thus, according to Apogee, the MAP file is a derivative work fixed on the CD and violates Apogee's right to distribute derivative works. The Ninth Circuit has rejected this exact position in *Galoob and* the case on which both Nintendo, and now Apogee, relied.

Galoob involved a product called the "Game Genie," which was designed to plug into Nintendo's enormously popular video game console to modify Nintendo games.'[6] The Game Genie — like the *Nuke It* MAP files — allowed a player to alter a game by altering data from the Nintendo game cartridge and replacing data in the Nintendo game cartridge with its own data created by the player. *Galoob,* 964 F.2d at 967. The Game Genie like the *Nuke It* MAP files "[could not] produce an audiovisual display; the underlying display must be produced by a Nintendo... game cartridge." *Id.* at 968. The Game Genie — like the *Nuke it* MAP files — "merely enhance[d] the audiovisual display (or underlying data bytes) that originate in the Nintendo game cartridges." *Id.* In essence, the purchaser could play the Nintendo game, viewing Nintendo's audiovisual display but temporarily change the game by using the Game Genie. The Game Genie like the *Nuke It* MAP files did not alter data that was stored in Nintendo's game cartridges, but merely changed the audiovisual images the Nintendo game displayed on the television screen for the duration of the game. *Id.*

The Game Genie did not create a derivative work. *Id.* at 968-969. This Court's reasoning in *Galoob* applies with equal force regarding *Nuke ft.*

> The Game Genie can only enhance, and cannot duplicate or recast, a Nintendo game's output in some concrete or permanent form, nor does it supplant demand for Nintendo game cartridges. Such innovations rarely will constitute infringing derivative works under the Copyright Act.

---

[6] An extensive recitation of the facts and reasoning in *Galoob* that was ultimately adopted by the Ninth Circuit can be found in the district court's opinion in the case, 780 F.Supp. 1283 (N.D.Cal. 1991), *affirmed,* 964 F.2d 965 (9th Cir. 1992).

Galoob, 964 F.2d at 969.

The three decisive reasons for holding that no derivative work was created in *Galoob* are all present here. Like the Game Genie, the MAP files do not physically incorporate a portion of the copyrighted work. All of the copyrightable elements of *Duke Nukem 3D,* if any, observed on the video screen when playing the *Nuke It* MAP files are contained on the Duke Nukem 3D program files. Like the Game Genie, the *Nuke It* MAP files do not supplant the demand for *Duke Nukem 3D. Id.* at 969. A purchaser of Nuke It must own a copy of the registered version of Duke Nukem 3D. Like the Game Genie, the MAP files on *Nuke It* are useless by themselves, they can only enhance *Duke Nukem 3D's* output, not replace the game itself. *Id.* Finally, the only information contained in the MAP files is generic data, not programming.[7] The data is not copyrightable. *See Feist,* 499 U.S. at 344 (facts are not copyrightable)."[8]

---

[7] Technically, the *Nuke It* MAP files only substitute for data in the *Duke Nukem 3D* program. Instead of executing data contained in the *Duke Nukem 3D* program, the *Duke Nukem 3D* program merely executes the data contained on the *Nuke It* CD to draw the audiovisual images on the user's screen. No MAP file, either in the *Duke Nukem 3D* program or on the *Nuke It* CD, can generate any visual images. Only *Duke Nukem 3D* can create those images.

[This is good stuff. But why is Micro Star putting it in a footnote? It seems to me that this is the heart of the comparison with *Galoob*? It thus should be prominent in the main body of the text. Also, it needs record references. Without references to the record, most judges will ignore it.

Also, why start this key paragraph with the apologetic "Technically"? Use of the word "Technically" belittles the significance of what comes after it, and may even induce some judges to skim the paragraph, mistakingly surmising that this paragraph is just to tie up some loose "technical" ends, and thus need not be read closely. These are important facts that show that the Micro Star CD is very similar to the game-altering device in *Galoob*; they should be proclaimed, not hidden away in a footnote.]

[8] The word processor again provides an apt analogy to the current case. Corel has a copyright for Wordperfect, one of the most popular wordprocessors. If the Court uses Wordperfect to author an opinion (which is stored in Wordperfect's data file format), that opinion, which is a data file, is useless unless it is viewed with Wordperfect. Clearly, the Court's written opinion, created with Wordperfect, is not a derivative work of Wordperfect.
[This, too, should not be in a footnote.]

Apogee's analysis proposes that the altered audiovisual displays created when *Duke Nukem 3D* reads the MAP files are the derivative works, and that these works are permanently incorporated on the *Nuke It* CD.[9] This precise argument, and the principal case on which Apogee relied, was directly rejected by *Galoob. Galoob,* 964 F.2d at 969 ("It cannot be a derivative work... A derivative work must incorporate a protected work in some concrete or permanent form. ***We cannot ignore the actual source of the Game Genie's display.")*** (emphasis added). The MAP files do not incorporate the protected work, period.[10]

In *Galoob,* Nintendo "relied heavily on *Midway Mfg. Co. v. Arctic* [*sic*—**"Artic"**] *International, Inc.*, 704 F.2d 1009 (7th Cir.), *cert denied,* 464 U.S. 823 (1983)." *Galoob,* 964 F.2d at 969. Apogee contends that this Court distinguished *Midway* on the ground that the "economic impact" on the copyright holder "was key." In fact, however, *Midway* was a standard application of the rule just laid down in *Galoob.* In *Midway,* the defendant "substantially copied and replaced the chip that was originally distributed by Midway." *Galoob,* 964 F.2d at 969. The chip physically incorporated the protected work in the chip, and therefore was a derivative work. Even so, the Seventh Circuit recognized that the definition of "derivative work must be stretched to accommodate speeded up video games." *Id.* The Ninth Circuit declined to stretch the definition — as Apogee now requests — any further. *Id.*

[Up to here, Micro Star is making a powerful argument, based on recent Ninth Circuit precedent in an analogous case, and one on which the district court relied in deciding not to enjoin Micro Star from selling its CD. This material should have been Micro Star's *first* argument. Micro Star should have used it to ram home its

---

[9] Contrary to Apogee's frequent assertions sprinkled throughout its Brief, the district court determined that "the layout, narrative and juxtaposition of elements" are not protected, and are not found on the MAP files.

[10] Apogee contends that the "MAP files contain hundreds of fixed, specific instructions that ... embody the narrative and specific juxtapositions of images that make up a particular level." This statement is a mere word game. As Apogee knows, the data in the MAP files are no more instructions than a Dewey Decimal number in the Library of Congress is an instruction. *See* Johnson-Laird Declaration (E.R. 420-422).

point that its CD merely enhances the "Duke Nukem 3D" game, as the device in *Galoob* enhanced the Nintendo game.

But the points scored by Micro Star's argument, with which the district court agreed, that *Galoob* is controlling, is weakened significantly by the following paragraph.]

> Finally, and again contrary to the record in the district court, Apogee contends that the district court abused its discretion by misapplying *Galoob*. Apogee's Brief, p. 18. However, a glance at the district court's Memorandum Order shows that the district court simply and correctly found that the MAP files did not contain protected expression of *Duke Nukem 3D* and that Apogee had not carried its burden of proving that the data format of the MAP files was protectible. The district court did not state that *Galoob* mandated those findings, although as set forth above, the court easily and correctly could have. Thus, the district court neither abused its discretion nor made clearly erroneous findings of fact in denying the requested injunction.

[Micro Star says: "The district court did not state that *Galoob* mandated those findings." Huh? Why back away from *Galoob*? Why treat it as an uncouth cousin you did not want invited to the party? The district court *did* of course rely on *Galoob*; it spent a significant part of its written decision discussing *Galoob*. And, it should be pointed out, the district court's decision was sent to West for publication in the F. Supp. reports; this was no file-drawer decision, hastily scribbled to dispose of a case.]

IV.

> <u>EVEN IF THE COURT WAS WILLING TO MAKE THE LEAP OF LOGIC REQUESTED BY APOGEE, THE *NUKE IT* MAP FILES ARE A "FAIR USE"]</u>

[Aside the being difficult to read because the caption is all in uppercase caps and underlined, this is an "even if" argument that should never be made. As discussed previously, both here and in *The "How-To-Win" Trial Manual*, using the "even if" argument is bad for two reasons. First, it is perceived as conceding the point (why say "even if 'X' is true" if you are confident in your position that "X" is not true?) Second, both at

the trial and appellate levels you hurt your credibility by making arguments that are inconsistent. Using the phrase "but even if" or some variant, you are making the reader see the two arguments as being *inconsistent*, even though, in fact, they might not be. Simply put, Micro Star's position that the MAP files are not subject to copyright protection is not inconsistent with its secondary position that their use of the MAP files meets all of the elements of "fair use."]

> The district court's factual findings, the fact that there was no copying of protected portions of *Duke Nukem 3D,* and the related fact that the MAP files are not derivative works all show that there was no abuse of discretion in denying the injunction. However, even if the MAP files were derivative works, injunctive relief should still be denied pursuant to the fair use doctrine, 17 U.S.C. § 107.

[This paragraph should be revised to eliminate the "but even if argument":

> **"The district court's factual findings that Micro Star did not copy protected portions of *Duke Nukem 3D,* and that the MAP files are not derivative works all show that there was no abuse of discretion in denying the injunction. Moreover, Micro Star's use of the MAP files satisfies each and every element of the 'fair use' doctrine."**

Also, 17 U.S.C. § 107 should be set out. Every time you use a statute to support your argument, you should set out its text. After all, how can the reader analyze your statutory argument unless the statute is presented so the reader can use it as a framework?

17 U.S. C. § 107 provides:

> **Notwithstanding the provisions of sections 106 and 106A, the fair use of a copyrighted work, including such use by reproduction in copies or phonorecords or by any other means specified by that section, for purposes such as criticism, comment, news reporting, teaching (including multiple copies for classroom use), scholarship, or research, is not an infringement of copyright. In**

determining whether the use made of a work in any particular case is a fair use the factors to be considered shall include--

(1) the purpose and character of the use, including whether such use is of a commercial nature or is for nonprofit educational purposes;

(2) the nature of the copyrighted work;

(3) the amount and substantiality of the portion used in relation to the copyrighted work as a whole; and

(4) the effect of the use upon the potential market for or value of the copyrighted work.

The fact that a work is unpublished shall not itself bar a finding of fair use if such finding is made upon consideration of all the above factors.]

The doctrine of fair use allows a holder of the privilege to use copyrighted material without the consent of the copyright holder. The fair use doctrine "calls for a case-by-case analysis" guided by the criteria articulated by Congress at 17 U.S.C. § 107 weighed together in order to resolve the question of fair use. *Campbell v. Acuff-Rose Music Co.*, 510 U.S. 569, 114 S.Ct. 1164, 1170, 127 L.Ed.2d 500 (1994). The "fair use" defense is subject to this Court's *de novo* review. *Lewis Galoob Toys, Inc. v. Nintendo of America, Inc.*, 964 F.2d 965, 969 (9th Cir. 1992), *cert. denied* 113 S.Ct. 1582 (1993); *Fisher v. Dees,* 794 F.2d 432, 435 (9th Cir. 1986). Apogee, as the moving party, bears the burden of showing that it is likely to prevail on any affirmative defenses raised by Micro Star, including Micro Star's affirmative defense of fair use. *Dr. Seuss Enterprises L.P. v. Penguin Books USA, Inc.*, 924 F. Supp. 1559, 1562 (S.D.Cal. 1996); *Religious Technology Center,* 923 F. Supp. at 1241.

A. *Nuke It* Is A Transformative, Albeit Commercial Use.

The first fair use factor is the "purpose and character of the use." 17 U.S.C. §107(1). As the Supreme Court recently explained:

> The central purpose of this investigation is to see.., whether the new work merely supersedes the objects of the original creation [] or instead adds something new, with a further purpose or different character, altering the first with new expression, meaning or message; it asks, in other words, whether and to what extent the new work is 'transformative.' [] Although such transformative use is not absolutely necessary for a finding of fair use, [] the goal of copyright to promote science in the arts, is generally furthered by the creation of transformative works.

Cambell, 114 S.Ct. at 1171 (interior quotes and citations omitted). Under this test, *Nuke It* qualifies as a "transformative work;" as an add-on game, *Nuke It* "adds something new" to *Duke Nukem 3D.* Indeed, the compilation of the add-on levels not only provides a public service, but is also independently copyrightable by Micro Star. *Feist,* 499 U.S. at 344. Thus, this factor favors Micro Star. *Accord, Sega,* 977 F.2d at 1522-23 (first factor weighs in favor of defendant where use led to increase in availability of compatible video games).

In addition to examining whether the work is transformative, courts also examine whether the use is commercial. The relevant inquiry here should be directed at the end user, not Micro Star, since the end user actually creates the derivative work, if at all. *Galoob,* 964 F.2d at 970. The end users, *i.e.,* the purchasers of Nuke It, are engaged in a "non-commercial, non-profit activity." *Id.* Even if this Court focused on Micro Star, commercial use does not dictate against a finding of fair use, as most of the uses listed in the statute as "generally conducted for profit in this country." *Campbell,* 114 S.Ct. at 1169. As in *Sega,* considerations of public benefit can also outweigh the fact that an alleged infringer may gain commercially. *Sega,* 977 F.2d at 1523. In *Sega,* the court upheld a competitor's use of Sega's proprietary source code to allow the competitor's product to be played on Sega's best-selling video game console as a fair use. As the Ninth Circuit noted, Accolade's use of the Sega source code

> led to an increase in the number of independently designed video game programs offered for use with the Genesis console. It is precisely this growth of creative expression, based on the dissemination of other

> creative works and the unprotected ideas contained in those works, that the Copyright Act was intended to promote.

Id. In a similar vein, the Ninth Circuit in *Galoob* noted that even though "the derivative works created by the Game Genie are comprised almost entirely of Nintendo's copyrighted displays," Galoob's use of the derivative works was a protected fair use. *Galoob,* 964 F.2d at 971. Furthermore, the Ninth Circuit noted that the purchasers of the Game Genie did not view Nintendo's derivative works without first paying Nintendo for the privilege, which militated in favor [*SIC* **of**] a fair, albeit commercial, use. *Id.*

In this case, the analysis and the result are the same. The registered version of *Duke Nukem 3D* is analogous to the console in *Sega* and *Galoob.* The add-on levels are analogous to the new games being marketed by Accolade for use in the Sega console and the "Game Genie" marketed in *Galoob.* The derivative works created by the MAP files are presumptively a "fair use." *Galoob,* 964 F.2d at 970. The purchasers of *Duke Nukem 3D* have already paid for the right to create and to play the derivative works using the *Duke Nukem 3D* "console" for non-profit, noncommercial purposes. *Id.*

[This is good, powerful stuff.]

B. The MAP files Are Unprotected Data or Function, And Thus The Nature Of The Copyrighted Work Weighs Against Copyright Protection.

The second fair use factor is the "nature of the copyrighted work." 17 U.S.C. § 107(2). This Court's holding in *Sega* governs the analysis of this statutory factor:

> The second statutory factor, the nature of the copyrighted work, reflects the fact that not all copyrighted works are entitled to the same level of protection. The protection established by the Copyright Act for original works of authorship does not extend to. . . the functional or factual aspects of the work. [] To the extent that a work is functional or factual, it may be copied. ...

Sega, 977 F.2d at 1524. The values in the *Nuke It* data files are not the protectible, expressive portion of the *Duke Nukem 3D* program; those values are "functional" aspects of the program that *Nuke It* (or any other add-on product) must be able to use to be compatible with *Duke Nukem 3D.* Since this data is "functional," and not protected by copyright, under *Sega,* its use in *Nuke It* is a fair use.

In addition, *Duke Nukem 3D* is published (as compared to unpublished), favoring fair use. *Religious Technology Center,* 923 F.Supp. at 1245. As discussed in the Moore Declaration and the Johnson-Laird Declaration, much of *Duke Nukem 3D* is merely a derivative work of two earlier games, *Doom* and *Wolfenstein.* While *Duke Nukem 3D* has creative elements, the majority of the game is functional. This factor also favors fair use.

[This is good as far as it goes. But don't force the judges to pick up the record understand your argument. This would have been a perfect place to quote from the declarations and argue from them. As discussed in the first part of this book, I recommend a paraphrase and then the supporting quote. Here, we have a weak paraphrase (more of a mere reference, actually) and no quote. As a judge reading this brief, I want to see what the declaration actually says, and whether it, in fact, supports the inference Micro Star is seeking to have me draw. Too many times, I have pulled out the record, examined the referenced material, only to find that the brief's "spin" on the material was so extreme that it bordered on misrepresentation. At this point in reading Micro Star's brief, I have no idea whether or not there is misrepresentation here. My assumption is that there is not; but my experience with reading thousands of briefs gives me a certain degree of skepticism. It is your job to make certain that the judge reading your brief has that skepticism defused by you.]

C. The Amount and Substantiality of the Portion Used in Relation to the Copyrighted Work.

The third statutory factor focuses on "the amount and substantiality of the portion used in relationship to the copyrighted work as a whole." 17 U.S.C. §107(3). As discussed *supra,* Apogee has not made any showing concerning (1) what elements of Duke Nukem 3D are copyrighted, and which of those elements are being used in the MAP files on the *Nuke It* CD. Moreover, there are no portions of the copyrighted work used in the MAP files on Nuke It. Since no portion of the copyrighted work has been used, this element is either entitled to no weight, or weighs in favor of fair use.

[Good point. But it can be made more clear: "FormGen has not shown that *any* of the elements of "Duke Nukem 3D" that are

properly copyrighted are being used in the *Nuke It* MAP files. Indeed, there are *no* portions of the copyrighted work used in the MAP files on *Nuke It*. Since no portion of the copyrighted work has been used, subsection (3) militates in a finding of fair use here."]

D. *Nuke It* Has No Effect On The Potential Market For *Duke Nukem 3D*.

The fourth fair use factor is the "effect on the potential market for the copyrighted work." *Sega,* 977 F.2d at 1523. This factor is "the most important, and indeed, central fair use factor." *Galoob,* 964 F.2d at 971 quoting *Stewart v. A bend,* 495 U.S. 207, 238, 110 S.Ct. 1750, 109 L.Ed.2d 184 (1990). It weighs strongly in favor of finding fair use because *Nuke It* cannot possibly harm the demand for *Duke Nukem 3D* since, for every *Nuke It* CD sold, there must be a corresponding sale of the *registered* version of *Duke Nukem 3D.* No consumer can purchase *Nuke It* instead of *Duke Nukem 3D.* Thus, *Nuke It* can neither diminish potential sales of *Duke Nukem 3D,* interfere with its marketability, nor usurp the market. *Sega,* 977 F.2d at 1523; Johnson-Laird Declaration, ¶¶ 57-63 (E.R. 433-435) (expert testimony refuting any market harm). As this Court stated in *Sega,*

> Accolade did not attempt to "scoop" Sega's release of any particular game or games, but sought only to become a legitimate competitor in the field of Genesis-compatible video games. Within that market, it is the characteristics of the game program as experienced by the user that determine the program's commercial success.

Id. Nuke It has only sought to provide a legitimate service in the field of *Duke Nukem 3D*—compatible games.[11] Neither the MAP files nor use of the

---

[11] As set forth in the Moore Declaration, ¶ 5, although the add-on levels on the *Nuke It* CD are available on the Internet, it would take a user much of a day to obtain all of the data files, assuming that he knew where to look. (E.R. 413). There is also a significant problem with viruses in game files on the Internet. *Id.* The user of *Nuke It* does not have to worry about viruses in the files. (E.R. 413). The user of *Duke Nukem 3D* may not even have access to the Internet at all. *Id.* Therefore, *Nuke It* provides a service that the public clearly desired. The fact that Micro Star had the idea to market such a product months before Apogee did is no reason for attempted monopolization. *See e.g., Sega,* 977 F.2d at 1523.

[This is good, but why put it in a footnote. It should be woven with the argument that Micro Star is merely facilitating what FormGen envisioned, saving the gamers from having to take the time, energy, and risk of downloading the files from the internet.]

file format is unfair. *Sega,* 977 F.2d at 1523 (use enabling the copier to enter the market for works of the same type is fair use).

The role of the court "is to distinguish between" products that "suppress demand" and "copyright infringement, which usurps it." *Campbell,* 114 S.Ct. at 1178. The fact that *Nuke It* may impair the market for Apogee's planned "professional" add-on product by effective competition "is no more relevant under copyright than the like threat to the original market." *Id.*

Even if it were a consideration, there is no basis for assuming that Nuke It has significantly affected the market for any add-on levels marketed by Apogee.

[The dreaded "but even if" argument again! Let's recast it: FormGen has not shown how or to what extent Micro Star's CD will hurt its projected sales of its own projected compilations—any more than the internet postings have and will do. Indeed, by encouraging gamers who play the "Duke Nukem 3D" game to post additional levels on the internet, FormGen recognized that such free availability of add-ons not produced by it help, rather than hurt, its profitability.]

> In any event, any attempt to monopolize the market by making it impossible for others to compete runs counter to the statutory purpose of promoting creative expression and cannot constitute a strong equitable basis for resisting the invocation of the fair use doctrine. the fourth statutory factor weighs in Accolade's, not Sega's favor, notwithstanding the minor economic loss Sega may suffer.

Sega, 977 F.2d at 1524.

Nothing prevents Apogee from introducing its own "official" add-on levels for *Duke Nukem 3D.* As this Court [*sic* **said**] in *Sega,* it does not "seem unlikely that a consumer particularly interested in *[Duke Nukem 3D]* might purchase both [add-on products]." *Sega,* 977 F.2d at 1523. In fact, other than Apogee's own self-serving statement that *Nuke It* would affect sales of its own add-on product, there is no evidence of any market harm whatsoever in the record. The functional aspects of computer video games "do not merit protection" under the Copyright Act.[12] *Sega,* 977 F.2d at 1527. Just as Sega could not prevent the release of Genesis-compatible games in *Sega,* Apogee may not prevent the release of *Duke Nukem 3D* compatible add-on disks here.

V.

APOGEE HAS WAIVED ANY CONTROL OVER THE MAP FILES BY IMPLIEDLY LICENSING, WAIVING OR ABANDONING IT RIGHTS

As fully discussed in Micro Star's Opening Brief, pp. 32-35, Apogee has waived its right to control the data files by granting permission (or a non-exclusive license) to *Duke Nukem 3D's* fans to create and distribute new add-on levels. *See e.g., I.A.E., Inc. v. Shaver,* 74 F.3d 768, 775 (7th Cir. 1996). Determining the scope of Apogee's written license is purely a matter of contract interpretation for the court. It rests on viewing the contract in the context of the undisputed facts. The legal conclusion that there was no implied license or waiver of the right of commercial distribution is subject to *de novo* review. *See Fleischman Distilling Corp. v. Maier Brewing Co.,* 314 F.2d 149, 152 n.2 (9th Cir. 1963).

Apogee specifically programmed its data files so that the users could alter and exchange different *Duke Nukem 3D* scenarios on the Internet. To this end, Apogee provided level editors and templates which give the *Duke Nukem 3D* player the instructions and ability to create their own new files or scenarios. Apogee admits that it actively encourages the development of different levels and the exchange of these levels over the Internet. Apogee cannot now assert copyright claims on the data which it encouraged *Duke Nukem 3D* players to use, alter and distribute.[13]

---

[12] The four statutory factors are not exclusive. This Court should also weigh the fact that the Apogee has not only failed to protect its alleged "franchise," but has actually encouraged users to distribute the MAP files around the world. Their exhortations support applying the fair use doctrine to some one who has merely taken Apogee up on its offer.

[Again, this and some of the other substantive footnotes, should be woven in with the main text.]

[13] Apogee did not even create the new add-on levels. It is simply complaining that the *Nuke It* levels are better than its own proposed product. The very function of the marketplace is to permit consumers to decide which product they prefer.

Apogee contended, and the district court found (albeit regarding the screen shots that are the subject of Micro Star's appeal), that Apogee did not intend to license commercial use.[14] But as the 7th Circuit noted in *I.A.E.* when dealing with an identical argument from the licensor in that case, the "intent relevant in contract matters is not the party's subjective intent, but their outward manifestation of it". 74 F.3d at 776. (Citations omitted). See also, *Hadady Corp. v. Dean Witter Reynolds, Inc.* 739 F.Supp. 1392, 1398 (C.D.Cal. 1990). (Copyright holders' subjective intent did not control when holder's objective acts evidenced clear intent to permit unlimited reproduction).

Apogee has reaped its rewards of their plan to let the world create and alter data files. By having third parties create different files, it does not have to expend its own resources to satisfy that demand. Here, Apogee not only is aware that MAP files are being created and distributed, but it has given the public the tools to do it, encouraged the public to create such files and then encouraged wide-spread distribution. Apogee has therefore licensed, waived or abandoned its right to restrict the creation and distribution of new data files. *National Comics Publications v. Fawcett Publications,* 191 F.2d 594, *598* (2nd Cir. 1951); *Lopez v. Electrical Rebuilders, Inc.*, 416 F.Supp. 1133, 1135 (C.D. Cal. 1976).

Apogee has not only waived its rights; it also misused what limited rights it had. Its inequitable and bad faith conduct, such as threatening to impound *Nuke It* if vendors carried the product when Apogee knew that there were no audiovisual elements contained in the MAP files also bars its claim, to the extent the claim was otherwise viable.[15] *See Qad, Inc. v. ALN Associates, Inc.*, 770 F.Supp. 1261, 1266 (N.D.IL. 1991), *affirmed* 974 F.2d 834 (7th Cir. 1992). "No party can use the limited grant that a copyright confers to gain control of components over which it has no such right." *Id.* "When a copyright holder attempts to use legal proceedings to protect an improper

---

[14] There is no finding, however, that the license was enforceable against purchasers. *Compare,* Apogee Brief at p. 41 (asserting License is enforceable against users).

[15] Apogee continues to insist that it had a valid registration when it filed its motion for preliminary injunction. It did not. Filing an application for registration is not the equivalent of having a registration certificate. *Pamfiloff v. Giant Records, Inc.*, 1992 Copy.L.Dec. CCH ¶ 26,865, 1991 WL 334916 (N.D.Cal. 1991); *Hudson 's Bay Co. of New York v. Seattle Fur Exchange, Inc.*, 15 U.S.P.Q. 1316, 1317 (S.D.N.Y. 1990); *Dodd v. Ft. Smith Special School District*, 666 F.Supp. 1278, 1282 (W.D. Ark. 1987). Simply because a Certificate is subsequently issued with the date on which the application was filed does not mean that there was a valid copyright registration when the motion was filed. *See* Apogee Brief, p. 35,n. 11.

extension of a copyright, the court may refuse to enforce the copyright." *Id.* Additionally, the purported grant-back provisions of the alleged license are a separate ground for copyright misuse. *Transparent-Wrap Machine Corp. v. Stokes & Smith Co*, 329 U.S. 637, 646, 67 S.Ct. 610, 91 L.Ed. 563 (1947) (grant back provisions in patent cases may be a ground for finding of misuse). The purpose and policy of patent misuse applies to copyright. *Sony Corp. of America v. Universal City Studios, Inc.*, 464 U.S. 417, 439, 104 S.Ct. 774, 787, 78 L.Ed.2d 574.

Each separate issue is a reason in and of itself to deny the requested injunction. Taken collectively, the factual and legal support for the district court's denial of Apogee's requested injunction is compelling.

[I am omitting material from Micro Star's brief that concerns the screen savers, the Micro Star CD packaging material, and a discovery dispute.

Although it has some good points, and is persuasive at times, Micro Star's brief is, as you've seen, not sufficiently focused to be as persuasive as, in my view, it might have been. By now, I am confident that *you* would do a far better job if forcefully arguing Micro Star's case.]

— — —

The following is FormGen's reply brief, which as I've mentioned, I'm presenting without my comments or suggestions. It is *your* turn now. Consider the following:

- how effective are its responses?
- should those responses have been anticipated by Micro Star?
- if so, how?
- do its analogies hold water?
- has FormGen left any of Micro Star's arguments unrebutted?
- if so, what affect that might have on a court?

Additionally, be alert to legal jargon and other things that detract from persuasive writing. Also, consider whether, if you were the judge deciding the case, you would want:

- the statute quoted at the spot where it is referenced;
- excerpts from the record quoted, rather than merely paraphrased or, worse, just referenced;
- specific supporting language from the cited cases set out—either in a parenthetical or in a block quote;
- whether there are any "make-weight" arguments of dubious validity that detract from the party's legitimate arguments;
- whether there is anything else that bothers you, or makes your analysis more difficult than it should be, or makes you do extra work that the brief-writer could have avoided by making things easier for you.

After you do all of this in connection with FormGen's reply brief, you will be well on your way to making *your* briefs, better, more persuasive, and more effective. As I've mentioned, your analysis of FormGen's reply brief will be the most valuable exercise you will do in the course of reading this book: it will give you a chance to apply the winning principles in a real life situation—an exercise that will, I trust, get you in the habit of going through that analysis in every one of *your* appeals to make *your* briefs better. Here is FormGen's reply brief:

Movants submit this Reply Brief in response to Appellant's and Cross-Appellee's Answering and Reply Brief (Ans. Br." or "Br.").

PRELIMINARY STATEMENT

Micro Star cannot escape the central truth of this case: it is selling a product containing additional scenarios in the saga of Duke Nukem comprised of Movants' protected expression. Despite the evasions, distortions, contradictions, and hyperbole throughout Micro Star's answering brief, Micro Star recognizes as much:

> Nuke It *contains* 300 additional levels of play for Duke Nukem 3D. . . . The characters are generally the same or similar, with the same

> rules of play, but the levels *contain* different layouts, combinations of elements and/or differing degrees of difficulty.

Ans. Br. 2 n.2 (emphasis added). Because the user-created levels contain Movants' protected expression -- including both the audiovisual elements and file structure of Duke Nukem 3D ("DN3D") -- Nuke It infringes Movants' copyright in DN3D.

The true nature of Nuke It -- an unauthorized reproduction and distribution by sale of user-created levels incorporating DN3D's protected audiovisual elements and file structure -- defeats Micro Star's fair use defense. Micro Star alleges for the first time (Ans. Br. 34) that its mechanical copying of DN3D levels yields a "transformative work ... independently copyrightable by Micro Star" and that Nuke It provides a "legitimate service in the field of *Duke Nukem* 3D-compatible games' (Br. 38). There is nothing transformative about Nuke It -- it merely reproduces existing user-created levels. Nor may Nuke It be termed a "service" in the "field" of DN3D compatible games: Nuke It invades the market for authorized DN3D products, and the concept of compatibility has no application to a single game like DN3D.

Many of Micro Star's scattershot arguments rest on a principal fallacy: that Movants have no right to seek a 'monopoly" over Duke Nukem-related products embodying protected expression from DN3D. The Copyright Act, in § 106. *does* grant such a right to authors to reward and encourage their creative efforts. The ability to block all uses of protected expression may have outer limits, as this Court explored in *Sega Enters. Ltd. v. Accolade Inc.*. 977 F.2d 1510 (9th Cir. 1992) *("Sega v. Accolade"),* where intermediate copying for reverse engineering purposes was deemed a fair use because it facilitated new creative expression by other parties. But Micro Star has engaged in no independent creativity entitled to any protection or deference by this Court; it has not brought to the marketplace a new game of its own creation to compete with DN3D. Instead, as Micro Star has repeatedly admitted, Nuke It consists only of hundreds of user-created MAP files downloaded from the Internet. That is not competition, but copying. Micro Star is in no position to accuse Movants of seeking a "free ride" from the users of DN3D. Ans. Br. 3.

Micro Star attempts to sidestep the questions presented on this cross-appeal (Movants' Br. 1) by characterizing the rulings below as fact findings. But the District Court's decision not to enjoin the reproduction and distribution by sale of user-created levels reflected two erroneous legal holdings on issues of paramount importance to the entertainment software industry, discussed in the Argument below. At the very least, the District

Court's rulings are reviewable *de novo* because they require the Court "to consider legal concepts in the mix of fact and law and to exercise judgment about the values that animate legal principles.' *Harper House. Inc. Thomas Nelson, Inc.*, 889 F.2d 197, 201 (9th Cir. 1989) (scope of copyright protection for organization and format of schedule organizers reviewed de novo) (citation omitted).

ARGUMENT

I. THE REPRODUCTION AND DISTRIBUTION BY SALE OF USER-CREATED MAP FILES INFRINGE THE COPYRIGHT IN MOVANTS' PROTECTED AUDIOVISUAL EXPRESSION

Micro Star devotes a scant five pages to the first of the two questions presented on this appeal: whether the District Court erred in concluding that *Lewis Galoob Toys. Inc. v. Nintendo of America, Inc.*, 964 F.2d *965* (9th Cir. 1992), *cert. denied*, 507 U.S. 985 (1993), compelled a finding that Nuke It did not infringe Movants' audiovisual expression.

Micro Star does not contest the basic principles set forth in Movants' opening brief (at 16-18) that establish copyright protection for the audiovisual display and characters of computer games. It is also not seriously disputed that DN3D's characters, artwork, and sounds are entitled to copyright protection in whatever setting they are reproduced or that, when Nuke It is played, DN3D's protected expression is displayed.[1] Micro Star's only potential escape from liability is to press its argument that all copyright protection was lost because of the way 'he game was designed by Apogee.

There can be little question that Nuke It's use of MAP files would be an infringement if Apogee had taken the more cumbersome route of causing all the data needed to draw each audiovisual element to be loaded into each and every MAP file -- that is, to enable MAP files to cause the display of DN3D's audiovisual elements without running the DN3D program. The more efficient method actually used of having the MAP files interact with an "image library" in the DN3D program to produce the total audiovisual display does not change the manner in which the game is experienced by users. It is "the characteristics

---

1 Micro Star suggests that DN3D is entitled to thin protection because it allegedly bears certain similarities to Doom, another popular computer game. Ans. Br. 27. But Micro Star is confusing the unprotected *idea* of a "first person shooter" -- a popular genre that has yielded numerous variations -- and the protected *expression of* that idea in DN3D, whose audiovisual elements were created by Apogee.

of the game program as experienced by the user that determine die program's commercial success," *Sega v. Accolade,* 977 F.2d at 1523, and Micro Star marketed Nuke It by advertising the audiovisual display. Micro Star's argument, accepted below, that this technical distinction in game design robs DN3D of protection has no support in logic or law, save to the extent *Galoob* is stretched beyond its limits.[2]

Micro Star does not meaningfully respond to Movants' detailed analysis (Br. 18-26) of the fundamental differences between *Galoob* and the present case. Key among these distinctions is that the Nuke It CD, unlike the Game Genie in *Galoob,* contains the output of the DN3D game in permanent data files.[3] The MAP files embody entire scenarIos, like chapters in a book. Unlike the Dewey decimal analogy of which Micro Star is so fond, the data in the MAP files are not mere citations but instructions that cause the display of DN3D's protected expression in particular arrangements and sequences. The screen display is the sum total of those instructions and the additional information contained in the game engine: Remove the Nuke It files from a PC and the 300 additional levels are gone, even if the original DN3D game (with its "image library") remains installed. Thus, the Nuke It MAP files do "contain or produce [DN3D's] output in some concrete or permanent form." *Galoob,* 964 F.2d at 969. This is unlike a library catalog card, which serves no purpose once the reader has retrieved the referenced book.

Micro Star also fails to refute that the juxtaposition of audiovisual elements and the resulting "storyline" of each level are embodied in the sequence of instructions in each MAP file. Micro Star claims, without citation (Br. 31 n.20), that the District Court determined that such narrative expression is not protected, but the court made no such finding. Micro Star itself recognizes that the levels "contain different layouts, combinations of elements and/or differing degrees of difficulty" *(id.* 2 n.2), but fails to explain where such expression is fixed if not in the MAP files.

---

[2] Micro Star seeks to distance the District Court's holding from *Galoob* (Br. 32), but the court's opinion makes clear that *Galoob* was the basis for its holding. (E.R. 1068-69.) This is part of Micro Star's larger effort to turn the court's legal ruling into a fact determination entitled to deference. Because there is no disagreement on the underlying technical facts, the question is whether *Galoob* controls on these undisputed facts. In view of the court's rulings in Movants' favor on fair use, waiver, and irreparable harm, it was only the erroneous application of *Galoob* that led the District Court to deny a broader injunction.

[3] The other pivotal distinction -- the absence in *Galoob* of economic harm to the copyright owner -- is analyzed in Part IIIA below, which addresses fair use.

Micro Star's own expert confirms that with the DN3D Build Editor a user "creates new levels and stores the details of those levels in individual computer data files, known as 'MAP' files." Johnson-Laird Decl. ¶ 8 (E.R. 420). Contrary to Micro Star's insistence that the MAP files do not contain instructions (Br. 31 n.2 1), Mr. Johnson-Laird confirms that the definitions contained in the MAP files "cause the game to create" various images and "make the Duke Nukem program to create [sic] appropriate views of the specified images." Johnson-Laird Decl. ¶10 (E.R. 420-21). The storing of these instructions in the MAP files constitutes a tangible and fixed output of the DN3D game -- satisfying any fixation requirement imposed by *Galoob* and demonstrating that the unlicensed sale of DN3D levels is a violation of Movants' copyright in the game's audiovisual display.

Micro Star's attempt to denigrate the MAP files as meaningless "data" recalls the Supreme Court's holding in *White-Smith Music Pub. Co. v. Apollo Co.*, 209 U.S. 1 (1908), that a perforated player piano music roll was not a "copy" of a musical composition and therefore did not infringe the copyright in the underlying musical work. Recognizing that evolving technology may result in expression being physically reproduced in new and different media, Congress, in the 1976 Copyright Act, eliminated the "artificial and largely unjustifiable distinctions" of such cases as *White-Smith*. H. R. Rep. No. 1476, 94th Cong., 2d Sess. 52 (1976); S. Rep. No. 473, 94th Cong. 1st Sess. 51 (1975). It provided that infringement may occur any time a protected work is reproduced in "any tangible medium of expression, now known or later developed, from which [the work] can be perceived, reproduced or otherwise communicated, either directly or with the aid of a machine or device." 17 U.S.C. § 102(a) 1978). *See also* 1 WILLIAM F. PATRY, COPYRIGHT LAW AND PRACTICE 168 (1994). Thus, that fixed expression is represented by digital data read by a machine -- whether included in a music CD or a computer game CD-ROM -- does not deprive it of copyright protection.

Micro Star attempts unsuccessfully to distinguish *Midway Mfg. Co. v. Artic Int'l*, 704 F.2d 1009 (7th Cir.), *cert. denied*, 464 U.S. 823 (1983). Here, as in *Midway* (but unlike in *Galoob*),output of the copyrighted work is physically incorporated in a new product causing economic harm to the copyright owner. The need to "stretch" (Ans. Br. 32) the definition of a derivative work to encompass a product that merely speeds up play is of no concern here, where the additional levels are classic derivative works -- different game levels with the same audiovisual elements.

II. THE REPRODUCTION AND DISTRIBUTION BY SALE OF MAP FILES INFRINGE MOVANTS' COPYRIGHT IN TILE DISTINCTIVE STRUCTURE OF THOSE FILES

Micro Star is more expansive, but no more persuasive, in addressing the second and alternative ground of infringement -- the unauthorized commercial use of the MAP file structure. It is well settled that non-literal aspects of computer programs, including the structure of data files, are copyrightable when they constitute not an "idea" but the *expression* of an idea. *See, e.g., Johnson Controls, Inc. v. Phoenix Control Systems, Inc.*, 886 F.2d 1173, 1175-76 (9th Cir. 1989); *CMAX/Cleveland, Inc. v. UCR, Inc.*, 804 F. Supp. 337 (M.D. Ga. 1992). Contrary to this authority, Micro Star declares that "file formats cannot be copyrighted." Br. 22. It cites only *Baker v. Selden,* 101 U.S. 99 (1880), which stands for the classic distinction between idea and expression. Just as the copyrighted of bookkeeping methods in that case did not give its author patent-like protection over the underlying ideas about ledger systems, the copyright in DN3D does not give Movants a monopoly on the idea of a first person shooter game or the idea of a data file. But this begs the question whether the *particular* structure of the MAP files embodies protected expression that cannot be copied without authorization.

Movants presented detailed and unrefuted evidence that the file structure devised by Apogee's designers involved a multitude of creative choices and therefore constituted a particular expression of the idea of a data file for a computer game. *See* Movants' Br. 27-28. Without discussing this evidence or making any findings that the file structure came within any other exceptions to copyright protection *(e.g.*, that it constituted a "method of operation" or was dictated by compatibility with other software or hardware systems), the District Court simply held, apparently as a matter of law, that "the data sequence in the Nuke It MAP files" is not subject to copyright protection. (E.R. 1069.) Micro Star's attempts to provide a rationale for this conclusory holding are unavailing.[4]

---

[4] Micro Star erroneously alleges (Br. 7) that Movants' only "claimed for the first time in [their] Reply papers . . . that the file 'format' of the MAP files was copyrighted." To the contrary, Movants alleged copyright protection for the MAP file structure in their counterclaims filed on August 9, 1996 (E.R. 369); in their initial brief in support of the preliminary injunction motion filed the same day (at 5, 11); and in the initial Blum declaration (at ¶ 10) (E.R. 57). Micro Star's repeated suggestion (Br. 7-8, 9) that the DN3D copyright may not cover the file structure is also wrong. Apogee filed a single registration form covering authorship of "computer program Duke Nukem 3D and other audiovisual elements." (E.R. 750.) File structure is undeniably an aspect of the computer program.

A. The MAP File Structure Is Not a "Method of Operation"

Micro Star argues that the MAP file structure is a purely functional "method of operation because it is a 'critical component" and an "integral part" of causing the computer to display the DN3D game. Br. 21. But all computer programs are "functional" in that sense, and Congress has nevertheless provided that they are to be protected. *Sega v. Accolade,* 977 F.2d at 1519-20.

The question, therefore, is not whether the file is important to running the computer. Rather, the question is whether the *structure* of the file was dictated by functional concerns or, as the unrefuted evidence shows, was designed by Apogee's programmers from a multitude of creative choices. *See id.* at 1524 (program structure and design may be protected where "there are many possible ways of accomplishing a given task" and programmers' choices are therefore "creative and idiosyncratic"); David W.T. Daniels. *Comment, Learned Hand Never Played Nintendo: A Better Way to Think About the Non-Literal, Non-Visual Software Copyright Cases.* 61 U. Chi. L. Rev. 613, 637-38 (1994) (advocating protection for "program elements which display exercise of the programmer's art" in selecting among different design choices, in contrast to ideas that can be expressed only in "one structural configuration" and therefore cannot be copyrighted without conveying "patent-like protection").

Apple Computer, Inc. v. Franklin Computer Corp., 714 F.2d 1240 (3d Cir. 1983), cited by Micro Star, expressly *rejected* the argument that computer operating systems are inherently utilitarian and unprotectible. Noting that both operating systems and application programs "instruct the computer to do something" *(Id.* at 1251), the court held that protectibility of an operating system is to be judged by the same idea/expression dichotomy as any other program. *Id.* at *1253.*

Nor does *Lotus Dev. Corp. v. Borland Int'l,* 49 F.3d 807 (1st Cir. 1995), *aff'd by an equally divided court,* 116 S. Ct. 804 (1996), establish that the MAP file structure is a "method of operation." *Lotus* concerned not a data file structure selected from a multitude of choices but a hierarchy of generic menu commands *(e.g.,* "print," "edit") that the First Circuit deemed to be a purely functional "method of operation," like the buttons on a VCR. *Id.* at 815. *Lotus* has been criticized for failing to apply traditional analysis to determine whether the menu hierarchy constituted an idea or the expression of the idea. *See* ANTHONY L. CLAPES, SOFTWARE, COPYRIGHT AND COMPETITION: THE USE OF ANTITRUST THEORY TO UNDERCUT COPYRIGHT PROTECTION FOR

COMPUTER PROGRAMS, at 553, 571-72 (PLI Literary Property Course Handbook Series No. G4-3 942, 1995). The *Lotus* court also acknowledged (49 F.3d at 819 n. 14) that its holding was inconsistent with language from this Circuit. *See Brown Bag Software v. Symantec Corp.*, 960 F.2d 1465, 1477 (9th Cir.) (protection may be afforded for a computer program's "screens, menus, and key strokes"), *cert. denied,* 113 S. Ct. 198 (1992). Expanding *Lotus* to declare that a computer file structure is as a matter of law, a 'method of operation" regardless of the creativity that went into it would be an unwarranted change in the law.

Micro Star further argues that the file structure is "merely functional" because "a MAP file originally created for *Doom* is identical to a MAP file created for *Duke Nukem 3D.*" Ans. Br. 8 & n.8. This misrepresents the record. Micro Star alleged below only that DN3D includes a program to *convert* "Wad" files created for Doom into the distinctive DN3D file structure so that these levels can be played on DN3D. Moore Decl. ¶8 (E.R. 414-15). This hardly establishes (but, rather, disproves) that the original file structures for the two games are identical -- much less does it show that the DN3D file structure involves no protectible creativity. Nor does Micro Star explain why alleged similarities in the screen formats and underlying ideas of Doom and DN3D (Br. 8) have any relevance to the protectible nature of the non-literal expression embodied in the data file structure.

. **The MAP File Structure Was Not Dictated by <u>Compatibility Requirements</u>**

Micro Star also alleges that the file structure is not protected because it was dictated by compatibility requirements. Aspects of program design dictated by the need to interface with hardware or other software programs are not copyrightable because they are functional and do not involve creative choices. *See Computer Assocs. Int'l v. Altai, Inc.*, 982 F.2d 693, 709-10 (2d Cir. 1992), *cert. denied,* 115 S. Ct. 1176 (1995). But DN3D's file structure is not dictated by compatibility with any other hardware or software. Of course, once Apogee's designers settled on a data structure for the MAP files, new MAP ides had to conform to that structure for the game to operate properly. But this does not establish that any aspect of that file structure was dictated by external compatibility concerns.

Micro Star's efforts to distinguish *CMAX* are unavailing. *CMAX* expressly held a data file structure to be protected because "[the selection and arrangement of the field definitions within the files . . . are the expression of an idea." 804 F. Supp. at 354. The court, in dicta, discussed programs that convert file formats not as part of any holding that such formats are unprotected, but to demonstrate that the same data could be stored in differently structured files and, therefore, that the structure selected reflected creativity. *Id.* Because here, as in *CMAX,* the DN3D file structure "is not dictated by the industry" but was selected 'from a myriad of possible options and alternatives" *(id.* at 354-55), it is expression rather than an idea and hence protectible.[5]

C. Affording Copyright Protection for DN3D's File Structure Would Not Violate the Policies Underlying the Copyright Act

Micro Star argues that protecting DN3D's file structure would have "enormous consequences" by granting programmers a "monopoly of information." Ans. Br. 25-26. Micro Star also suggests that recognizing the copyright in Movants' computer game file structure would wreak havoc in the software industry, causing innovators in word processing and other fields to be "ruined overnight." Ans. Br. 25.

The short answer is that no such consequences would occur if the Court were to enjoin Micro Star's unfair use of Movants' file structure. *See* Point IIIA below. This unfair use is easily distinguished from the examples of appropriate use of other programs offered by Micro Star. Notably, no relief is sought against users of DN3D, who are permitted to make and exchange new levels for non-commercial purposes incorporating the protected file structure.

Micro Star makes factual assertions not in the record, including the assumption that a right to unfettered access to file structure and other programming governing inter-operability is universally accepted in the software industry. To the contrary, if the Court is to engage in extra-record speculation, it is more plausible to assume that manufacturers of software

---

[5] Micro Star attempts a misleading analogy to *Lotus* and other cases that appear to accept, in dicta, programs that translate documents into different file structures. *Lotus* referred only to the use of menu commands to allow macros to be translated *out* of a competitor's format into the format of the new software. *See* 49 F.3d at 809-10, 818. This does not implicate the issue of selling files that copy a competing *file* structure. Similarly, *Engineering Dynamics, Inc. v. Structural Software, Inc.,* 46 F.3d 408, 409 (5th Cir. 1995), merely stated the basic rule that user interfaces are protected "to the extent that the selection of variable inputs from the universe of potential inputs reflects non-functional judgments." The court then discussed programs used to "read" the file formats of other programs to achieve inter-operability -- again, not addressing the creation or sale of documents structured in the copyright-protected format of a competitor. Neither case is relevant to the question whether DN3D's file structure was dictated by compatibility concerns.

products for which inter-operability is an important feature -- such as Microsoft's Windows environment or the WordPerfect wordprocessing program -- *choose* to make available, through public disclosure or more controlled licensing arrangements, the information necessary for compatible products to interface. That does not mean that file structure is *per se* unprotectible. The ruling sought by Movants would not disturb those practices.[6]

In situations where a copyright owner seeks to block compatibility by competing products, issues might be presented as to whether the product has become so much of an industry standard that fair use, implied license, or some other limit on copyright protection gives other software manufacturers the "right" to inter-operability. *See Lotus*, 49 F.3d at 819-21 (Boudin, J., concurring) (suggesting that decision finding structure of command hierarchy unprotected was driven by "the concern with fencing off access to the commons," because of Lotus 1-2-3's position as "the *de facto* standard for electronic spreadsheet commands"). Since the policy favoring standardization must be weighed against the need to protect the value of original authorship, it has been suggested that no "right" to inter-operability exists unless and until a software interface has taken on the status of a "standard." Timothy S. Teter, *Note, Merger and the Machines: An Analysis of the Pro-Compatibility Trend in Computer Software Copyright Cases*, 45 Stan. L. Rev. 1061, 1088 (1993) ("elements of a user interface should lose protection only after becoming *de facto* standards").

Sega v. Accolade is consistent with this approach. There, a minimal 20-byte interface code was deemed unprotected. *See* 977 F.2d at 1524 n.7. *Sega* appears to treat the popular Genesis game system hardware as an industry standard and to conclude that competing software developers therefore had the right to create games that could run on the Sega platform. *See* ARTHUR R. MILLER, COPYRIGHT PROTECTION FOR COMPUTER PROGRAMMERS,

---

[6] Micro Star repeatedly invokes inapt analogies to wordprocessing programs. Br. 8 n.8, 18 n.13, 31 n.19. For example, Micro Star contends that an opinion of this Court composed with WordPerfect is "useless unless it is viewed with Wordperfect." Br. 31 n. 19. However, the purpose of WordPerfect is to create a document -- be it an opinion, a brief, or a letter -- that is printed out and distributed as a discrete item, no longer tied to the wordprocessor that created it. The storage of that document in a computer data file, or its reproduction by disk or modem transfer for copying and editing, does not involve the reproduction and distribution by sale of WordPerfect's data file format. Such "copying" of WordPerfect's file structure is part and parcel of the basic use of the product, does not involve any commercial impact on WordPerfect, and in any event is likely to be embraced by license or by fair use. The relief sought in this appeal simply does not threaten conventional uses of wordprocessors.

DATABASES, AND COMPUTER-GENERATED WORKS: IS ANYTHING NEW SINCE CONTU?, 106 Harv. L. Rev. 977, 1020 (1993) ("The underlying premise that led the Ninth Circuit to declare a 'market' in Sega cartridges, and to encourage competition in it, was probably Sega's success in the home entertainment field.").

These policy concerns are not implicated here. DN3D is not a piece of hardware with which software programs must interact. Nor was it either conceived or promoted as a "platform"-type software product, like Windows, whose inter-operability is an inherent feature. There is no need to "read" or reproduce DN3D's file structure to create a competing game that runs on popular computer systems. Protecting Movants' internal data file structure in this case will have no adverse industry consequences, other than for infringers wishing to use protected expression for profit.[7]

III. MICRO STAR IS UNLIKELY TO PREVAIL ON ANY OF ITS AFFIRMATIVE DEFENSES

If the District Court erred either in its application of *Galoob* or its holding that DN3D's data file structure is not protectible, Movants are entitled to a preliminary injunction against the unauthorized sale of user-created levels. None of Micro Star's affirmative defenses would block that result.

A. Nuke It Is Not a Fair Use of Movants' Protected Expression

Movants' opening brief (at 28-31) amply demonstrates that Micro Star's purely commercial, non-transformative exploitation of DN3D's protected expression, competing with Movants head to head in the market for authorized derivative DN3D products, does not come close to satisfying the criteria for a finding of fair use. Micro Star's new arguments are unavailing.

1. The Four Statutory Factors All Cut Against Fair Use

Micro Star now claims for the first time on appeal that Nuke It is a transformative (and even independently copyrightable) work. Br.34. But Micro

---

[7] Micro Star argues (Br. 27) that the purported similarities it has identified between the concepts and screen formats of DN3D and those of Doom somehow rebut the admitted presumption of originality in the MAP file format. But the expression contained in the structure of the MAP files – the selection and arrangement of specific parameters -- does not correspond to the purported similarities Micro Star discusses. Micro Star does not identify any similarity in data file structures between the two games, and its expert has not done so on this record.

Star has admitted that it contributed no original creativity to the marketplace; it simply downloaded hundreds of levels from the Internet, reproduced them on a CD in extremely rough alphabetical order (E.R. 58), and put the disk into stores to be marketed alongside DN3D. (E.R. 414-15.) Such a use is non-transformative under the cases cited by Movants (at 29) and ignored by Micro Star.

Micro Star's claim that Nuke It is "transformative" is an attempt to come within the limited rule of *Sega v. Accolade*, which held that *intermediate* copying of protected expression may be a fair use where necessary to discover unprotected compatibility information that will allow new expressive works to be run on popular game hardware. Key to the holding of *Sega v. Accolade*, as Micro Star recognizes (Br. 39), was the public policy favoring *new* creative expression. Unlike Accolade, Micro Star has not designed its own competing game; it has merely copied and sold elements of DN3D. This Court's decision in *Triad Sys. Corp. v. Southeastern Express Co.*, 64 F.3d 1330, 1336-37 (9th Cir. 1995), distinguishing *Sega* where a competitor copied protected expression for commercial purposes and "invented nothing of its own," is the controlling authority. That purchasers of DN3D have already paid for the original game *(see* Ans. Br. 36) has no bearing -- no more than it would matter that purchasers had paid for a book when someone other than the book's author wanted to publish an unauthorized sequel.

Contrary to Micro Star's suggestion (Br. 34-35), the fair use analysis properly focuses on Micro Star rather than the users. Unlike *Galoob*, in which only contributory infringement was alleged, this case concerns direct infringement by Micro Star. Focusing on the end user here would render meaningless the distinction between commercial and non-commercial uses. *See Lotus Dev. Corp. v. Borland Int'l*, 831 F. Supp. 223, 242 (D. Mass 1993) (focus on end user in direct infringement case could allow bookstore to claim right to sell unauthorized copies of "Gone With The Wind" based on non-commercial use by customers), *rev'd on other grounds,* 49 F.3d 807 (1st Cir. 1995), *aff'd by an equally divided court*, 116 S. Ct. 804 (1996).

With respect to the second fair use factor, the nature of the infringed work, Micro Star simply recycles its argument on copyright protection, declaring (Br. 36) that 'the Nuke It data files are not the protectible, expressive portion of the Duke Nukem 3D program." But the fair use analysis proceeds on the assumption that the sale of Nuke It's MAP files *has* been held to infringe Movants' creative expression. In any event, Micro Star's statement that "the majority of the game is functional" (Br. 37) is false. DN3D is a creative work entitled to the highest level of protection; Micro Star ignores *Galoob*'s express holding on this point cited in Movants' brief (at 30). While it harps on genre-specific similarities to other games, Micro Star admits that DN3D's fanciful audiovisual displays are new. (E.R. 411.)

On the third factor, Micro Star similarly restates its argumentative conclusion that "there are no portions of the copyrighted work used in the MAP files on Nuke It." Br. 37. But if the MAP files are held to infringe DN3D's creative expression, they obviously use substantial portions of that expression, since the levels are made up entirely of material from DN3D. Moreover, Nuke It's MAP files copy the entire structure of those files -- including dozens of creatively selected parameters -- rather than the few bytes of initialization code addressed in *Sega v. Accolade*. The suggestion that Movants have somehow failed to identify the protected expression involved (Br. 37) is frivolous. *See* Movants' Brief at 6-11.

Micro Star recognizes that the fourth factor, harm to the commercial exploitation of the copyright, is the most important, but persists in its assertion that Nuke it will not harm demand for the original DN3D game. Br. 38. Micro Star misrepresents *Campbell v. Acuff-Rose Music, Inc.*, 510 U.S. 569 (1994), as holding that unauthorized competition with legitimate "add on" products does not constitute harm under the fourth factor. Br. 39. *Campbell* in fact stands for the opposite proposition -- that harm to the market for licensed derivative products *must* be considered. *See* 510 U.S. at 590.

The distinction drawn in *Campbell* between "suppression" and "usurpation" of demand is of no help to Micro Star. *Campbell* addressed the *suppression* of demand that may flow from a devastating parody that harms the reputation or market appeal of the original without actually taking away sales. It contrasted this with the *usurpation* caused by products (including derivative products), marketed in the same niches as authorized products, that actually shift sales from the copyright owner to the infringer. Thus, while reputational harm to the copyright owner flowing from a parody may itself not be cognizable, the *Campbell* Court found it relevant to analyze whether the parody also might occupy a market niche in which the copyright owner could be expected to license its own derivative works (in that case, the market for rap versions of a pop song). *See* 510 U.S. at 592-93.

Thus, *Campbell* cuts against Micro Star here: Nuke It directly usurps sales in a narrow market niche -- the market for additional levels for DN3D using DN3D's protected expression. Unlike in *Sega*, where the Court thought it likely that consumers would buy Accolade's independently produced games in addition to the different games marketed by Sega *(see* 977 F.2d at 1523), the market niche for a single game is much narrower, and it can be presumed that the thousands of copies of Nuke It sold have directly usurped sales of Movants' authorized products containing similar (or identical) user-created levels. This Court made clear in *Sega* that if the competing games threatened to usurp sales in that manner, "all other considerations might be irrelevant." *Id.* at 1523. For that reason there is no merit to Micro Star's suggestion (Br.40) that the record contains "no evidence" of market harm.

It is beside the point that sales of Nuke It may, as Micro Star alleges, minimally stimulate sales for the underlying DN3D game. Purchase of the original DN3D game is necessary to run *any* add-on levels. Therefore, any positive impact on the sale of DN3D can be accomplished through the sale of *authorized* add-on levels, for which Movants collect licensing fees. In Micro Star's view of copyright, the producers of the film version of "The English Patient" would not have to pay any fee to the author of the underlying novel, since their derivative work does not hurt sales of the novel and in fact has catapulted it to the top of the paperback best seller list. The law does not countenance such a bizarre result. To the contrary, in *Twin Peaks Prods., Inc. v. Publications Int'l*, 996 F.2d 1366 (2d Cir. 1993), a book containing detailed plot summaries from the "Twin Peaks" television program was held not to be a fair use because it used protected expression to compete in markets for derivative works in which the original copyright owner had "a legitimate interest" -- notwithstanding that the book might provide helpful publicity and thereby tend to confer economic benefit on the copyright holder." *Id.* at 1377. Thus, the *Twin Peaks* court rejected the same fair use argument raised by Micro Star.

2. *Fair Use Does Not Convey an Automatic Right to Compete By Creating "Compatible" Products*

Micro Star maintains (Br. 38) that it is seeking only "to provide a legitimate service in the field of Duke Nukem 3D-compatible games." But there is no such "field." Nuke It is not the same "type" of game as DN3D (Br. 39) -- it is levels of the same game. If Micro Star were correct, then nothing would prevent a publisher from issuing an unauthorized collection of passages from various John Grisham novels, defending it as a fair use because it constitutes a "legitimate service" in the "field" of Grisham-compatible books.

Nor does this Court's discussion in *Sega* create any such unbridled "fair use" right to create "compatible" products using a competitor's protected expression. *Sega* stands only for the proposition that independent creative effort may excuse intermediate copying when that is the only way to discover unprotected functional aspects of a program. It is simply inapplicable to Micro Star's wholesale copying and sale of protected expression, admittedly with no additional creative contribution.

Of course, Movants cannot monopolize the field of first person shooters, and Micro Star is free to create its own game in this genre. It has not done so. There is no public policy or other reason to grant a "right" of inter-operability with DN3D itself. First, Movants do not control the platform on which new games may run. *See* Point IIC, above. The console at issue in *Sega* is a game system attached for years to millions of television sets to which other game designers seek access to meet the demand for new games. DN3D is just one game. Second, Movants have limited opportunity to profit from this game. Micro Star's own president testified that "[u]sually, computer games have a shelf life of about a year." (E . R. 402.) Movants showed the importance of avoiding market saturation in the effort to maximize revenues from a successful game and related products. (E.R. 390.) Congress intended that copyright owners, through exploitation of their § 106 rights, would be rewarded for their creativity and thereby would be motivated to publish additional works. *See Twentieth Century Music Corp. v. Aiken*, 422 U.S. 151, 156 (1975). That is the policy that should control.

B. The District Court Correctly Rejected Micro Star's Waiver and Implied License Argument

Micro Star's affirmative defense based on waiver and implied license fails for the simple reason that there is no evidence in the record of any objective manifestation by Movants of an intention to abandon or give away the right to commercial exploitation of the protected expression in DN3D. Whether or not the User License included with the game is enforceable against the users themselves, the absence of such affirmative objective evidence itself defeats Micro Star's defense. Once again, Micro Star does not take issue with a single authority cited by Movants for this fundamental conclusion. *See* Movants' Brief 40-44.[8]

---

[8] The Court need not decide whether the User License is enforceable against users, since the License does not govern Micro Star's rights and becomes even theoretically relevant as a limitation on commercial exploitation only if other statements by Movants somehow gave away more than non-commercial rights in the first place. Micro Star falsely accuses Movants of "surreptitiously" adding a computer command to their demonstrative video to fool the lower court into thinking that the User License automatically appears at the conclusion of each level. Br. 11-12 n. 11. But the cited transcript (E.R. 796-97) shows that Movants' witness was simply showing the court (during a live demonstration, not on the videotape) how it was possible to move from the Build Editor (not from a level) to the User License.

In view of the total absence of any evidence that Movants expressed an intention to abandon their commercial rights, the District Court found as a matter of fact that no waiver or implied commercial license had been granted. (E.R. 1072-74.) Whether or not a course of conduct has created a contract or led to a waiver of rights is purely a question of fact, reviewed on appeal only for clear error. *See Kern Oil & Refining Co. v. Tenneco Oil Co.*. 840 F.2d 730, 736 (9th Cir. 1988) (conclusions on waiver and extrinsic fact questions related to contract reviewed under clearly erroneous standard), *cert. denied*, 488 U.S. 948 (1988). Micro Star tries to transform this determination into a legal question (Br. 4041) by pretending that the court was construing a written contract -- the User License. This is an odd argument, since Micro Star's position is that the User License was a nullity. In fact, the court never decided whether the User License was enforceable, and so had no occasion to construe it legally. It merely referenced the User License as well as Movants' other public statements to find that there was no objective evidence of an intention to give away commercial rights in DN3D. (E.R. 1065-66, 1072-74.)

Micro Star complains on behalf of the users whose interests it does not represent that Movants provided all the ingredients "to make the movie," and now "claim[] ownership of the movie." Br. 3. But in addition to "movie-making" equipment. Movants provided users with access to a large selection of conspicuously copyrighted audiovisual expression. Users were encouraged to employ that expression to make the equivalent of "home movies" for non-commercial entertainment purposes. No reasonable user could have believed that he or she had thereby been granted the right to commercial exploitation of that material. In this sense, DN3D is no different from the familiar products now available that allow children to make 'Lion King" or "Barbie" party invitations, clothing, or even cartoons for personal use or to share with friends. Micro Star could not reproduce and sell those items at F.A.O. Schwarz in competition with Disney and Mattel.

In any event, Movants' action against Micro Star does not focus on any claim to ownership of "the movie," *ie.*, the new levels themselves. Movants seek to enforce only their rights in the underlying expression -- the original audiovisual elements, portions of the narrative juxtaposition lifted from the original levels, and the file structure. As established by authority cited in Movants' opening brief (at 44) and not refuted by Micro Star, ownership (or copyright-protected status) of the new levels themselves is irrelevant. Even if the new levels were, as Micro Star has argued without basis, in the public domain, Movants' rights to the underlying expression would remain intact.

C. Movants Have Not Misused Their Copyright

Micro Star's repeated baseless accusations of "copyright misuse' are a regrettable attempt to divert attention from its own inequitable conduct.[9] As noted in Movants' opening brief (at 35 n.11), Micro Star has repeatedly acknowledged the good faith basis of Movants' copyright claim. Needless to say, the District Court made no finding of "misuse."[9]

CONCLUSION

For the foregoing reasons and those stated in their opening brief, Movants respectfully request the Court to reverse the District Court's erroneous legal rulings that reproduction and distribution by sale of user-created levels does not infringe the DN3D copyright, to remand the case for entry of an appropriate additional injunction and recall order, and to affirm the injunctive relief granted by the District Court.

Now the moment we've all been waiting for: the decision by the United States Court of Appeals for the Ninth Circuit. Before you read it, though, think about how and why you would decide the case. Perhaps jot down some brief thoughts—covering all the factors that *you* believe an appellate court should consider and those that you would consider if you were on the panel. This exercise, too, will help to make you a better appellate advocate. Putting yourself in the position of the tribunal that will decide your case—be that tribunal a jury of folks from the community, a single judge or administrative law judge sitting as a fact-finder, or an appellate court—will help you immensely in representing your clients.

---

[9] As part of this diversion, Micro Star continues to make irrelevant insinuations about Movants' copyright registration, now implying (Br. 43 n.26) that Movants are falsely claiming to have had a registration certificate at the time the suit was commenced. This accusation is unaccompanied by citation. As explained in Movants' opening brief (at 35 n.11), Apogee filed an expedited application for copyright registration prior to the filing of Movants' answer and compulsory counterclaims. While Micro Star suggests that an application is "not the equivalent" of a certificate (Br. 43 n.26), it does not refute the authority in Movants' opening brief holding that filing an application is sufficient to convey subject matter jurisdiction. In any event, a valid certificate effective as of August 8, 1996 was in the record of the case a month before the hearing even commenced in the District Court, rendering the issue moot. (E.R. 1120, 1127-30.)

Micro Star v. Formgen, Inc.

United States Circuit Court for the Ninth Circuit
(1998)

(All footnotes are the court's.)
[I will have one comment, in footnote 4.]

Kozinski, Circuit Judge.

Duke Nukem routinely vanquishes Octabrain and the Protozoid Slimer. But what about the dreaded Micro Star?

I

FormGen Inc., GT Interactive Software Corp. and Apogee Software, Ltd. (collectively FormGen) made, distributed and own the rights to Duke Nukem 3D (D/N-3D), an immensely popular (and very cool) computer game. D/N-3D is played from the first-person perspective; the player assumes the personality and point of view of the title character, who is seen on the screen only as a pair of hands and an occasional boot, much as one might see oneself in real life without the aid of a mirror.[1] Players explore a futuristic city infested with evil aliens and other hazards. The goal is to zap them before they zap you, while searching for the hidden passage to the next level. The basic game comes with twenty-nine levels, each with a different combination of scenery, aliens, and other challenges. The game also includes a "Build Editor," a utility that enables players to create their own levels. With FormGen's encouragement, players frequently post levels they have created on the Internet where others can download them. Micro Star, a computer software distributor, did just that: It downloaded 300 user-created levels and stamped them onto a CD, which it then sold commercially as Nuke It (N/I). N/I is packaged in a box decorated with numerous "screen shots," pictures of what the new levels look like when played.

Micro Star filed suit in district court, seeking a declaratory judgment that N/I did not infringe on any of FormGen's copyrights. FormGen counterclaimed, seeking a preliminary injunction barring further production and distribution of N/I. Relying on *Lewis Galoob Toys, Inc. v. Nintendo of Am., Inc.*, 964 F.2d 965 (9th Cir.1992), the district court held that N/I was not a derivative work and therefore did not infringe FormGen's copyright. The district court did, however, grant a preliminary injunction as to the screen

---

[1] This form of play was pioneered by a company called id Software with its classic Wolfenstein 3D character.

shots, finding that N/I's packaging violated FormGen's copyright by reproducing pictures of D/N-3D characters without a license. The court rejected Micro Star's fair use claims. Both sides appeal their losses.

II

A party seeking a preliminary injunction must show "either a likelihood of success on the merits and the possibility of irreparable injury, or that serious questions going to the merits were raised and the balance of hardships tips sharply in its favor." *Johnson Controls, Inc. v. Phoenix Control Systems, Inc.*, 886 F.2d 1173, 1174 (9th Cir.1989). Because "in a copyright infringement claim, a showing of a reasonable likelihood of success on the merits raises a presumption of irreparable harm," *id.*, FormGen need only show a likelihood of success on the merits to get the preliminary injunction it seeks (barring the manufacture and distribution of N/I) and to preserve the preliminary injunction it already won (barring the screen shots on N/I's packaging).

III

To succeed on the merits of its claim that N/I infringes FormGen's copyright, FormGen must show (1) ownership of the copyright to D/N-3D, and (2) copying of protected expression by Micro Star. *See Triad Systems Corp. v. Southeastern Express Co.*, 64 F.3d 1330, 1335 (9th Cir.1995). FormGen's copyright registration creates a presumption of ownership, see id., and we are satisfied that FormGen has established its ownership of the copyright. We therefore focus on the latter issue.

FormGen alleges that its copyright is infringed by Micro Star's unauthorized commercial exploitation of user-created game levels. In order to understand FormGen's claims, one must first understand the way D/N-3D works. The game consists of three separate components: the game engine, the source art library and the MAP files.[2] The game engine is the heart of the computer program; in some sense, it is the program. It tells the computer when to read data, save and load games, play sounds and project images onto the screen. In order to create the audiovisual display for a particular level, the game engine invokes the MAP file that corresponds to that level. Each MAP file contains a series of instructions that tell the game engine (and, through it, the computer) what to put where. For instance, the MAP file might say scuba

---

[2] So-called because the files all end with the extension ".MAP":. Also, no doubt, because they contain the layout for the various levels.

gear goes at the bottom of the screen. The game engine then goes to the source art library, finds the image of the scuba gear, and puts it in just the right place on the screen.[3] The MAP file describes the level in painstaking detail, but it does not actually contain any of the copyrighted art itself; everything that appears on the screen actually comes from the art library. Think of the game's audiovisual display as a paint-by-numbers kit. The MAP file might tell you to put blue paint in section number 565, but it doesn't contain any blue paint itself; the blue paint comes from your palette, which is the low-tech analog of the art library, while you play the role of the game engine. When the player selects one of the N/I levels, the game engine references the N/I MAP files, but still uses the D/N-3D art library to generate the images that make up that level.

FormGen points out that a copyright holder enjoys the exclusive right to prepare derivative works based on D/N-3D. See 17 U.S.C. § 106(2) (1994). According to FormGen, the audiovisual displays generated when D/N-3D is run in conjunction with the N/I CD MAP files are derivative works that infringe this exclusivity. Is FormGen right? The answer is not obvious.

The Copyright Act defines a derivative work as a work based upon one or more preexisting works, such as a translation, musical arrangement, dramatization, fictionalization, motion picture version, sound recording, art reproduction, abridgment, condensation, or any other form in which a work may be recast, transformed, or adapted. A work consisting of editorial revisions, annotations, elaborations, or other modifications which, as a whole, represent an original work of authorship, is a "derivative work." *Id.* § 101. The statutory language is hopelessly overbroad, however, for "[e]very book in literature, science and art, borrows and must necessarily borrow, and use much which was well known and used before." *Emerson v. Davies*, 8 F. Cas. 615, 619 (C.C.D.Mass.1845) (No. 4436), *quoted in* 1 NIMMER ON COPYRIGHT, § 3.01, at 3-2 (1997). To narrow the statute to a manageable level, we have developed certain criteria a work must satisfy in order to qualify as a derivative work. One of these is that a derivative work must exist in a "concrete or permanent form," *Galoob*, 964 F.2d at 967 (internal quotation marks omitted), and must substantially incorporate protected material from the preexisting work, see *Litchfield v. Spielberg*, 736 F.2d 1352, 1357 (9th

---

[3] Actually, this is all a bit metaphorical. Computer programs don't actually go anywhere or fetch anything. Rather, the game engine receives the player's instruction as to which game level to select and instructs the processor to access the MAP file corresponding to that level. The MAP file, in turn, consists of a series of instructions indicating which art images go where. When the MAP file calls for a particular art image, the game engine tells the processor to access the art library for instructions on how each pixel on the screen must be colored in order to paint that image.

Cir.1984). Micro Star argues that N/I is not a derivative work because the audiovisual displays generated when D/N-3D is run with N/I's MAP files are not incorporated in any concrete or permanent form, and the MAP files do not copy any of D/N-3D's protected expression. It is mistaken on both counts.

The requirement that a derivative work must assume a concrete or permanent form was recognized without much discussion in *Galoob*. There, we noted that all the Copyright Act's examples of derivative works took some definite, physical form and concluded that this was a requirement of the Act. See *Galoob*, 964 F.2d at 967-68; see also EDWARD G. BLACK & MICHAEL H. PAGE, ADD-ON INFRINGEMENTS, 15 HASTINGS COMM. ENT. L.J. 615, 625 (1993) (noting that in *Galoob* the Ninth Circuit "re-examined the statutory definition of derivative works offered in section 101 and found an independent fixation requirement of sorts built into the statutory definition of derivative works"). Obviously, N/I's MAP files themselves exist in a concrete or permanent form; they are burned onto a CD-ROM. See *ProCD, Inc. v. Zeidenberg*, 86 F.3d 1447, 1453 (7th Cir.1996) (computer files on a CD are fixed in a tangible medium of expression). But what about the audiovisual displays generated when D/N-3D runs the N/I MAP files--i.e., the actual game level as displayed on the screen? Micro Star argues that, because the audiovisual displays in *Galoob* didn't meet the "concrete or permanent form" requirement, neither do N/I's.

In Galoob, we considered audiovisual displays created using a device called the Game Genie, which was sold for use with the Nintendo Entertainment System. The Game Genie allowed players to alter individual features of a game, such as a character's strength or speed, by selectively "blocking the value for a single data byte sent by the game cartridge to the [Nintendo console] and replacing it with a new value." *Galoob*, 964 F.2d at 967. Players chose which data value to replace by entering a code; over a billion different codes were possible. The Game Genie was dumb; it functioned only as a window into the computer program, allowing players to temporarily modify individual aspects of the game. See *Lewis Galoob Toys, Inc. v. Nintendo of Am., Inc.*, 780 F.Supp. 1283, 1289 (N.D.Cal.1991).

Nintendo sued, claiming that when the Game Genie modified the game system's audiovisual display, it created an infringing derivative work. We rejected this claim because "[a] derivative work must incorporate a protected work in some concrete or permanent form." *Galoob*, 964 F.2d at 967 (internal quotation marks omitted). The audiovisual displays generated by combining the Nintendo System with the Game Genie were not incorporated in any permanent form; when the game was over, they were gone. Of course, they could be reconstructed, but only if the next player chose to reenter the same codes.[4]

Micro Star argues that the MAP files on N/I are a more advanced version of the Game Genie, replacing old values (the MAP files in the original game) with new values (N/I's MAP files). But, whereas the audiovisual displays created by Game Genie were never recorded in any permanent form, the audiovisual displays generated by D/N-3D from the N/I MAP files are in the MAP files themselves. In Galoob, the audiovisual display was defined by the original game cartridge, not by the Game Genie; no one could possibly say that the data values inserted by the Game Genie described the audiovisual display. In the present case the audiovisual display that appears on the computer monitor when a N/I level is played is described--in exact detail--by a N/I MAP file.

This raises the interesting question whether an exact, down to the last detail, description of an audiovisual display (and--by definition--we know that MAP files do describe audiovisual displays down to the last detail) counts as a permanent or concrete form for purposes of *Galoob*. We see no reason it shouldn't. What, after all, does sheet music do but describe in precise detail the way a copyrighted melody sounds? See 1 WILLIAM F. PATRY, COPYRIGHT LAW AND PRACTICE 168 (1994) ("[A] musical composition may be embodied in sheet music...."). To be copyrighted, pantomimes and dances may be "described in sufficient detail to enable the work to be performed from that description." *Id.* at 243 (citing *Compendium II of Copyright Office Practices* § 463); *see also Horgan v. Macmillan, Inc.*, 789 F.2d 157, 160 (2d Cir.1986). Similarly, the N/I MAP files describe the audiovisual display that is to be generated when the player chooses to play D/N-3D using the N/I levels. Because the audiovisual displays assume a concrete or permanent form in the MAP files, *Galoob* stands as no bar to finding that they are derivative works.

---

[4] A low-tech example might aid understanding. Imagine a product called the Pink Screener, which consists of a big piece of pink cellophane stretched over a frame. When put in front of a television, it makes everything on the screen look pinker. Someone who manages to record the programs with this pink cast (maybe by filming the screen) would have created an infringing derivative work. But the audiovisual display observed by a person watching television through the Pink Screener is not a derivative work because it does not incorporate the modified image in any permanent or concrete form. The Game Genie might be described as a fancy Pink Screener for video games, changing a value of the game as perceived by the current player, but never incorporating the new audiovisual display into a permanent or concrete form.

[This is a wonderful way to visualize the complex concept. This is what good lawyering and judging is all about. Keep it in mind when you analyze your cases and when you write your briefs.]

In addition, "[a] work will be considered a derivative work only if it would be considered an infringing work if the material which it has derived from a preexisting work had been taken without the consent of a copyright proprietor of such preexisting work." *Mirage Editions v. Albuquerque A.R.T. Co.*, 856 F.2d 1341, 1343 (quoting 1 NIMMER ON COPYRIGHT § 3.01 (1986)) (internal quotation marks omitted). "To prove infringement, [FormGen] must show that [D/N-3D's and N/I's audiovisual displays] are substantially similar in both ideas and expression." *Litchfield v. Spielberg*, 736 F.2d 1352, 1356 (9th Cir.1984) (emphasis omitted). Similarity of ideas may be shown by comparing the objective details of the works: plot, theme, dialogue, mood, setting, characters, etc. *See id.* Similarity of expression focuses on the response of the ordinary reasonable person, and considers the total concept and feel of the works. See *id.* at 1356-57. FormGen will doubtless succeed in making these showings since the audiovisual displays generated when the player chooses the N/I levels come entirely out of D/N-3D's source art library. *Cf. Atari, Inc. v. North Am. Philips Consumer Elec. Corp.*, 672 F.2d 607, 620 (7th Cir.1982) (finding two video games substantially similar because they shared the same "total concept and feel").

Micro Star further argues that the MAP files are not derivative works because they do not, in fact, incorporate any of D/N-3D's protected expression. In particular, Micro Star makes much of the fact that the N/I MAP files reference the source art library, but do not actually contain any art files themselves. Therefore, it claims, nothing of D/N-3D's is reproduced in the MAP files. In making this argument, Micro Star misconstrues the protected work. The work that Micro Star infringes is the D/N-3D story itself--a beefy commando type named Duke who wanders around post-Apocalypse Los Angeles, shooting Pig Cops with a gun, lobbing hand grenades, searching for medkits and steroids, using a jetpack to leap over obstacles, blowing up gas tanks, avoiding radioactive slime. A copyright owner holds the right to create sequels, *see Trust Co. Bank v. MGM/UA Entertainment Co.*, 772 F.2d 740 (11th Cir.1985), and the stories told in the N/I MAP files are surely sequels, telling new (though somewhat repetitive) tales of Duke's fabulous adventures. A book about Duke Nukem would infringe for the same reason, even if it contained no pictures.[5]

---

[5] We note that the N/I MAP files can only be used with D/N-3D. If another game could use the MAP files to tell the story of a mousy fellow who travels through a beige maze, killing vicious saltshakers with paper- clips, then the MAP files would not incorporate the protected expression of D/N-3D because they would not be telling a D/N-3D story.

Micro Star nonetheless claims that its use of D/N-3D's protected expression falls within the doctrine of fair use, which permits unauthorized use of copyrighted works "for purposes such as criticism, comment, news reporting, teaching (including multiple copies for classroom use), scholarship, or research." 17 U.S.C. § 107; *see Narell v. Freeman*, 872 F.2d 907, 913 (9th Cir.1989). Section 107 instructs courts "determining whether the use made of a work in any particular case is a fair use" to consider four factors: (1) the purpose and character of the use, including whether it is commercial in nature; (2) the nature of the copyrighted work; (3) the amount and substantiality of the copied material in relation to the copyrighted work as a whole; and (4) the effect of the use on the potential market for the copyrighted work. 17 U.S.C. § 107.

As a preliminary matter, Micro Star asks us to focus on the player's use of the N/I CD in evaluating the fair use claim, because-according to Micro Star-the player actually creates the derivative work. In *Galoob*, after we assumed for purposes of argument that the Game Genie did create derivative works, we went on to consider the fair use defense from the player's point of view. *See Galoob*, 964 F.2d at 970. But the fair use analysis in Galoob was not necessary and therefore is clearly *dicta*. More significantly, Nintendo alleged only contributory infringement--that *Galoob* was helping consumers create derivative works; FormGen here alleges direct infringement by Micro Star, because the MAP files encompass new Duke stories, which are themselves derivative works.

Our examination of the section 107 factors yields straightforward results. Micro Star's use of FormGen's protected expression was made purely for financial gain. While that does not end our inquiry, *see Campbell v. Acuff-Rose Music, Inc.*, 510 U.S. 569, 584 (1994), "every commercial use of copyrighted material is presumptively an unfair exploitation of the monopoly privilege that belongs to the owner of the copyright." *Sony Corp. of Am. v. Universal City Studios, Inc.*, 464 U.S. 417, 451 (1984).[6] The Supreme Court has explained that the second factor, the nature of the copyrighted work, is particularly significant because "some works are closer to the core of intended copyright protection than others, with the consequence that fair use is more difficult to establish when the former works are copied." *Campbell*, 510 U.S.

---

[6] Of course, transformative works have greater recourse to the fair use defense as they "lie at the heart of the fair use doctrine's guarantee of breathing space within the confines of copyright ... and the more transformative the new work, the less will be the significance of other factors, like commercialism, that may weigh against a finding of fair use." *Campbell*, 510 U.S. at 579 (citations omitted). N/I can hardly be described as transformative; anything but.

at 586. The fair use defense will be much less likely to succeed when it is applied to fiction or fantasy creations, as opposed to factual works such as telephone listings. *See United Tel. Co. v. Johnson Publ'g Co.*, 855 F.2d 604, 609 (8th Cir.1988); *see also Stewart v. Abend*, 495 U.S. 207 (1990). Duke Nukem's world is made up of aliens, radioactive slime and freezer weapons-clearly fantasies, even by Los Angeles standards. N/I MAP files "expressly use[ ] the [D/N-3D] story's unique setting, characters, [and] plot," *Stewart*, 495 U.S. at 238; both the quantity and importance of the material Micro Star used are substantial. Finally, by selling N/I, Micro Star "impinged on [FormGen's] ability to market new versions of the [D/N-3D] story." *Stewart*, 495 U.S. at 238; *see also Twin Peaks Productions, Inc. v. Publications Int'l, Ltd.*, 996 F.2d 1366, 1377 (2d Cir.1993). Only FormGen has the right to enter that market; whether it chooses to do so is entirely its business. "[N/I] neither falls into any of the categories enumerated in section 107 nor meets the four criteria set forth in section 107." *Stewart*, 495 U.S. at 237. It is not protected by fair use.

Micro Star also argues that it is the beneficiary of the implicit license FormGen gave to its customers by authorizing them to create new levels. Section 204 of the Copyright Act requires the transfer of the exclusive rights granted to copyright owners (including the right to prepare derivative works) to be in writing. See 17 U.S.C. § 204(a); *Effects Assocs., Inc. v. Cohen*, 908 F.2d 555, 556 (9th Cir.1990). A nonexclusive license may, however, be granted orally or implied by conduct. *See Effects*, 908 F.2d at 558. Nothing indicates that FormGen granted Micro Star any written license at all; nor is there evidence of a nonexclusive oral license. The only written license FormGen conceivably granted was to players who designed their own new levels, but that license contains a significant limitation: Any new levels the players create "must be offered [to others] solely for free." The parties dispute whether the license is binding, but it doesn't matter. If the license is valid, it clearly prohibits commercial distribution of levels; if it doesn't, FormGen hasn't granted any written licenses.[7]

In case FormGen didn't license away its rights, Micro Star argues that, by providing the Build Editor and encouraging players to create their own levels, FormGen abandoned all rights to its protected expression. It is well settled that rights gained under the Copyright Act may be abandoned. But abandonment of a right must be manifested by some overt act indicating an

---

[7] We would have no reason to sever the limitation from the license; the limitation is plainly stated in the User License, unambiguous, and not the least bit unreasonable. Indeed, it is precisely the sort of term we would expect to see in such a license.

intention to abandon that right. See *Hampton v. Paramount Pictures Corp.*, 279 F.2d 100, 104 (9th Cir.1960). Given that it overtly encouraged players to make and freely distribute new levels, FormGen may indeed have abandoned its exclusive right to do the same. But abandoning some rights is not the same as abandoning all rights, and FormGen never overtly abandoned its rights to profit commercially from new levels. Indeed, FormGen warned players not to distribute the levels commercially and has actively enforced that limitation by bringing suits such as this one.

IV

Because FormGen will likely succeed at trial in proving that Micro Star has infringed its copyright, we reverse the district court's order denying a preliminary injunction and remand for entry of such an injunction. Of course, we affirm the grant of the preliminary injunction barring Micro Star from selling N/I in boxes covered with screen shots of the game.[8]

AFFIRMED in part, REVERSED in part, and REMANDED. Micro Star to bear costs of both appeals.

2. *Fair Play, Due Process, and Common Sense—The Appeal of a Criminal Case.*

Admittedly, the *Micro Star v. FormGen* case was complicated, and the appeal presented legal issues that are, at their edges, far from being settled. That's one reason why, of course, each party believed that it had a shot of winning. Indeed, one judge out of four who considered the case sided with the party that ultimately lost. Would the result have been different if the panel were different? Perhaps. Anyone who does not believe that it makes a difference which judge hears what case is living in a make-believe world. By honing arguments until they are sharp and persuasive, and by hitting the so-called judicial "hot buttons," however, the effective appellate lawyer can either minimize the adverse effect of a judge's predilections or use them as but another tool of persuasion.

---

8 Micro Star raises various other claims alleging copyright misuse and abuse of the discovery process. However, nothing indicates that FormGen abused its copyright. See *Triad Systems Corp. v. Southeastern Express Co.*, 64 F.3d 1330, 1337 (9th Cir.1995). And we are at a loss to understand why Micro Star complains about the discovery process; certainly the district court did not abuse its discretion. *See Sopcak v. Northern Mountain Helicopter Serv.*, 52 F.3d 817, 819 (9th Cir.1995).

As I write this, the United States Court of Appeals for the Seventh Circuit has just upheld the constitutionality of laws in Illinois and Wisconsin forbidding so-called "partial-birth abortions." *The Hope Clinic v. Ryan*, ___ F.3d. ___ (7th Cir. 1999). The case was heard *en banc*, and the vote was six to four. Judge Frank Easterbrook wrote the majority opinion; Chief Judge Richard Posner wrote the dissent. Both opinions are sparkling, laced with wit and erudition, and forceful. But they reach opposite conclusions—not only on the underlying news-media-focus of outcome, but also on approach and judicial philosophy.

Judge Easterbrook's majority opinion, and the court's mandate, requires the district judges in the two cases to issue injunctions prohibiting enforcement of the laws beyond their core-concern of banning a method of terminating a pregnancy that Judge Easterbrook notes is an "uncommon procedure known to the medical community as 'intact dilation and extraction' or just 'dilation and extraction (D & X),' and to the public as 'partial-birth abortion.'"[41] Admitting that the majority's use of judicial construction to, in effect, have a federal court re-write and thus "save" the state statutes, is "an example of brute force," he responds with an insouciance that undoubtedly belies the spirited discussions: that "well, courts do it all the time."

Judge Posner, on the other hand is aghast at what he derides as "an evasion of judicial duty, a violation of Article III, and an affront to federalism," by the court's "forbidding the states to enforce state statutes that the court has not found to be invalid." Although acknowledging that "[c]ompromise holds seductive allure for a court faced with a hot issue" such as abortion, Judge Posner believes that on the merits of the vagueness-challenge, the statutes are constitutionally deficient:

> "If a woman told by her physician that her fetus will be a Down's baby or a Tay-Sachs baby or will be born without arms or legs, or that her own health or even life will be endangered if she carries the fetus to term, decides nevertheless against abortion, I would be the last to criticize her decision. I might consider her a heroine or a saint. But what is at stake in these cases is whether the people who feel that way are entitled to coerce a woman who feels differently to behave as they would in her situation. The Constitution as interpreted by the

---

[41] Judge Easterbrook, like most lawyers and judges, loves to use abbreviations. D & X is cumbersome and distracting; it reminds me of a possible title to an *avant garde* movie. For the life of me I don't understand why he could not have used the simple phrase "dilation and extraction," over which our eyes can pass quickly, without having to translate the abbreviation.

Supreme Court in decisions that we are not free to palter with answers this question 'no.'"

The issues thrashed out in *The Hope Clinic* will, undoubtedly, be decided by the United States Supreme Court—there is a significant split among the circuits. It will be interesting to see how the various predilections of the justices shake out. One thing is certain, the clarity of position as articulated on the one hand by Judge Easterbrook and on the other by Judge Posner will be lost in the prism-like mist of multiple decisions, as most of the justices write their pieces, joining this or that part of a colleague's concurrence or dissent. The result will be a scattered rainbow of light, the colors of the various concepts blending and bleeding into one another.

Can advocacy make a difference in this type of case? Did advocacy make a difference in *Micro Star v. FormGen*? Skeptics may say "no"—that the individual judges use and used the parties' arguments as springboards to, in Nizer's description of the Cardozo approach to judicial decision-making quoted in the beginning of this book, the judges' "subsequent research and reasoning to justify" the judges' initial "instinctive reaching of a conclusion."

I believe that advocacy can and *does* make a difference—I've seen it not only in my own practice as a lawyer, but also in my privileged role to be privy to, and a participant in, the decision-making process.

Let us move now to the second of the two cases we use to help us dissect the art of winning on appeal. It is a criminal case: *McGuire v. Estelle*.

Unlike the complex copyright case, *McGuire* presents simple and straightforward issues with which most, if not all, lawyers will have some familiarity. Just as the copyright case challenged us to cut through the jargon of an arcane field in order to make the arguments understandable and persuasive, *McGuire* will, in contrast, challenge us to take routine issues in a criminal case that may appear to some as open and shut, and craft winning arguments for either side.

What makes *McGuire* so intriguing is that the judges along the way—trial courts in both the state and federal systems, appellate panels, and finally the United States Supreme Court, viewed the case differently and reached different bottom-line results on the fairly simple concepts involved. In its essence, the case pits what some might view as the type of common sense that, on one hand, we tell jurors to take with them into the jury room and, on the other hand, a technical approach to the law that is justified by many as the only way to preserve a criminal justice system that truly protects the innocent.

We now turn to *McGuire*. We pick it up with the decision by the United States Court of Appeals for the Ninth Circuit, which reversed a decision by a district court not to grant *McGuire* a new trial *via* federal *habeas corpus*. The briefs we will analyze are the government's brief for a re-hearing *en banc*, and McGuire's response in opposition.

As you read the panel decision in *McGuire*, put yourself in the parties' shoes, and see what issues you would argue if you were seeking a rehearing *en banc*, and how you would oppose those arguments if you represented McGuire. First, however, let's review briefly the criteria for getting a rehearing *en banc* by a United States Court of Appeals.

Rule 35 of the Federal Rules of Appellate Procedure governs the procedure for seeking a rehearing *en banc* (I am omitting purely technical requirements, such as the number of copies that have to be filed, etc.) :

(a) *When Hearing or Rehearing En Banc May Be Ordered.* A majority of the circuit judges who are in regular active service may order that an appeal or other proceeding be heard or reheard by the court of appeals *en banc*. An *en banc* hearing or rehearing is not favored and ordinarily will not be ordered unless:

(1) *en banc* consideration is necessary to secure or maintain uniformity of the court's decisions; or

(2) the proceeding involves a question of exceptional importance.

(b) *Petition for Hearing or Rehearing En Banc.* A party may petition for a hearing or rehearing en banc.

(1) The petition must begin with a statement that either:

(A) the panel decision conflicts with a decision of the United States Supreme Court or of the court to which the petition is addressed (with citation to the conflicting case or cases) and consideration by the full court is therefore necessary to secure and maintain uniformity of the court's decisions; or

(B) the proceeding involves one or more questions of exceptional importance, each of which must be concisely

> stated; for example, a petition may assert that a proceeding presents a question of exceptional importance if it involves an issue on which the panel decision conflicts with the authoritative decisions of other United States Courts of Appeals that have addressed the issue.

Keep these criteria in mind as we read the panel decision in *McGuire v. Estelle*, 902 F.2d 749 (9th Cir. 1990) (I omitting from the decision, and from the parties' briefs, the discussion of whether McGuire sufficiently exhausted his state-court remedies, which turned out to be, essentially, a dead issue. All footnotes are the court's.):

WIGGINS, Circuit Judge:

Mark McGuire ("McGuire") appeals from the district court's denial of his petition for a writ of habeas corpus under 28 U.S.C. § 2254(a). McGuire was convicted of second degree murder and is now serving a fifteen year to life sentence in a California state prison. McGuire contends that the admission of evidence of prior acts against him at his trial, coupled with an instruction that permitted the jury to consider those prior acts as evidence of his guilt of the crime charged, were errors that denied him due process of law under the Fourteenth Amendment. We find that his contention has merit and REVERSE.

FACTS AND PROCEEDINGS BELOW

Because a proper consideration of McGuire's due process claim requires weighing the prejudice to him of the error he alleges, we examine the trial testimony in some detail.

At about 9:00 p.m., on July 7, 1981, McGuire and his wife brought their six month old baby girl to the emergency room of a hospital in Hayward, California. The baby was bluish in color and was not breathing. The hospital staff were unable to save the baby and she was pronounced dead at about 9:45 p.m.

The father, McGuire, was charged with the second degree murder of his child.

At trial, the prosecution called Dr. Levine, the doctor who examined the baby at the hospital. She testified that the child was essentially lifeless and without vital signs when she was brought into the hospital. The doctor also testified that the baby had a large and relatively recent bruise on the upper left chest area with multiple bruise marks around it, black and blue marks on her ears, and scar tissue indicating a healed tearing around the anus. Doctor Levine opined that the rectal tear was not caused by constipation or fecal impactment. She testified that such scarring probably resulted from the forceful insertion of a finger or some other foreign object. The doctor also testified that the baby had suffered from seven earlier rib fractures.

A different doctor performed an autopsy on the baby and testified that there were at least 17 contusions on the baby's chest and 29 more on her abdomen. He testified that his examination of the internal organs revealed that the liver was split in half, her pancreas was lacerated and split apart, her lower right lung and large vein from the heart were damaged, and part of her intestine was lacerated. The doctor also testified to rectal tearing at least six weeks old and to evidence of several partially healed rib fractures approximately seven weeks old.

McGuire made timely objection to all evidence of prior injuries as not being connected to him. The objections were overruled.

None of the foregoing evidence of injury to the child included evidence of who caused the injuries to her.

The prosecution also called a witness who had overheard McGuire talking to his wife in the emergency room of the hospital. The witness stated that McGuire's wife asked him "what really had happened?" and McGuire is reported to have responded that the baby had fallen from the couch.

A police officer was called by the prosecution. He testified that McGuire had told him that the child had fallen from the couch. The officer then told McGuire that the baby's injuries were inconsistent with a fall from the couch. McGuire thereupon responded that "maybe some Mexicans came in while I was upstairs."

McGuire's wife was next called as a witness by the prosecution. She was granted transactional immunity for her testimony although she had made no statement to the prosecutor prior to the trial. When asked about the circumstances of the baby's death, she testified that she, and not her husband, had beaten the baby. She gave a confused account of having struck the baby in the afternoon of July 7, 1981 and that the child did not move, cry, or cough thereafter.

McGuire's wife testified that on the afternoon of the 7th, after she struck the child, she left the house for about ten minutes and when she returned, the child was not breathing. She stated that she asked her husband what had happened and he said the child had fallen from the couch and struck the walker. She also testified that several weeks prior to the baby's death, she inserted her finger into the baby's rectum in an attempt to relieve her of constipation. She also testified to staying at a neighbor's house for four days prior to the 7th and had made inquiries about a battered woman's shelter.

The prosecution introduced evidence that a fall from a couch could not have produced the injuries causing the baby's death. The prosecution also introduced evidence that McGuire had treated the baby roughly in the past.

The defense countered with witnesses who testified they had never seen McGuire abuse the child. McGuire did not testify in his own defense.

On March 19, 1982, the jury returned a verdict of second degree murder against McGuire. On January 15, 1985, the California Court of Appeal affirmed his conviction. McGuire petitioned for a hearing before the California Supreme Court. On March 21, 1985, the California Supreme Court issued a "postcard denial" of the petition. It did so without any citation or comment.

On August 30, 1985, McGuire filed a petition for writ of habeas corpus in federal district court under 28 U.S.C. § 2254(a). Order to show cause issued on February 26, 1986. In its original response, the state of California did not answer on the merits but argued that McGuire had failed to exhaust his state remedies. The district court, relying on *Maxwell v. Sumner*, 673 F.2d 1031, 1034 n. 1 (9th Cir.), *cert. denied,* 459 U.S. 976 (1982), ruled against the state on the exhaustion issue and ordered it to answer on the merits. After the state did so, the district court denied McGuire's petition on July 15, 1987. It held that the admission of the evidence of the prior injuries to the child, and a jury instruction relating to that evidence, was proper under California evidence rules. The court also found that the evidence was relevant to contradict a pretrial statement made by McGuire, and offered at trial by the prosecution, that the baby's injuries were caused by her falling off a couch. The court also rejected McGuire's fifth amendment prosecutorial misconduct and denial of discovery claims. McGuire timely appealed. We have jurisdiction under 28 U.S.C. § 1291.

[Discussion of exhaustion of state-court remedies omitted.]

II. THE CONSTITUTIONALITY OF APPELLANT'S CONVICTION

We review the district court's denial of a petition for a writ of habeas corpus de novo. *Weygandt v. Ducharme,* 774 F.2d 1491, 1492 (9th Cir.1985). A state prisoner is entitled to habeas relief only if he is held in violation of the constitution, laws, or treaties of the United States. *Engle v. Isaac*, 456 U.S. 107, 119 (1982); 28 U.S.C. § 2254(a). McGuire contends that the procedures used to convict him in state court violated his fourteenth amendment right to due process. U.S. CONST. AMEND XIV. We agree.

A claim for deprivation of due process will succeed only if the trial court's errors rendered the trial arbitrary or fundamentally unfair. *Pennywell v. Rushen*, 705 F.2d 355, 357 (9th Cir.1983). In the instant case we find that the aggregate effect of the admittance of irrelevant, highly prejudicial evidence, compounded by the trial court's instruction to use that evidence in the most prejudicial manner possible, rendered appellant's trial arbitrary and fundamentally unfair.

A. THE ADMITTANCE OF IRRELEVANT, PREJUDICIAL EVIDENCE

The trial court admitted extensive evidence of prior physical abuse the baby had suffered, including evidence of possible sexual abuse. However, that evidence has no relevance to appellant because the prosecution did not establish that appellant inflicted those injuries.

In order for evidence to be relevant, it must have some probative value. See, e.g., FED.R.EVID. 401 (evidence to be relevant must make the determination of the action more probable or less probable than it would be without the evidence). Evidence cannot have probative value unless a party connects it to the defendant in some meaningful way. *See, e.g., United States v. Hooten*, 662 F.2d 628, 635 (9th Cir.1981), cert. denied, 455 U.S. 1004 (1982) (in order for prior act evidence to be admissible under the FED.R.EVID. it must be "similar and close enough in time to be relevant"); *People v. Rivera*, 41 Cal.3d 388, 392, 710 P.2d 362, 364, 221 Cal.Rptr. 562, 564 (1985) (in bank) ("In order for evidence of a prior [act] to have a tendency to prove the defendant's identity as the perpetrator of the charged offense, the [prior act and the charged offense] must have enough shared characteristics to raise a strong inference that they were committed by the same person... It is not enough that the two acts contain common marks.").

In the instant case, the prosecution made no such connection. The prosecution elicited evidence that McGuire was rough with the baby, and that on one occasion McGuire had squeezed the baby's cheeks. Daisy McGuire also stated that she feared leaving the baby alone with McGuire. We recognize the temptation to find that such evidence is enough to infer that McGuire caused the prior rectal tearing and the broken ribs. However, we cannot permit a jury that temptation. Evidence of McGuire's petty meanness does not establish that he committed, or is even capable of, the extensive physical abuse inflicted on the child. It is precisely because anyone, including Daisy McGuire, could have inflicted those injuries that makes the prior injury evidence irrelevant.

We emphasize that the trial court's error was not simply that it admitted the prior evidence under the wrong evidentiary theory. Nor do we dispute that there are constitutionally permissible uses for admitting evidence of prior bad acts. *See* FED.R.EVID. 404(b) (evidence of other crimes, wrongs or acts may be admissible to prove motive, opportunity, intent, preparation, plan, knowledge identity, or absence of mistake or accident); *United States v. Lewis*, 837 F.2d 415, 418-419 (9th Cir.), *cert. denied*, 488 U.S. 923 (1988) (evidence of prior child abuse properly admitted to show intent). However, acts which the prosecution did not connect to appellant cannot be characterized as his prior bad acts.

Furthermore, we find the introduction of such prior injury evidence highly prejudicial. The prosecution introduced evidence of prior injuries to the baby to establish that appellant was a child abuser, and for no other purpose, in a murder trial for the death of his child. The trial court incorrectly admitted the evidence pursuant to California law allowing past injury evidence to establish the "Battered Child Syndrome." The Battered Child Syndrome allows proof of past injuries to prove the child's present injuries did not occur accidentally. *See People v. Jackson*, 18 Cal.App.3d 504, 506, 95 Cal.Rptr. 919, 921 (1971); *Landeros v. Flood*, 17 Cal.3d 399, 409, 551 P.2d 389, 393, 131 Cal.Rptr. 69, 73 (1976).

However, in the instant case, no claim was made that the child died accidentally. The prosecution attempted to prove Mark McGuire deliberately did it. The defense attempted to prove Daisy McGuire deliberately did it. Although the prosecution did not succeed in proving that the appellant caused the prior injuries, we cannot ignore that a trial of the grisly murder of an innocent baby implicates highly charged emotions. The unproven characterization of appellant as a child abuser maximized the prejudice flowing from the irrelevant evidence. See *Dudley v. Duckworth, 854 F.2d 967*

(7th Cir.1988) (granting habeas relief where prejudicial effective evidence so outweighed probative value that result was a denial of fundamental fairness); *Osborne v. Wainwright*, 720 F.2d 1237 (11th Cir.1983) (reversing and remanding a denial of habeas corpus petition on basis that prejudicial effect of evidence might have risen to such magnitude as to deny fundamental fairness); *Bisaccia v. Attorney General of State of New Jersey*, 623 F.2d 307 (3d Cir.1980) (same).

B. IMPROPER JURY INSTRUCTIONS

The trial court did not merely admit irrelevant, highly prejudicial evidence without comment. The trial court instructed the jury to use that evidence in the most improper way possible. We assume that the jury followed its instructions. *Aspen Skiing Co. v. Aspen Highlands Skiing Corp.*, 472 U.S. 585, 604 (1985). The trial court's jury instructions stated:

> Evidence has been introduced for the purpose of showing that the defendant committed acts similar to those constituting a crime other than that for which he is on trial. Such evidence, if believed, was not received, and may not be considered by you to prove that he is a person of bad character or that he had a disposition to commit crimes. Such evidence was received and may be considered by you only for the limited purpose of determining if it tends to show three things:
>
> 1) The impeachment of Daisy McGuire's testimony that she had no cause to be afraid of the defendant,
>
> 2) To establish the battered child syndrome, and
>
> 3) Also a connection between the other two offense (sic) and the one of which the defendant is accused so that *it may be logically concluded that if the defendant committed other offenses, he also committed the crime charged in the case*. You are not permitted to consider evidence for any other purpose. (emphasis added).

Subsection 3 of the instruction is erroneous.[1] It permits the jury to make a direct determination of guilt by concluding that appellant committed prior bad acts. The rejection of such use of circumstantial character evidence in criminal

---

[1] It appears that the trial court's erroneous instruction was the result of an incorrect reading of CALJIC 2.50 (1979 Revision). This standard jury instruction has been clarified to avoid the misunderstanding which occurred here. See CALJIC 2.50 (1987 Revision).

cases has become "so deeply imbedded in our jurisprudence as to assume almost constitutional proportions...." Fed.R.Evid. 404(a) advisory committee's note.

Not only have we never condoned an instruction which permits a finding of guilt based on a conclusion that the appellant committed prior bad acts, we have consistently stressed the importance of a limiting instruction to confine the use of prior bad act evidence to the proper purpose for which the court admitted it. *See United States v. Green,* 648 F.2d 587, 593 (9th Cir.1981) (admission of bad act evidence in conjunction with failure of trial judge to provide limiting instruction following admission of bad act evidence required reversal); *cf. Butcher v. Marquez,* 758 F.2d 373, 378 (9th Cir.1985) (no due process violation resulted from wrongful admission of prejudicial evidence where instructions limited use of that evidence to find intent); *United States v. McCown*, 711 F.2d 1441, 1454 (9th Cir.1983) (no due process violation resulted from admission of prior bad acts evidence where prejudice was minimal and trial judge offered to give a limiting instruction).

The damage done by subsection 3 is not limited by a qualifying instruction by the court. Nor is subsection 3 limited by the preceding subsections of the instruction. The first subsection simply warned the jury not to use the evidence of prior bad acts to find that McGuire was a bad person and therefore infer that McGuire was likely to have committed this crime. Subsection 3, however, informed the jury that it may find McGuire guilty of the offense charged if it logically concluded that he committed the other earlier offenses. For these reasons, the faulty instruction considered along with the admittance of the prejudicial evidence "so infected the entire trial that the resulting conviction violate[d] due process." *Cupp v. Naughten,* 414 U.S. 141, 147 (1973). Nor do we believe that this error can be considered harmless beyond a reasonable doubt. *See Chapman v. California*, 386 U.S. 18, 24 (1967). Although there was evidence suggesting McGuire's guilt, this evidence was certainly not overwhelming. *See Dudley v. Duckworth*, 854 F.2d 967, 972 (7th Cir.1988) (error not harmless even when evidence of petitioner's guilt was "impressive but not overwhelming.").

III. CONCLUSION

We find that the jury instruction which permitted the direct determination of guilt from evidence of prior injuries not connected to McGuire denied him due process. The severity of these errors sets this case apart from arguably similar cases in which we rejected claims that evidentiary error rendered a trial fundamentally unfair. For example, in *Lewis*, we found no due process error where the trial court admitted evidence of prior child abuse in a defendant's trial for the murder of his son. 837 F.2d at 418-19. However, *Lewis* suffered from neither of the errors we find determinative in the instant case. In *Lewis*, the testimony of two witnesses connected the defendant to the infliction of the prior injuries, and the trial court provided a limiting instruction. *Id.* at 419.

Because the prejudicial effect of the errors discussed above amount to a denial of due process, we grant McGuire's habeas petition. However, we are also not blind to the fact that apart from those errors, only the barest threads connect McGuire to the crime. True, given the pattern of most child abuse cases, it is not unreasonable to assume that one or both of the baby's primary care givers were responsible for the baby's injuries and death. We are also mindful that in the emergency room, McGuire answered unconvincingly in response to Daisy McGuire's accusation that McGuire bore responsibility for the baby's injuries leading to death. And evidence existed that McGuire had treated his wife and the baby roughly in the past. But these are mere shadows of guilt which leave ample room for reasonable doubt. Due process requires more than a simple intuitive feeling that the father may be guilty. It requires convincing proof.

We REVERSE and REMAND for a new trial.

— — —

The panel in *McGuire* concluded unanimously that McGuire was denied due process because: 1) in its view, there was no evidence to connect him with the baby's earlier horrendous injuries, and that, therefore, admission of evidence of those injuries was error; and 2) the trial court's instruction on use of the prior-injury evidence was error. What are the competing interests that the parties should consider in either seeking or opposing an *en banc* hearing by the court?

As *Berger v. United States*, 295 U.S. 78, 88 (1935), reminds us, the purpose of our criminal law is two fold: "that guilt shall not escape nor innocence suffer." The state prosecutor sees the panel decision as permitting a guilty man to "escape." McGuire's lawyer sees the panel decision as upholding the rightful burden that the law imposes on the government, to paraphrase Justice Oliver Wendell Holmes's famous phrase, to turn the corners square when seeking to convict a defendant, so that innocence does not suffer.[42] But there must be more—a mere error by a panel is not enough to justify *en banc* review. The State must show that there is a "question of exceptional importance" that makes *en banc* review warranted. The State must also motivate the judges of the circuit to *want* to overturn the panel's decision. On the other hand, McGuire must persuade the judges that the case is not worthy of their attention, and, moreover, that the panel was correct.

As you read the briefs, think about the strength of the parties' arguments, the clarity and forcefulness of their presentations, and whether you believe they are either omitting a good argument or larding the briefs with weak arguments. Also, think about how you would do a better job. As with the panel's decision, I am omitting all discussion of whether McGuire exhausted his state-court remedies. Again, my comments will be in brackets and in **Univers bold**. All footnotes are the brief's.

Petition of the State of California for a rehearing *en banc*:

PETITION FOR REHEARING AND SUGGESTION FOR REHEARING EN BANC

INTRODUCTION

In an opinion filed on May 8, 1989, a panel of this Court reversed the District Court's order denying a petition for writ of habeas corpus, and ordered the State of California to grant petitioner a new trial. A petition for rehearing and suggestion for rehearing en banc was filed on May 19, 1989. On April 23, 1990, the panel withdrew and vacated its 1989 opinion.

A second opinion was filed by the panel on May 4, 1990. It again reversed the order denying habeas corpus relief. This petition for rehearing and suggestion for rehearing en banc is filed within 14 days, as required by Federal Rules of Appellate Procedure [FRAP] 40.

[This is procedural background to bring the rest of the judges up-to-speed. But there is something incredibly important missing. What? What fact or series of facts will, from California's standpoint, give the circuit judges reading its petition a sense that justice has miscarried? Here, as in every case, you must show the proverbial "bloody shirt." Tragically, the "shirt" here is

[42] "Men must turn square corners when they deal with the Government." *Rock Island, etc., R. Co. v. United States*, 254 U.S. 141, 143 (1920).

both metaphorically and literally true. I would put the following first, right at the top:

> **This is a tragic case. First, as even the panel recognized, Tori McGuire's six months of life was racked with pain and torture. Beaten to death, her life ended on a midsummer's night. But there is more. Here is the panel's description:**
>
> > **"[Tori] was essentially lifeless and without vital signs when she was brought into the hospital. ... [Tori] had a large and relatively recent bruise on the upper left chest area with multiple bruise marks around it, black and blue marks on her ears, and scar tissue indicating a healed tearing around the anus. ... [Tori] ... had suffered from seven earlier rib fractures. ... there were at least 17 contusions on the baby's chest and 29 more on her abdomen. ...[Tori's] liver was split in half, her pancreas was lacerated and split apart, her lower right lung and large vein from the heart were damaged, and part of her intestine was lacerated. [Tori also had] ... rectal tearing at least six weeks old and to evidence of several partially healed rib fractures approximately seven weeks old."]**

Respondent believes that a rehearing is necessary in order to address material points of fact and law overlooked in the decision. Specifically, the panel held: (1) that evidence was improperly admitted in petitioner's state court murder trial; and, (2) that a limiting instruction was improper, based in part on its conclusion that such evidence would not have been admissible in a federal prosecution under the Federal Rules of Evidence. Those holdings ignore the inapplicability of the federal rules to state prosecutions, fail to comport with the limited review function appropriate to habeas corpus, and are inconsistent with a recent United States Supreme Court decision on the scope of due process when potentially prejudicial evidence is admitted in a criminal trial.

[These are mere glimmerings of issues that might make the case *en-banc* worthy: 1) federal rules of evidence don't apply in California state courts; 2) the panel exceeded the proper scope of *habeas-corpus* review; and 3) a misapplication of the fairly

elastic concept of "due process." Is this enough? Is it persuasive? Why is *en-banc* review required? Stated another way, why can't the judges of the circuit just let this arguably erroneous panel decision sit, along with others with which they might also disagree?

It is the job of the petitioner, California, to persuade the judges that this case is different from all the others with which they might disagree.

In my view, the crux of California's best argument is that the panel decision is a *usurpation* that will significantly change the way state-court convictions are reviewed by the federal courts in the Ninth Circuit. In other words, the panel decision sanctions second-guessing by the federal courts of state-court evidentiary rulings and *this* puts at risk almost *every* state criminal conviction.

The following would be my syllogism:

- The universal standard used to review evidentiary decisions by trial courts is whether the trial court has abused its discretion. The panel's decision ignores that, and indeed, did not even use the *word* "discretion." Rather, it applied an amorphous standard of review that it did not even articulate, but one that smells like review *de novo*.

- This is a sea change—a highly significant departure, a rogue decision that threatens not only the whole constitutional fabric of federalism that protects against federal-court interference with state-court convictions unless the State has violated the defendant's federal constitutional rights.

- Although the panel's decision uses the phrase "due process," that phrase is but the veneer applied to its underlying disagreement with the

evidentiary rulings by the state trial court and the affirmance of those rulings by the California appellate process.

- **Unless overturned, district courts in the entire Ninth Circuit will be bound by *McGuire* and will, as a result, be reviewing state-court evidentiary rulings *de novo*. Further, the rulings of the district courts in these *habeas corpus* matters will, themselves, be reviewed *de novo* by the court of appeals. We now continue with California's brief.]**

Respondent additionally suggests, pursuant to FRAP 35, that rehearing en banc is appropriate for two reasons. First, it is necessary to secure uniformity of decision within the Circuit. Other panels have recognized the substantial showing necessary to find a violation of due process based on the improper admission of evidence or the giving of inadequate jury instructions. The panel decision is inconsistent with that line of cases. Second, the question of when issues are viewed as exhausted by this Court is of exceptional importance to the State of California.

[Rule 35 requires the listing of decisions with which the panel's decision is alleged to conflict. The petition ignores this requirement. Judges reviewing the petition will conclude that there are none. Also, so far, the petition ignores what I see as the strongest ground for acceptance of *en-banc* review: the radical departure from established rules for the review of state-court convictions.]

II.

THE PANEL'S HOLDING THAT IT WAS ERROR TO INTRODUCE EVIDENCE DEMONSTRATING PRIOR INCIDENTS OF CHILD ABUSE AND TO GIVE AN INSTRUCTION ON THE USE OF THAT EVIDENCE IMPROPERLY RELIES UPON THE POSSIBLE INADMISSIBILITY OF SUCH EVIDENCE IN A FEDERAL PROSECUTION, WHILE IGNORING ITS CONCEDED ADMISSIBILITY UNDER STATE LAW AND FAILS TO CONSIDER THE EXTENT TO WHICH THE EVIDENCE AND INSTRUCTION RESULTED IN THE DENIAL OF A FUNDAMENTALLY FAIR TRIAL.

The panel concluded that petitioner was prejudiced by the admission of evidence demonstrating prior acts of child abuse and by a jury instruction relating to that evidence. Although the analysis has been modified and some of the language changed, this is otherwise identical to the conclusion reached in the first opinion. The decision remains factually and legally inaccurate and should be reconsidered.[1]

[Ordinarily, this would be a weak beginning. But here, the panel withdrew its first decision in response to an earlier petition for rehearing *en banc*. This paragraph is thus, in my view, appropriately designed to alert the judges who will vote on the State's petition that, in essence, nothing has changed even though the earlier opinion was withdrawn.]

"The writ of habeas corpus has limited scope; the federal courts do not sit to re-try state cases *de novo* but, rather, to review for violation of federal constitutional standards." *Milton v. Wainwright*, 407 U.S. 371, 377 (1972). When reviewing a state criminal judgment on habeas corpus, a federal court does not act "as a 'super state supreme court.'" *Payne v. Janaz,* 711 F.2d 1305, 1310 (6th Cir. 1983). The panel decision ignores these limitations on federal habeas corpus jurisdiction.

[This is good. It is clear, concise, and to the point. Note how we see quotes from the decisions in the context of a powerful, coherent argument that the scope of review by the federal courts of state-court convictions is exceedingly limited. There is, however, something missing.

Recall that one of the criteria for granting a rehearing *en banc* is that "the proceeding involves a question of exceptional importance." The State's "Introduction" does say that "the question of when issues are viewed as exhausted by this Court is of exceptional importance to the State of California," but does not argue, either there or here, that the panel has dramatically changed the law by, in essence, sanctioning and, indeed,

---

[1] Although given less emphasis in the second opinion, the panel continues to characterize the evidence of prior physical abuse suffered by the six-month old murder victim as "including evidence of possible sexual abuse." Slip opn. at 4363. Assuming this refers to evidence that the victim sustained damage to her anus, we repeat that there was never any suggestion in the testimony or argument that this injury was sexual in nature. There is simply no basis in the state court record for concluding that the jury viewed this evidence as demonstrating sexual abuse of the child.

requiring, *de novo* review of state-court evidentiary rulings in criminal cases, and that this, too, presents a question of "exceptional importance" to all the courts within the Ninth Circuit—both federal *and* state.]

The admission in a state criminal trial of other crimes evidence will not justify federal habeas corpus relief unless the admission of that evidence was "arbitrary or fundamentally unfair." *Terrovona v. Kincheloe,* 852 F.2d 424, 428 (9th Cir. 1988); *Colley v. Sumner,* 784 F.2d 984, 990 (9th Cir. 1986). The petitioner must demonstrate that use of the evidence rendered his trial fundamentally unfair and thus denied him his constitutional right to due process. *Gordon v. Duran,* 895 F.2d 610, 613 (9th Cir. 1990); *Butcher v. Marquez,* 758 F.2d 373, 378 (9th Cir. 1985). The District Court relied upon these standards in denying the petition. A-15-A-16. The panel did not. It ruled, instead, that the evidence of prior physical abuse to the victim was not admissible under the Federal Rules of Evidence and was "incorrectly admitted . . . pursuant to California law. . . Slip opn. at 4363-4364. Neither holding is correct; neither is a proper basis for federal habeas corpus relief.

[This gets into the merits of the panel's decision. But the argument is tautological. The panel believed that it was not fair to saddle McGuire with crimes to which he was not linked. As a concept, there is nothing unusual or wrong about that. Certainly, if there were *nothing* from which a jury could reasonably conclude that McGuire *did* inflict those horrendous earlier injuries on the baby, permitting the jury to consider that evidence would be error—perhaps even of constitutional dimension. So what does the State have to demonstrate? That the state trial judge acted within the proper scope of his discretion, and, therefore, there was no due-process violation. How do you do this? By showing that there *is* a connection between McGuire and the baby's earlier catastrophic injuries. Does the State do this? No. Can it? Of course. I offer the following outline:

- **Section 1101 of the California Evidence Code provides:**

  (a) Except as provided in this section and in Sections 1102, 1103, 1108, and 1109, evidence of a person's character or a trait of his or her character (whether in the form of an opinion, evidence of reputation, or evidence of specific

> **instances of his or her conduct) is inadmissible when offered to prove his or her conduct on a specified occasion.**
>
> **(b) *Nothing in this section prohibits the admission of evidence that a person committed a crime, civil wrong, or other act when relevant to prove some fact (such as motive, opportunity, intent, preparation, plan, knowledge, identity, absence of mistake or accident*, or whether a defendant in a prosecution for an unlawful sexual act or attempted unlawful sexual act did not reasonably and in good faith believe that the victim consented) other than his or her disposition to commit such an act.**

(Emphasis added.) Rule 404(b) of the Federal Rules of Evidence similarly provides that: "Evidence of other crimes, wrongs or acts ... may ... be admissible ... as proof of motive, opportunity, intent, preparation, plan, knowledge, identity, or absence of mistake or accident ..." The rules are, insofar as material here, almost identical;

- **The determination of whether the "other acts" were committed by the person alleged to have committed them is, under federal law, made by the jury, after the trial court first decides under Rule 104(b) of the Federal Rules of Evidence that there is "evidence sufficient to support" a finding that the person did commit those acts. *See Huddleston v. United States*, 485 U.S. 681, 689–691 (1988). Although there are no California cases specifically adopting *Huddleston*, the *Huddleston* standard obviously comports with due process.**

- **The panel's conclusion that there was no evidence to "connect" McGuire to the baby's earlier injuries is wrong:**

  — McGuire and his wife were the only two persons who had access to the baby when the baby suffered those horrendous injuries.

— Parents innocent of abuse causing those injuries would have 1) sought medical treatment for their baby: and 2) would have reported the abuse to the police. The McGuires did neither.

— The wife's questions and comments to McGuire at the hospital indicated that she suspected him of abusing the child. Moreover she had moved out of the house, for four days, before the baby was beaten to death, and had asked about a battered woman's shelter. Additionally, even the panel described her testimony claiming blame for the baby's death as being "a confused account." In light of all this, there was sufficient evidence for the jury to reasonably conclude that she 1) did not commit the abuse that night; 2) was afraid of McGuire; and 3) suspected that McGuire, based on her awareness of what he had done in the past, was the abuser.

— McGuire's inculpatorily false responses to his wife, both at home and at the hospital, was evidence that he had beaten the baby that day, and that this was but one incident in a pattern of beatings that included the prior injuries.

- There was sufficient evidence under Rule 104(b) of the Federal Rules of Evidence and *Huddleston* for a jury to find that McGuire inflicted those earlier injuries; accordingly, there was sufficient evidence to "connect" McGuire to the prior incidents of abuse. This means that *the only reason* that the panel gave for holding that the state trial court erred in admitting the evidence falls away.

Additionally, the State's brief glides over the important point that needs to be trumpeted (because *en banc* review will not be granted to merely correct an erroneous decision by a panel): the panel usurped the state courts in their interpretation of their own evidence codes, and that this usurpation has to be nipped in the

bud. Stated another way, the panel's decision is but the proverbial camel's nose in the tent—once the nose enters, the camel is not far behind. As the United States Supreme Court observed more than one-hundred years ago in a different context, "illegitimate and unconstitutional practices get their first footing ... by silent deviations from legal modes of procedure." *Boyd v. United States,* 116 U.S. 616, 635 (1886).]

The panel cites as support for its conclusion that the other crimes evidence was not admissible Federal Rules of Evidence 401 and 404. However, those rules are not constitutionally based. *Dowling v. United States,* ___ U.S. ___ 110 S.Ct. 668, 674 (1990). As such, violation of the rules alone could not constitute a federal constitutional violation. The Supreme Court has "defined the category of infractions that violate 'fundamental fairness' very narrowly." *Dowling, supra.* "Rules of evidence are designed in the interest of fair trials. But unfairness in result is no sure measure of unconstitutionality." *United States v. Augenblick,* 393 U.S. 348, 352 (1969). Moreover, the rules generally do not prohibit the introduction of evidence, but rather limit the purpose for which it may be used. *Huddleston v. United States,* 485 U.S. 681, 687 (1988). It is clear that when it enacted the rules Congress was less concerned with the potential prejudicial effect of other crimes evidence "as it was with ensuring that restrictions would not be placed on the admission of such evidence." *Huddleston, supra,* at 688-689. Simply put, it is not at all clear that the panel's interpretation of the federal rules is correct. Even if it were, however, the erroneous admission of evidence which results in a conviction is not sufficient to support a finding of federal constitutional error. *Dowling, supra.*

[Again, the dreaded "but even if" argument.]

More importantly, a federal court has "no supervisory authority over state judicial proceedings." *Smith v. Phillips,* 455 U.S. 209, 221 (1982). It was inappropriate for the panel to attempt to impose the limitations of federal evidentiary rules on a state court proceeding. This is particularly true given that the degree of error necessary to justify a reversal on habeas corpus is even greater than the showing required to establish plain error on direct appeal. *Henderson v. Kibbe,* 431 U.S. 145, 154 (1977); *Payne v. Janaz, supra,* 711 F.2d at 1310. In *Huddleston, supra,* the court recognized that "unduly prejudicial evidence might be introduced" under the federal rule allowing for evidence of prior acts, but concluded that protection against such "unfair prejudice" emanated from requirements in the rules that the evidence be admitted for a proper purpose, that it be relevant, that the trial court weigh probative value against undue prejudicial effect, and that a limiting instruction be given upon request. 485 U.S. at 691-692. All of these conditions were satisfied under equivalent state rules of evidence in petitioner's trial. Disagreement over the determination of relevance, clearly a question of state law, is not an issue which a federal court may reach on habeas corpus.

[This is confusing for two reasons. First, it concedes that the evidence *was* not admissible under the Federal Rules of evidence. This is a concession that, as we've seen, the State does not have to make. Second, the error warranting *en banc* review is *not* that the panel used federal authorities to interpret state evidence law, which generally tracks the federal rules anyway. Indeed, as we've seen, section 1101(b) of the California Evidence Code is almost identical, as material here, to Rule 404(b) of the Federal Rules of Evidence. The error warranting *en banc* review is that the panel seized for itself the *fact* of review and, additionally, did not give to the state trial court's ruling the required abuse-of-discretion deference. This is the danger to orderly process and constitutionally mandated federalism that warrants *en banc* review and reversal because, and this is critical, the panel's errors extend and have controlling influence well beyond McGuire and the specific facts of this case.]

The panel's conclusion that admission of the other crimes evidence to support a diagnosis of Battered Child Syndrome was incorrect under California state law is erroneous for several reasons. First, the state trial and appellate court concluded that the evidence was admissible under state law. The panel had no basis for disputing that conclusion. *Clemons v. Mississippi,* ___ U.S. ___, 110 S.Ct. 1441, 1449—1450 (1990).

Second, the diagnosis of Battered Child Syndrome "has been judicially recognized in [California]." *People v. Steger,* 16 Cal.3d 539, 549, n.4 (1976). The diagnosis is not an opinion that any particular person caused the injuries (or death), but relates solely to the likelihood that the number and degree of injuries were accidentally inflicted. *People v. Jackson,* 18 Cal.App.3d 504, 507 (1971). Thus, evidence of other injuries sustained by the child is relevant not because of its direct linkage to the specific defendant on trial, but because of its use in support of the Battered Child diagnosis. That diagnosis is relevant both to establish death by a criminal agency and to rebut any suggestion of accidental cause for the fatal injuries. Those uses are proper under state law, and are not precluded by any provision in the United States Constitution.

Finally, the panel suggests that the Battered Child diagnosis, and thus the evidence in support of it, was irrelevant because petitioner did not claim that the child died accidentally. The panel overlooks the fact that no such argument was presented to the state trial court in support of the motion to exclude the prior injuries. State defense counsel argued only that the evidence was more prejudicial than probative and should be excluded for that reason. RT 71-72. Counsel did not suggest that the Battered Child Syndrome lacked relevance, because petitioner admitted that the victim was intentionally injured. Moreover, defense counsel reserved her opening statement, RT 12, thus requiring the state to overcome the accidental death defense proffered in petitioner's statements to the police.[2] Admission of the previous injuries in support of testimony demonstrating that petitioner's version of the events was impossible did not violate any federal right.

[This argument ignores the following: McGuire claimed that the injuries were accidental or non-intentional—he said initially that the baby fell from the couch. If true, he was not guilty. If not true, the jury could reasonably conclude that he was guilty because otherwise he would have no reason to make up such a story. The prior acts, therefore, are admissible under both section 1101(b) of the California Code and Rule 404(b) the Federal Rules of Evidence to show lack of accident. (Battered Child Syndrome is but a name applied to evidence admissible to show either intent or lack of accident under section 1101(b)).

Moreover, because his theory also encompassed his denial that he was the abuser (claiming first that it was some "Mexicans," and, later, his wife) the "identity" of the abuser was at issue, and the signature pattern of abuse was probative of the abuser's identity—this pointed to McGuire and neither a "Mexican" nor his wife as that person. Thus, the "other acts" that made up that signature pattern of abuse were also admissible under both section 1101(b) the California Evidence Code and Rule 404(b) the Federal Rules of Evidence.]

---

2 Even in argument defense counsel did not concede that the death was intentional. She argued primarily that petitioner's wife caused the injuries, but that they were exacerbated by a fall from the couch as described in petitioner's statements. RT 713. Counsel also asserted that the prior injuries did not establish that the victim was a battered child, RT 716, and suggested that whoever killed the victim, the crime was at most involuntary manslaughter. RT 718-720.

The panel's additional holding that a limiting instruction on the use of other crimes evidence was prejudicial is equally erroneous. A jury instruction must itself infect the entire trial in order to establish a violation of due process. *Henderson v. Kibbe, supra,* 431 U.S. at 154; *Van Pilon v. Reed, supra,* 799 F.2d at 1342. It is not enough to show that the instruction was undesirable, erroneous, or condemned; it must violate some due process right protected by the Fourteenth Amendment. *Prantil v. State of California,* 843 F.2d 314, 317 (9th Cir. 1988). The state trial record does not present such a showing.

The instruction allowed the jury to consider evidence of prior similar acts to impeach the testimony of petitioner's wife, to establish the Battered Child Syndrome, and to find that petitioner committed the present offense if it could logically be concluded that he committed the other offenses. The panel concludes, again in reliance on the Federal Rules of Evidence, that the evidence of prior injury to the victim was not explicitly connected to petitioner and therefore could not be used to permit an inference of guilt in this case. This precise objection was rejected by the state trial court, which noted that if the jury found from the evidence of prior injuries that the victim was a battered child, it could then conclude that her death was not accidental. Once it made that finding, the jury could consider petitioner's contrary assertions to his wife and to the police that the death was accidental to be lies indicating a consciousness of guilt, and further infer that petitioner murdered his baby. RT 645-652. This use of the evidence was proper under state law and neither petitioner nor any citation in the panel opinion suggests a constitutional basis for challenging the instruction.

[The last several sentences are good-but should be expanded on, with citation to both California and federal case law. Moreover, the instruction accurately reflected the law: if the jury found that McGuire inflicted the earlier injuries, and the jury concluded that, therefore, the "pattern" of abuse established the "identity" of McGuire as the abuser (rather than a "Mexican" or his wife) because that type of abuse was his "signature," the jury could logically conclude that he also battered her on July 7. *See United States v. Beasley*, 809 F.2d 1273 (2d Cir. 1987) ("The pattern serves as the signature that enables the jury to determine that this offense, too, was committed by the defendant. *See* the summaries in McCormick on Evidence 449 (Cleary ed. 1972), and 2 J. Weinstein & M. Berger, Weinstein's Evidence ¶ 404[16] (1986 rev.)") Note: although it does not appear that the "signature" equals "identity" rationale was argued to the California trial

court, or was the basis for its decision to admit the evidence, it is universally recognized that an appellate court may affirm a trial court where the trial court reached the right result for the wrong reason. *See Union CATV v. City of Sturgis*, 107 F.3d 434, 442 (6th Cir.1997).]

CONCLUSION

For the reasons stated above, respondent respectfully submits that a rehearing or rehearing en banc should be granted.

— — —

Now we turn to the response by Mark McGuire in opposition.

What does McGuire have to do to persuade the judges not to grant California's petition for an *en banc* hearing? As mentioned earlier, McGuire must persuade the judges that the case is not worthy of their attention, and, moreover, that the panel was correct. And, he has to proclaim his innocence. As we read his brief, we'll see if he does these things. (Again, I am omitting discussion of the "exhaustion" issue. All footnotes are the brief's.).

I

INTRODUCTION

The Attorney General argues, in his latest Petition for Rehearing that: (1) the California State Court claims were not exhausted as the State Court was not properly apprised of the federal due process violation; and (2) that this Panel erred in its decision regarding jury instructions and evidence of prior injuries relied on federal rather than state precedent.[1]

---

[1] If this were a habeas petitioner instead of the Attorney General, it could be argued that these successive, redundant claims should be dismissed under the Federal Rules Governing §2254 Cases, Rule 9(b) which states:

> A second or successive petition may be dismissed if the judge finds that it fails to allege new or different grounds for relief and the prior determination was on the merits or, if new and different grounds are alleged, the judge finds that the failure to assert those grounds in a prior petition constitutes abuse of the writ.

There is no necessity for rehearing on the basis of either issue asserted. The first issue raised, the question of exhaustion, has been fully determined and decided by this Panel on two prior occasions.

As to the second issue, the Attorney General, in his previous Petition for Rehearing to this Panel, specifically requested rehearing on the ground that the Panel "overlooks federal authority recognizing the admissibility of such evidence."[2]

The very cases cited by the Attorney General in his previous brief were the authorities relied upon and cited by this Panel in rendering its decision. What the Attorney General now argues is that the Panel, "improperly relies upon the possible inadmissibility of such evidence in a federal prosecution, while ignoring its conceded admissibility under state law . . .". (PR2, 9)

The essence of the second argument is that the federal cases did not support the Attorney General's position and therefore his new analysis concludes that the Panel improperly relied on the federal precedent cited by him. This argument is obviously the reverse of his position taken on the prior Petition for Rehearing. The Panel correctly relied on both federal and state cases in rendering its decision.

[This is, essentially, a "what's new?" argument, and can be effective, especially when the opponent is seeking discretionary review—such as review by a state's highest court, when that court can decline to hear cases; an interlocutory review by any court, and, of course review by the United States Supreme Court.]

California Evidence Code §1101(b) and the Federal Rules of Evidence §404(b) govern the admissibility of prior injuries and prior bad acts. No authority exists in any jurisdiction which permits the introduction of evidence of prior injuries without linking the prior injuries to the defendant. In this case the prosecution introduced evidence of prior injuries in its case in chief, ostensibly to rebut a defense of accident. As stated by this Panel, "However, in the instant case, no claim was made that the child died accidentally."

---

[2] PR1 refers to the Attorney General's prior petition for rehearing; PR2 refers to the present petition for rehearing.

(Slip Opn. page 4364.) This evidence, combined with the improper jury instruction, denied McGuire due process. As the Panel stated in its opinion, "the trial court did not merely admit irrelevant, highly prejudicial evidence without comment. The trial court instructed the jury to use that evidence in the most improper way possible." (Slip Opn. page 4365). The evidence was improperly admitted, the jury was instructed to convict based on the improperly admitted evidence. The Panel correctly held that the foregoing errors denied McGuire the right to a fair trial and due process of law under the 14th Amendment of the United States Constitution.

[This is a recitation of what the panel did. Judges reading the petition will say: "Yes, I know this. I read the panel decision. Tell me why I should not vote to grant the rehearing *en banc*."]

II

B. THE PANEL CORRECTLY DECIDED THE ISSUES OF (A) ADMISSIBILITY OF PRIOR INJURY EVIDENCE; AND (B) THE JURY INSTRUCTIONS ON THE USE OF THAT EVIDENCE.

The Panel cited both state and federal precedent for the proposition that there must be a connection between the evidence admitted and the defendant. (Slip Opn. page 4363.)

The Attorney General misquotes the Panel's decision and characterizes the evidence as concededly admissible under state law.[3] This misrepresents the opinion. What the Panel stated:

> The trial court incorrectly admitted the evidence pursuant to California law allowing past injury evidence to establish the "Battered Child Syndrome."

This is not an, "attempt to impose the limitations of federal evidentiary rules on a state court proceeding." (PR2, 11.)

There is no question that evidence regarding the Battered Child Syndrome is admissible under California law. The more accurate

---

[3] It is argued that the panel ruled "that the evidence of prior physical abuse to the victim was not admissible under the Federal Rules of Evidence and was 'incorrectly admitted . . pursuant to California law . . . .' Slip Opn. at 4363—4364." (PR2, 10)

question is whether it was admissible in this trial under these circumstances against this defendant for the purpose it was used. The question was answered by the California Supreme Court in People v. Alcala, 36 Cal.3d 604, where the court stated:

> The rule excluding evidence of criminal propensity is nearly three centuries old in the common law. [citation] Such evidence is deemed objectionable . . . because . . . it tempts the tribunal . . . to take proof of it as justifying a condemnation, irrespective of guilt of the present charge.

In this case, the prior crimes were introduced, without a link to McGuire, for the purpose of justifying his condemnation. As authority for its proposition that the Panel had no basis for disputing the legal admissibility of the evidence, the Attorney General cites Clemons v. Mississippi (1990) ____ U.S. ____, 110 S.Ct. 1441, 1449. In Clemons the court discusses legalities of "reweighing" sentencing considerations by an appellate court under state law. The issues presented and the court's decision in Clemons is inapplicable to this case.

The Battered Child Syndrome evidence in this matter was originally admitted at trial to rebut the defense of accident (A—45).[4] McGuire's "accident" statement, which was equivocal at best, and preceded by the words, "I don't know," was introduced by the prosecutor as part of his case in chief. It is now argued, in a novel turn, that by reserving her opening statement, counsel for defendant somehow opened the floodgates for rebuttal of a potential accidental death defense. There is no authority cited for this proposition nor can there be. (PR2, 13.) The Attorney General argues that:

> State defense counsel argued only that the evidence was more prejudicial than probative and should be excluded for that reason. RT 71-72.
>
> Counsel did not suggest that the Battered Child Syndrome lacked relevance, because petitioner admitted that the victim was intentionally injured.

---

[4] Reference is to Appellant's Excerpts of Record filed with AOB and referred to in Respondent's PR2 as RT 71-72.

McGuire's trial defense counsel clearly made her argument for inadmissibility of the evidence and against the jury instruction.

> That is I would also oppose the admission of the earlier injuries . . . in all of those cases the children involved have extensive histories of prior injuries and in those cases those injuries were much more closely tied to the defendant than they are in this case. (A4 5)

There was no admission of intentional injury as alleged by the Attorney General, nor was there a concession of admissibility. The prosecutor and the court then ignored the court's initial ruling limiting the admission of Battered Child Syndrome testimony and prior injuries and permitted instruction under CALJIC 2.50. (A-47.) Defense counsel argued against the CALJIC 2.50 instruction in part as follows:

> These injuries are not tied to my defendant, but you are going to ask the jury to say, well, because it, they occurred in the past, that that makes it more likely that he committed the injuries on July 7, 1981 and that because the injuries on July 7, 1981 were proceeded (sic) by the other injuries, then it is more likely that he committed all of the injuries. (A—46)

In addition to the preceding, McGuire's trial counsel also objected that the injuries were more prejudicial than probative in her objection to the CALJIC 2.50 instruction linking the injuries to the present crime. The prosecutor argued that §1101(b) of the California Evidence Code had no application in child murder cases. (A-52). This analysis is wrong under either state or federal authority. These issues were fully and fairly presented at trial, before the California Court of Appeal, the California Supreme Court, the United States District Court and to this Panel. The Panel's decision is correct and fully supported by the law.

[This is, in my view, effective on one of the prongs of a two-pronged argument that would help McGuire, namely that this is but one case out of many and mere disagreement with the panel is not a reason to grant the extraordinary remedy of an *en banc* hearing. True, McGuire does not actually say this, but the tone of the reply is mundane and routine. Whether intended or not, it

conveys in its subtext that this is not a very important case—at least as it may extend beyond the interests of the particular parties. As such, it is not a bad response to the State's petition. But I believe that McGuire could have made the response more effective and powerful.

First, although I do not have the trial transcript, as we will see later the jury's deliberation lasted three days and much of the trial transcript was read to it during the deliberations. The case must have appeared to the jury, therefore, as fairly close—it was not one of those open-and-shut cases where the jury returns right after they've had lunch or dinner. Thus, there *must* be powerful arguments that can be made in support of McGuire's innocence. Those, like the "bloody shirt" of Tori's tragic life, must be proclaimed as a positive aspect of McGuire's presentation to the judges considering the State's petition for an *en banc* hearing. Actual innocence—or, at the very least, a reasonable doubt as to guilt—is a persuasive filter though which judges consider the proffered legal arguments. *See Brewer v. Williams*, 430 U.S. 387, 416 (1977) ("Williams is guilty of the savage murder of a small child; no member of the Court contends he is not.") (Burger, C.J., dissenting).

Second, McGuire must limit the scope of the panel's decision by pointing out that the instruction that the state trial court gave has been revised, that none of the other states within the Ninth Circuit have jury instructions that could possibly run afoul of the panel's decision, and that the question of whether "other acts" under either Rule 404(b) of the Federal Rules of Evidence or its California equivalent were sufficiently connected to McGuire is, by definition, fact-specific to McGuire's case. Thus, the case is not one of the exceptional appeals that are worthy of *en banc* consideration.]

III

CONCLUSION

The California state courts were fully and fairly presented with the Constitutional arguments herein. Both federal and state authority justify reversal of this conviction on the grounds as stated by this Panel. There is no reason for rehearing -- the opinion should stand.

— — —

OK. We're now going to see what happened to California's petition. It was denied, with two judges, Alex Kozinski and Stephen Trott, dissenting. Judge Kozinski wrote the dissent and it is especially powerful. It may have been the reason the United States Supreme Court granted *certiorari* and reversed. As you will see, Judge Kozinski was not timid about showing the "bloody shirt." All footnotes are Judge Kozinski's.

McGuire v. Estelle, 919 F.2d 578 (9th Cir. 1990)

ORDER

The panel has voted to deny the petition for rehearing and reject the suggestion for rehearing *en banc*. Judges Kozinski and Trott would grant the suggestion for rehearing *en banc*.

The full court has been advised of the suggestion for an *en banc*. An active judge requested a vote on whether to rehear the matter *en banc*. The request failed to receive a majority of the votes of the nonrecused active judges in favor of *en banc* consideration. Fed.R.App.P. 35.

The petition for rehearing is denied and the suggestion for rehearing *en banc* is rejected.

KOZINSKI, Circuit Judge, with whom Circuit Judge TROTT joins, dissenting from the order rejecting the suggestion for rehearing en banc:

Six month old Tori McGuire died in a hospital emergency room, the victim of appalling internal injuries: her liver was split in half, her pancreas was lacerated and split apart, her lower right lung and the large vein from her heart were damaged, and part of her large intestine was lacerated. No, little Tori was not the victim of a hideous automobile accident; nor had she been extracted from the rubble of an earthquake. She had been beaten to death. Her lifeless body, with dozens of contusions on her chest and abdomen, was brought to the hospital by her parents who claimed they didn't know what could have happened to her. Perhaps, the father said, "the baby fell off the couch" or maybe "some Mexicans" broke in and abused her while he was out of the room. Not taken in by these transparent falsehoods, the state brought charges against the father, Mark McGuire. A state jury convicted him of second degree murder; the conviction was affirmed on appeal.

A panel of this court now overturns the conviction, quite possibly forever. In so doing, it not only reaches a result that is contrary to simple justice and common sense, but does so in a way that will seriously interfere with the authority and autonomy of the state courts in many other criminal proceedings. Most fundamentally, the panel overturns the state conviction because it disagrees with the state court on questions of state law.[1] Worse, the panel punishes the prosecution for introducing what the court deems to be unnecessary evidence of the defendant's intent, even though intent is clearly an element of the crime with which McGuire was charged. Finally, the panel misapplies the teachings of *Chapman v. California*, 386 U.S. 18 (1967), and *United States v. Hasting*, 461 U.S. 499 (1983), by failing to consider "the entire record prior to reversing a conviction for constitutional errors that may be harmless." *Id.* at 509 n. 7.

This opinion is markedly out of step with the law of the Supreme Court and this circuit governing these sensitive and important issues. While *en banc* procedures are cumbersome and time consuming, such considerations ought not deter us from maintaining uniformity in the law of the circuit, as well as correcting an obvious miscarriage of justice. Because my colleagues' decision not to take this case *en banc* lets stand what I consider to be a wholly unacceptable precedent, I must respectfully dissent.

Discussion

Tori McGuire's short life was the type of horror no sentient being should have to endure. In addition to the ghastly injuries that caused her death, the doctors who examined her discovered some earlier injuries—rectal tearing that was at least six weeks old and several partially healed rib fractures that were approximately seven weeks old. The prosecution introduced evidence of these earlier injuries, and the trial court instructed the jury as to the inferences it could draw therefrom. This evidence and these instructions lie at the heart of the panel's decision to overturn the conviction. A dispassionate review of the state court proceedings, however, reveals that no error at all was committed, much less

---

[1] A similar concern was raised by *Blair v. McCarthy*, 881 F.2d 602 (9th Cir.1989), *cert. granted*, 498 U.S. 807, *vacated as moot and remanded* ___ U.S. ___, (1990), where the first question presented was:

> "Has court below improperly and unduly expanded scope of federal habeas corpus relief by granting such relief in absence of any federal violation on sole basis of alleged violation of state procedural rule plus finding that it is 'reasonably probable' that different result would have occurred in absence of state law error?"

an error of constitutional dimensions, and that the disputed evidence was, in any event, not prejudicial given the overwhelming evidence of McGuire's guilt.

A. The Panel Second-Guessed the State Courts on Questions of State Law.

This is not an appeal from a federal criminal conviction; it is a state habeas corpus case. Our function is limited to determining whether the petitioner's constitutional rights were violated. *Engle v. Isaac*, 456 U.S. 107, 119 (1982); *Oxborrow v. Eikenberry,* 877 F.2d 1395, 1400 (9th Cir.), *cert denied* 493 U.S. 942 (1989); *Middleton v. Cupp*, 768 F.2d 1083, 1085 (9th Cir.1985), *cert. denied* 478 U.S. 1021 (1986). In making that determination, we do not review issues of state law, such as evidentiary rulings; we are bound by the state courts' interpretations of the law entrusted to them. The panel disregards this limitation entirely and overturns Mark McGuire's conviction because it disagrees with the way the state court resolved questions of state law concerning the admissibility of evidence and the wording of jury instructions.

On the evidentiary question, the state trial court admitted proof of prior injuries for three separate reasons, one of them being that it tended to establish that Tori was a battered child, pursuant to a theory known as the "Battered Child Syndrome." The state court of appeal affirmed:

> [P]roof of Tori's "prior injuries" tending to establish the "battered child syndrome" was patently proper.

People v. McGuire, No. AO17800, at 7 (Cal.App. Jan. 15, 1985), *citing and discussing People v. Bledsoe*, 36 Cal.3d 236, 203 Cal.Rptr. 450, 681 P.2d 291 (1984); *People v. Jackson*, 18 Cal.App.3d 504, 95 Cal.Rptr. 919 (1971); and *Landeros v. Flood,* 17 Cal.3d 399, 131 Cal.Rptr. 69, 551 P.2d 389 (1976). Our panel flatly disagrees with this determination:

> The trial court incorrectly admitted the evidence *pursuant to California law* allowing past injury evidence to establish the "Battered Child Syndrome." The Battered Child Syndrome allows proof of past injuries to prove the child's present injuries did not occur accidentally. *See People v. Jackson*, 18 Cal.App.3d 504, 506, 95 Cal.Rptr. 919, 921 (1971); *Landeros v. Flood*, 17 Cal.3d 399, 409, 551 P.2d 389, 393, 131 Cal.Rptr. 69, 73 (1976).

902 F.2d at 754 (emphasis added).

What can one possibly say about this? The panel not only expressly states that the state court erroneously admitted the evidence "pursuant to California law," but it relies on two of the same cases that the state court of appeal relied on in reaching the opposite conclusion. Until reading the panel's opinion, I had thought the federal courts were bound by state court interpretations of the state rules of evidence. Apparently, however, the panel has now declared open season on state court evidentiary rulings in the Ninth Circuit.

The panel makes precisely the same mistake when it concludes that "[s]ubsection 3 of the [prior bad acts] instruction is erroneous." 902 F.2d at 755. The panel's only explanation for this conclusion appears in a footnote:

> It appears that the trial court's erroneous instruction was the result of an incorrect reading of CALJIC 2.50 (1979 Revision). This standard jury instruction has been clarified to avoid the misunderstanding which occurred here. See CALJIC 2.50 (1987 Revision).

Id at 755 n. 2. Once again, the panel cites only state law in support of its conclusion that the state courts committed error.

The panel does ultimately conclude that "the faulty instruction considered along with the admittance of the prejudicial evidence 'so infected the entire trial that the resulting conviction violate[d] due process.'" 902 F.2d at 755 (*quoting Cupp v. Naughten*, 414 U.S. 141, 147 (1973)). This reference to the due process clause does not repair the damage done by the panel's earlier analysis. The problem is that, in order to conclude that there was a due process violation, one must first determine that the state trial court erred. The panel made that initial determination by relying almost exclusively on state law, which it reads in a way directly contrary to the state court's reading.[2]

---

[2] I say almost exclusively because the court does sprinkle in citations to federal law, particularly the Federal Rules of Evidence. See, for example, 902 F.2d at 754 (*citing* FRE 404(b) and *United States v. Lewis*, 837 F.2d 415 (9th Cir.), *cert. denied* 488 U.S. 923 (1988)); *id.* at 755 (citing FRE 404(a) Advisory Committee note and *United States v. Green*, 648 F.2d 587, 593 (9th Cir.1981)). The Federal Rules of Evidence, the Advisory Committee notes, and federal criminal cases are, of course, wholly irrelevant to a state habeas case, where the only issue is whether the trial violated constitutional norms. The panel's opinion in this case could well be construed as giving the Federal Rules of Evidence a constitutional cast. See *id.* at 755.

B. Evidence of Intent was Proper and Necessary

In concluding that the evidence of prior injuries was improperly admitted, the panel suggests that the evidence was not relevant. *Id.* at 754. As discussed above, the panel had no business second-guessing the state courts on a question of state law. Having started down this path, however, the panel makes a collateral error, one with grave constitutional implications.

As the panel recognizes, evidence is admitted pursuant to the Battered Child Syndrome theory to prove that the death was not accidental. *Id.* If the child has suffered a series of injuries as the result of child abuse, this tends to make it less likely that the injury in question resulted from a mishap. *People v. Jackson*, 18 Cal.App.3d 504, 507, 95 Cal.Rptr. 919, 921 (1971). The panel concludes that the evidence of prior injuries was irrelevant because "in the instant case, no claim was made that the child died accidentally." *Id.* According to the panel, the only issue at trial was who killed Tori, not whether the killing was intentional.

This passage in the panel's opinion has serious implications: It suggests that due process may be violated by the admission of evidence which clearly goes to an element of the offense charged if it turns out that the defense does not put that particular element in issue. This reasoning, if it stands as the law of the circuit, will present state prosecutors with an intractable problem: Just how are they to know whether the defendant intends to put a particular element of the crime in issue? After all, the prosecution must go first and bears the burden of establishing every element of the crime beyond a reasonable doubt—including, for second degree murder, malice aforethought, Cal. Penal Code §§ 187, 189 (West 1988). If the prosecution decides not to present proof of any element of the crime on the theory that the defense will not put that element in issue, the defendant automatically becomes entitled to a directed verdict of acquittal. JAMES W. MOORE AND JO D. LUCAS, 5A MOORE'S FEDERAL PRACTICE ¶ 50.02[1] at 50-16.1 to 50-17 (2d ed. 1990). The simple reality is that, in a criminal case, every element of the crime is in issue; the defense is free to sit back and see how the prosecution's case shapes up, and then focus its attack where the prosecution is weakest.

The panel's insistence that intent was not an issue in the case is contradicted not only by elementary principles of criminal procedure, but by the record in this case as well. As the panel recognizes, McGuire at one time claimed that the baby was injured when she fell off the couch. 902

F.2d at 751. He later suggested that "maybe some Mexicans came in while I was upstairs." *Id.* How on earth was the prosecutor to know that McGuire would not raise one of these defenses when his turn came to put on evidence?[3] More fundamentally, if the prosecutor decided to play it safe by introducing evidence in addition to the fatal injuries to prove that the death was not accidental, how can we say that the evidence was irrelevant? For the panel to look at the evidence after the case was closed and say that the prosecutor was too cautious in proving every element of the offense is nothing but 20/20 hindsight.[4]

What are state prosecutors in the Ninth Circuit supposed to do when presented with a situation such as that here? On the one hand, they face the possibility of a directed verdict or unfavorable jury instructions if they fail to prove an element of the case that somehow seems "obvious." On the other hand, under today's precedent, they face the possibility that a federal court—with the benefit of hindsight—will conclude that the evidence was not really necessary because that particular element of the crime was not contested by the defense. It is obvious that the McGuire prosecutor could not have guarded against this type of whipsaw; more troubling is that, even

---

[3] Indeed, early in the trial the prosecutor advised the court that he anticipated the defense would rely primarily on the "some Mexicans" theory, with "try[ing] to hang it on momma" a less likely alternative.
Reporter's Transcript on Appeal, *People of the State of California v. McGuire*, H 3748 (RT) 213-14 (Book II).

[4] As it turns out, the defense did raise the issue of intent, and very vigorously. Defense counsel objected to a jury instruction on second degree murder, stating "I don't think there is evidence of intent." RT 562 (Book V). She requested an involuntary manslaughter instruction, stating "my contention is that whoever killed the baby or hit the baby had no malice, had no intent to kill the baby." RT 619. With the agreement of both sides, the court instructed the jury that "[t]he unintentional killing of a human being is excusable and not unlawful when committed by accident," and that "[t]he burden is on the Prosecution to prove beyond a reasonable doubt that the homicide was not excusable." RT 762. During her closing argument, defense counsel argued that the prosecution had failed to establish intent:

> "Involuntary manslaughter ... is an unlawful killing of a human being where there is no intent to kill and no malice. That is what we have here, if anything."

RT 720. See also RT 718-19. In McGuire's motion for a new trial after the verdict came in, defense counsel asserted that the trial court had erroneously failed to instruct the jury on the requirement of specific intent. Clerk's Transcript on Appeal, *The People of the State of California v. McGuire*, H 3748 (CT) 155. Thus, while the panel appears to have labored under the misapprehension that McGuire had conceded or stipulated to intent, defense counsel was well aware of the state's burden of proof as to McGuire's state of mind, and pressed the issue forcefully.

with today's precedent in hand, no prosecutor will know when to withhold evidence or when to include it until he sees the defendant's evidence, by which time it will be too late. In common parlance, this is known as a Catch-22.

C. Panel's Harmless Error Analysis is Deficient

It is well established that errors, even constitutional ones, do not warrant overturning a state conviction unless it is determined that the errors are not harmless. *Chapman v. California*, 386 U.S. 18, 22 (1967). Except where the error is so fundamental that it is deemed harmful *per se*, which is not the case here, the federal court must examine the entire state court record to determine whether the jury would have reached a different conclusion absent the error. *United States v. Hasting*, 461 U.S. 499, 509 n. 7 (1983).

The panel here speaks the language of harmless error analysis but fails to perform the tasks associated therewith. The sum and substance of the panel's harmless error "analysis" is the following: "Although there was evidence suggesting McGuire's guilt, this evidence was certainly not overwhelming." 902 F.2d at 755. The panel does not state that it has reviewed, or even seen, the state court record; it does not discuss the evidence supporting guilt; and it does not analyze how the trial would have played out had the perceived errors been eliminated. Harmless error analysis that is so utterly devoid of analysis is no better than no harmless error analysis at all. At a bare minimum, it seems to me, the panel must represent that it has ordered the state court record, looked at it and undertaken the type of review mandated by the Supreme Court.

Quite frankly, it is impossible to review the record in this case and understand how the panel reached its conclusion. Take, for example, the error perceived by the panel as to the admission of the evidence under the Battered Child Syndrome. Even if the panel were correct in concluding that the evidence was improperly admitted for this purpose, it does not matter. The trial court found the evidence of prior injuries admissible for three distinct purposes: (1) to establish the existence of Battered Child Syndrome; (2) to show that McGuire had committed similar prior bad acts;[5] and (3) to

[5] The trial court treated Battered Child Syndrome and prior bad acts as separate evidentiary categories; it may be more accurate to say that evidence of Battered Child Syndrome is a subset of evidence of prior bad acts. For our purposes it makes no difference: A finding that evidence is inadmissible to prove Battered Child Syndrome says nothing about whether the evidence may be admitted for the broader purpose of showing prior bad acts.

impeach Mrs. McGuire's testimony that Mr. McGuire was kind to his daughter. RT 573-75 (Book V), 757. The state court of appeal found the evidence admissible on the first of these grounds, and so did not reach the other two. *People v. McGuire*, No. AO17800, at 5-7 (Cal.App. Jan. 15, 1985).

Where a trial court admits evidence for three independent reasons, and we find one of them insufficient, our job is hardly done.[6] All evidence is admissible for some purposes but inadmissible for others; we could reverse convictions any time we liked were we to focus on one purpose exclusively. Here, the panel did not find that the evidence was inadmissible on the other two grounds; therefore, it is bound to assume that the evidence would have been admitted in any event. In light of the indisputable record on this point, I fail to see how McGuire suffered any prejudice from the alleged error regarding admission of evidence of the Battered Child Syndrome, much less a denial of due process.

But there is more. Even were we to assume, with the panel, that admission of the evidence was prejudicial error, the panel was required to decide whether the jury would have convicted anyway. *See United States v. Hasting*, 461 U.S. at 510-11. A determination on this issue required the panel to weigh the prosecution's case, the likely effect of the wrongfully admitted evidence and the likelihood that the jury would have come to a different result. A review of the record leads to only one conclusion: The jury would have reached exactly the same verdict regardless of the errors perceived by the panel.

First, the record discloses that the prosecution's case was very strong indeed. In weighing the strength of that evidence, it must be kept in mind that there were only two plausible theories of the case: that the father abused Tori or that the mother did; no one else had access to the baby immediately prior to her death. While the 1500 page trial transcript contains a good deal of testimony establishing that the father did it, perhaps the strongest piece of evidence is the testimony of several witnesses who overheard a conversation between Mr. and Mrs. McGuire at the hospital while the couple was waiting to learn Tori's fate:

---

6 That the state court of appeal only considered one ground for admission is not, of course, dispositive. Having found the evidence admissible on one ground, the court of appeal had no need to examine whether the evidence was admissible on other grounds as well. To find the evidence inadmissible–and so highly prejudicial as to constitute a due process violation--we must make sure that it is not in fact admissible on any of the grounds relied on by the trial court.

> While Tori was being treated, and McGuire and his wife were seated together in a hospital waiting room, Mrs. McGuire several times insistently asked "what really happened?" McGuire replied that he "didn't know," and that he "guessed" the baby fell off the couch; his response was always the same. Finally Mrs. McGuire said, "You are responsible," to which he apparently made no reply.

People v. McGuire, No. AO17800, at 3 (Cal.App. Jan. 15, 1985).

This conversation makes no sense at all unless it was the father who abused the baby. Had the baby been alone with the mother at the time she suffered the injuries, as Mrs. McGuire claimed at trial, one would have expected the accusations at the hospital to point entirely the other way. Not only did McGuire fail to question or accuse his wife, he lamely suggested the baby "fell off the couch" and did not protest her accusation that "you are responsible." Short of a videotape of the crime, it's not clear what better evidence the prosecution might have presented.

The fact is, child abuse cases are inherently difficult to prove: the evidence is usually circumstantial and often ambiguous; eyewitnesses seldom come forward because of family considerations; and the victims often are dead or too young to speak. See, for example, *United States v. Boise*, 916 F.2d 497 (9th Cir.1990). It is rare indeed to have a case like this one, where the defendant makes what is tantamount to a spontaneous confession of his guilt. When this conversation is viewed in the context of all the other evidence presented to the jury, *see People v. McGuire* at 2-4, one must conclude that the prosecution's case was extremely strong.

Second, the prejudice flowing from any error would have been minimal. If I understand the panel's rationale correctly, it is that the prosecution failed to sufficiently prove McGuire's connection to the earlier acts of child abuse. Even if that were true--which it clearly is not[7]—how was the defendant

---

[7] The record contains ample evidence from which a rational jury could conclude that McGuire had been the perpetrator of the earlier injuries:

— Mrs. McGuire's statements to Detective Gillis to the effect that, when she bathed Tori, she noticed the child had bruises on her body. When asked how Tori might have gotten those bruises, Daisy responded:

McGuire: I don't really know, you know, I am not the only one who is taking care of her.

(continued)

prejudiced? Evidence of the earlier abuse could only harm the defendant to the extent the jury was convinced he committed those acts. If the jury was in doubt, or believed that someone else (for example, Mrs. McGuire) committed the bad acts, its outrage over them would not have been directed at Mark McGuire.

Finally, it is highly unlikely that, absent the error, the jury would have reached a not guilty verdict because to do so it would have had to adopt the defense's alternative theory--that the mother did it. Mrs. McGuire's "confession," made only after she was granted immunity and had the luxury of attempting to save her husband at no risk to herself, is halting and tentative, marked by evasion and lapses of memory, RT 333-39, 341-42, 351-58, 364, 385. It is also internally inconsistent, RT 353-56; contradicted by her earlier statements to the police and at the preliminary hearing, RT 370-75, 410-11, and by Mr. McGuire's own statements to the police, RT 209-10 (Book II), 251 (Book III); and inconsistent with the weight of the medical evidence.[8] The jury deliberated for three days and had extended passages of the trial transcript read back to it, including large portions of Mrs. McGuire's testimony. RT 254A (Book I), 777. This jury was clearly not inflamed by passion. McGuire got no worse than he deserved.

(continued)

Gillis: Well, who else is taking care of her?

McGuire: My husband, too, takes care of her. RT at 371.

— Testimony by a neighbor "that she had observed McGuire pick up the infant by 'one of her arms.' She had also seen him, when the baby was crying, roughly pinch her cheeks together, and do other 'bad things.' Mrs. McGuire, the witness said, was a 'very caring mother' toward Tori, who was never seen to 'abuse the child' in any way." *People v. McGuire*, No. AO17800, at 4 (Cal.App. Jan. 15, 1985).

— The fact that one of the injuries--rectal tearing--is sexual in nature, and of a type more likely made by a man than a woman.

[8] Mrs. McGuire claimed to have killed the baby some time in the afternoon, "[a] long time" before her husband returned home. RT 353; see also RT 348; *but see* RT 356 ("I beat my child when he, shortly before he comes home on that evening."). The infant most likely died within minutes of having been beaten. RT 139-40 (Book II). Yet when the McGuires took the baby to the hospital at nine in the evening, RT 87 (Book II), the doctors believed they had a chance of resuscitating the child because irreversible brain swelling had not yet begun, indicating that her death was very recent. RT 86, 98-99, 169-71 (Book II).

It is this type of inquiry, or something akin to it, that the panel was required to pursue under Chapman. Its unsubstantiated assertion that the evidence against McGuire "was certainly not overwhelming" simply does not do the job.

D. Reprosecution of McGuire may be Precluded

When a federal court grants a writ of habeas corpus, the state normally has the option of retrying the defendant. This is not the case, however, when there is a determination that the prosecution failed to meet its burden of proof on any element of the offense; under those circumstances, retrial is barred by the double jeopardy clause. *Burks v. United States*, 437 U.S. 1 (1978).

While the point is not entirely free from doubt, the opinion contains statements that could well preclude retrial of McGuire. Specifically, the panel casts aspersions on the prosecution's case by stating that "only the barest threads connect McGuire to the crime." 902 F.2d at 755. Worse still, the panel characterizes the state's evidence as suggesting no more than "mere shadows of guilt which *leave ample room for reasonable doubt*." *Id.* at 756 (emphasis added).

It is entirely possible that the state courts on remand will read these passages as holding that the prosecution failed to introduce sufficient evidence to meet its constitutional burden of establishing guilt beyond a reasonable doubt. Certainly it would be difficult to come up with language more clearly conveying this idea than that used by the panel. If the state court does construe the panel's opinion as precluding a retrial, there will be no possibility of correcting the error. Once McGuire is released, the prosecution has no mechanism for coming into federal court to complain, as the state is not entitled to collaterally attack the state judgment.

Conclusion

The panel has overturned a state conviction, and has done so in a manner that seriously and unjustifiably interferes with the authority of the state courts, hamstrings state prosecutors and may result in the permanent release of a defendant who was justly and properly convicted of a heinous crime. We make a grave mistake by failing to take the case en banc to correct these errors and set the law of the circuit back on course.

— — —

The decision by the United States Supreme Court: *Estelle v. McGuire*, 502 U.S. 62 (1991). All footnotes are Chief Justice Rehnquist's or, in her separate opinion, Justice O'Connor's.

Chief Justice REHNQUIST delivered the opinion of the Court.

Respondent Mark Owen McGuire was found guilty in a California state court of second-degree murder for the killing of his infant daughter. After unsuccessfully challenging his conviction on appeal in the state courts, McGuire sought federal habeas relief, and the United States Court of Appeals for the Ninth Circuit set aside his conviction. 902 F.2d 749 (1990). We hold that in so doing the Court of Appeals exceeded the limited scope of federal habeas review of state convictions.

McGuire and his wife brought their 6-month-old daughter, Tori, to a hospital in Hayward, California. The baby was bluish in color and was not breathing. The attending physician noticed a large and relatively recent bruise on Tori's chest with multiple bruises around it, as well as black and blue marks around her ears. Efforts to revive the child were unsuccessful; Tori died 45 minutes after being brought to the hospital. An autopsy revealed 17 contusions on the baby's chest, 29 contusions in her abdominal area, a split liver, a split pancreas, a lacerated large intestine, and damage to her heart and one of her lungs. The autopsy also uncovered evidence of rectal tearing, which was at least six weeks old, and evidence of partially healed rib fractures, which were approximately seven weeks old.

The police questioned McGuire and his wife. McGuire stated his belief that Tori's injuries must have resulted from a fall off the family couch. He told the police that when his wife went out to make a telephone call, he went upstairs, leaving Tori lying on the couch; when he heard the baby cry, he came back downstairs to find her lying on the floor. After a police officer expressed skepticism at this explanation, McGuire replied that "[m]aybe some Mexicans came in" while he was upstairs. *Id.*, at 751. During separate questioning, McGuire's wife stated that she had not hit Tori, and that she was unsure whether her husband had done so.

McGuire was charged with second-degree murder. At trial, the prosecution introduced both the statements made by McGuire to police and the medical evidence, including the evidence of prior rectal tearing and fractured ribs. Two physicians testified that Tori was a battered child, relying in part on the prior rib and rectal injuries, as well as on the more recent injuries. McGuire's neighbor testified that she had seen McGuire carry Tori by one of her arms to the car and roughly pinch her cheeks together when she cried. The neighbor added that McGuire's wife had expressed fear in leaving Tori alone with McGuire, because he had been rough with the baby and "did bad things" to her.

In addition, the prosecution called a witness who had overheard a conversation between McGuire and his wife in the hospital emergency room the night of Tori's death. According to the witness, McGuire's wife several times insistently asked, "What really happened?" McGuire replied that he "didn't know," and that he "guessed" the baby fell off the couch. His wife continued to press for an answer, stating, "I am very patient. I can wait a long time. I want to know what really happened." Finally, she told McGuire that "the baby was alright when I left. You are responsible." App. 44; Brief for United States as Amicus Curiae 3-4. McGuire's wife was called by the prosecution to testify at trial, after having been granted transactional immunity from future prosecution. In contrast to her prior statement to the police and her declarations at the hospital, she stated that she had beaten Tori on the day of her death before her husband arrived home. The jury convicted McGuire of second-degree murder.

The California Court of Appeal affirmed McGuire's conviction. The court observed that the evidence of prior rib and rectal injuries was introduced to prove "battered child syndrome." That syndrome exists when a child has sustained repeated and/or serious injuries by nonaccidental means. *People v. Bledsoe*, 36 Cal.3d 236, 249, 203 Cal.Rptr. 450, 458, 681 P.2d 291, 299 (1984). After reviewing California authority on the subject, the court concluded that "proof of Tori's 'prior injuries' tending to establish the 'battered child syndrome' was patently proper." App. 47. The California Supreme Court denied review.

McGuire then filed a petition for habeas corpus relief in the United States District Court for the Northern District of California. That court denied relief. The Court of Appeals for the Ninth Circuit reversed and granted McGuire's habeas petition. The court ruled that the prior injury evidence was erroneously admitted to establish battered child syndrome, because no evidence linked McGuire to the prior injuries and no claim had been made at trial that the baby died accidentally. In addition, the court believed that the trial court's instruction on the use of prior act evidence allowed a finding of guilt based simply on a judgment that McGuire committed the prior bad acts.[1] The court concluded that the admission of the evidence, in conjunction with the prejudicial instruction, "rendered [McGuire's] trial arbitrary and fundamentally unfair" in violation of due process. 902 F.2d, at 753. We hold that none of the alleged errors rise to the level of a due process violation, and so reverse.

I

We first consider whether the admission of the prior injury evidence justified habeas relief. In ruling that McGuire's due process rights were violated by the admission of the evidence, the Court of Appeals relied in part on its conclusion that the evidence was "incorrectly admitted ... pursuant to California law." *Id.*, at 754. Such an inquiry, however, is no part of a federal court's habeas review of a state conviction. We have stated many times that "federal habeas corpus relief does not lie for errors of state law." *Lewis v. Jeffers*, 497 U.S. 764, 780 (1990); *see also Pulley v. Harris*, 465 U.S. 37, 41 (1984). Today, we reemphasize that it is not the province of a federal habeas court to reexamine state-court determinations on state-law questions. In conducting habeas review, a federal court is limited to deciding whether a conviction violated the Constitution, laws, or treaties of

---

[1] The court instructed the jury:

"Evidence has been introduced for the purpose of showing that the Defendant committed acts similar to those constituting a crime other than that for which he is on trial. Such evidence, if believed, was not received, and may not be considered by you[,] to prove that he is a person of bad character or that he has a disposition to commit crimes. Such evidence was received and may be considered by you only for the limited purpose of determining if it tends to show three things:

"1. The impeachment of Daisy McGuire's testimony that she had no cause to be afraid of the Defendant,

"2. To establish the battered child syndrome, and

"3. Also a clear connection between the other two offense[s] and the one of which the Defendant is accused, so that it may be logically concluded that if the Defendant committed other offenses, he also committed the crime charged in this case.

"For the limited purpose for which you may consider such evidence, you must weigh it in the same manner as you do all other evidence in the case. You are not permitted to consider evidence for any other purpose." App. 40-41.

the United States. 28 U.S.C. § 2241; *Rose v. Hodges*, 423 U.S. 19, 21 (1975) (*per curiam*).[2]

We thus turn to the question whether the admission of the evidence violated McGuire's federal constitutional rights. California law allows the prosecution to introduce expert testimony and evidence related to prior injuries in order to prove "battered child syndrome." *People v. Bledsoe, supra*, 36 Cal.3d, at 249, 203 Cal.Rptr., at 458, 681 P.2d, at 299; *Landeros v. Flood*, 17 Cal.3d 399, 409, 131 Cal.Rptr. 69, 73, 551 P.2d 389, 393 (1976); *People v. Jackson*, 18 Cal.App.3d 504, 506-508, 95 Cal.Rptr. 919, 921-922 (1971). The demonstration of battered child syndrome "simply indicates that a child found with [serious, repeated injuries] has not suffered those injuries by accidental means." *Id.*, at 507, 95 Cal.Rptr., at 921. Thus, evidence demonstrating battered child syndrome helps to prove that the child died at the hands of another and not by falling off a couch, for example; it also tends to establish that the "other," whoever it may be, inflicted the injuries intentionally. When offered to show that certain injuries are a product of child abuse, rather than accident, evidence of prior injuries is relevant even though it does not purport to prove the identity of the person who might have inflicted those injuries. *See id.*, at 506-508, 95 Cal.Rptr., at 921-922; *People v. Bledsoe, supra*, 36 Cal.3d, at 249, 203 Cal.Rptr., at 458, 681 P.2d, at 299. Because the prosecution had charged McGuire with second-degree murder, it was required to prove that Tori's death was caused by the defendant's intentional act. Proof of Tori's battered child status helped to do just that; although not linked by any direct evidence to McGuire, the evidence demonstrated that Tori's death was the result of an intentional act by someone, and not an accident. The Court of Appeals, however, ignored the principle of battered child syndrome evidence in holding that this evidence was incorrectly admitted. For example, the court stated that "[e]vidence cannot have probative value unless a party connects it to the defendant in some meaningful way." 902 F.2d, at 753. We conclude that the evidence of prior injuries presented at McGuire's trial, whether it was directly linked to McGuire or not, was probative on the question of the intent with which the person who caused the injuries acted.

---

[2] In this regard, we observe that the Ninth Circuit reached a similar result in *Blair v. McCarthy*, 881 F.2d 602 (1989), *cert. granted*, 498 U.S. 807, *vacated as moot and remanded*, 498 U.S. 954 (1990). In that case, the Court of Appeals based its grant of habeas relief solely on a violation of state law that prejudiced the defendant. *Blair v. McCarthy, supra*, at 603-604. As our discussion above makes clear, such state-law violations provide no basis for federal habeas relief.

In holding the prior injury evidence inadmissible, the Court of Appeals also relied on the theory that, because no claim was made at trial that Tori died accidentally, the battered child syndrome evidence was irrelevant and violative of due process. *Id.*, at 754. This ruling ignores the fact that the prosecution must prove all the elements of a criminal offense beyond a reasonable doubt. In this second-degree murder case, for example, the prosecution was required to demonstrate that the killing was intentional. Cal.Penal Code Ann. §§ 187, 189 (West 1988). By eliminating the possibility of accident, the evidence regarding battered child syndrome was clearly probative of that essential element, especially in light of the fact that McGuire had claimed prior to trial that Tori had injured herself by falling from the couch. The Court of Appeals, however, ruled that the evidence should have been excluded because McGuire did not raise the defense of accidental death at trial. But the prosecution's burden to prove every element of the crime is not relieved by a defendant's tactical decision not to contest an essential element of the offense. In the federal courts, "[a] simple plea of not guilty ... puts the prosecution to its proof as to all elements of the crime charged." *Mathews v. United States*, 485 U.S. 58, 64-65 (1988). Neither the Court of Appeals nor the parties have given us any reason to think that the rule is different in California. The evidence of battered child syndrome was relevant to show intent, and nothing in the Due Process Clause of the Fourteenth Amendment requires the State to refrain from introducing relevant evidence simply because the defense chooses not to contest the point.

Concluding, as we do, that the prior injury evidence was relevant to an issue in the case, we need not explore further the apparent assumption of the Court of Appeals that it is a violation of the due process guaranteed by the Fourteenth Amendment for evidence that is not relevant to be received in a criminal trial. We hold that McGuire's due process rights were not violated by the admission of the evidence. *See Spencer v. Texas*, 385 U.S. 554, 563-564 (1967) ("Cases in this Court have long proceeded on the premise that the Due Process Clause guarantees the fundamental elements of fairness in a criminal trial.... But it has never been thought that such cases establish this Court as a rulemaking organ for the promulgation of state rules of criminal procedure") (citations omitted).

II

The Court of Appeals, however, did not rely solely on a finding that the admission of the evidence was unconstitutional. It based its decision in part on a belief that the instruction given by the trial court, set forth in n. 1, supra, allowed the jury to consider the prior injury evidence for more than simply proof of the battered child syndrome, and thereby violated McGuire's due process rights. McGuire focuses on the portion of the instruction explaining to the jury that the prior injury evidence "was received and may be considered by you only for the limited purpose of determining if it tends to show ... a clear connection between the other two offense[s] and the one of which the Defendant is accused, so that it may be logically concluded that if the Defendant committed other offenses, he also committed the crime charged in this case." App. 41.

McGuire argues that, despite the absence of any direct evidence showing that he caused the rib and rectal injuries, the instruction told the jury to find that he had committed those prior offenses. Furthermore, he argues, the instruction left the jury with the mistaken impression that it could base its finding of guilt on the simple fact that he had previously harmed Tori. Under McGuire's reading, the instruction is transformed into a propensity instruction, allowing the jury to consider as evidence of his guilt the fact that his prior acts show a disposition to commit this type of crime. This, he contends, violates the Due Process Clause.

In arguing his point, McGuire makes much of the fact that, in giving its instruction, the trial court deviated in part from standard jury instruction 2.50, 1 California Jury Instructions, Criminal (4th ed. 1979) (CALJIC).[3] As we have stated above, however, the fact that the instruction was allegedly incorrect under state law is not a basis for habeas relief. *See Marshall v. Lonberger*, 459 U.S. 422, 438, n. 6 (1983) ("[T]he Due Process Clause does not permit the federal courts to engage in a finely tuned review of the wisdom of state evidentiary rules"). Federal habeas courts therefore do not grant relief, as might a state appellate court, simply because the instruction may have been deficient in comparison to the CALJIC model. Nor do our habeas powers allow us to reverse McGuire's conviction based on a belief

---

[3] Meticulous compliance with CALJIC 2.50, as in effect at McGuire's trial, would have led the trial court to instruct the jury that the prior injury evidence

> "was received and may be considered by you only for the limited purpose of determining if it tends to show:
>
> "A characteristic method, plan or scheme in the commission of criminal acts similar to the method, plan or scheme used in the commission of the offense in this case which would further tend to show a clear connection between the other offense[s] and the one of which defendant is accused so that it may be logically concluded that if defendant committed the other offense[s] he also committed the crime charged in this case" (portion in italics was omitted from the actual jury instruction given at McGuire's trial).

that the trial judge incorrectly interpreted the California Evidence Code in ruling that the prior injury evidence was admissible as bad acts evidence in this case. See Cal.Evid.Code Ann. § 1101(b) (West 1988). The only question for us is "whether the ailing instruction by itself so infected the entire trial that the resulting conviction violates due process." *Cupp v. Naughten*, 414 U.S. 141, 147 (1973); *see also Henderson v. Kibbe*, 431 U.S. 145, 154 (1977); *Donnelly v. DeChristoforo*, 416 U.S. 637, 643 (1974) ("'[I]t must be established not merely that the instruction is undesirable, erroneous, or even "universally condemned," but that it violated some [constitutional right]' "). It is well established that the instruction "may not be judged in artificial isolation," but must be considered in the context of the instructions as a whole and the trial record. *Cupp v. Naughten, supra*, 414 U.S. at 147. In addition, in reviewing an ambiguous instruction such as the one at issue here, we inquire "whether there is a reasonable likelihood that the jury has applied the challenged instruction in a way" that violates the Constitution. Boyde v. California, 494 U.S. 370, 380, 110 S.Ct. 1190, 1198, 108 L.Ed.2d 316 (1990).[4] And we also bear in mind our previous admonition that we "have defined the category of infractions that violate 'fundamental fairness' very narrowly." *Dowling v. United States*, 493 U.S. 342, 352 (1990). "Beyond the specific guarantees enumerated in the Bill of Rights, the Due Process Clause has limited operation." *Ibid.*

McGuire first claims that the instruction directed the jury to find that he had caused the prior injuries, thereby effectively taking that question from the jury. One might argue that the "two offense[s]" referred to in the instruction were McGuire's pinching of the child's cheeks and the lifting of the child by her arm. When read in context, however, we conclude that the most likely interpretation is that the reference was to the rectal tearing and fractured ribs. McGuire argues that, despite the lack of any direct evidence linking him to those injuries, the instruction directed the jury to find that he

---

[4] We acknowledge that language in the later cases of *Cage v. Louisiana*, 498 U.S. 39 (1990), and *Yates v. Evatt*, 500 U.S. 391 (1991), might be read as endorsing a different standard of review for jury instructions. See Cage, supra, 498 U.S. at ("In construing the instruction, we consider how reasonable jurors could have understood the charge as a whole"); *Yates, supra*, 500 U.S. at 401 ("We think a reasonable juror would have understood the [instruction] to mean ..."). In *Boyde*, however, we made it a point to settle on a single standard of review for jury instructions–the "reasonable likelihood" standard--after considering the many different phrasings that had previously been used by this Court. 494 U.S. at 379-380 (considering and rejecting standards that required examination of either what a reasonable juror "could" have done or "would" have done). So that we may once again speak with one voice on this issue, we now disapprove the standard of review language in *Cage* and *Yates*, and reaffirm the standard set out in *Boyde*.

had committed them. This claim is clearly foreclosed, however, by the language of the instruction. The challenged portion of the instruction included the words "if the Defendant committed other offenses." App. 41. By including this phrase, the trial court unquestionably left it to the jury to determine whether McGuire committed the prior acts; only if the jury believed he was the perpetrator could it use the evidence in deciding whether McGuire was guilty of the crime charged. Therefore, if the jury did not believe McGuire caused the prior injuries, he was not harmed by the challenged portion of the instruction. To the extent that the jury may have believed McGuire committed the prior acts and used that as a factor in its deliberation, we observe that there was sufficient evidence to sustain such a jury finding by a preponderance of the evidence. Cf. *People v. Simon*, 184 Cal.App.3d 125, 134, 228 Cal.Rptr. 855, 858 (1986); *Huddleston v. United States*, 485 U.S. 681, 690 (1988). The proof of battered child syndrome itself narrowed the group of possible perpetrators to McGuire and his wife, because they were the only two people regularly caring for Tori during her short life. *See People v. Jackson*, 18 Cal.App.3d, at 507, 95 Cal.Rptr., at 921 ("Only someone regularly 'caring' for the child has the continuing opportunity to inflict these types of injuries; an isolated contact with a vicious stranger would not result in this pattern of successive injuries stretching through several months"). A neighbor testified that she had seen McGuire treat Tori roughly on two occasions, and that McGuire's wife was scared to leave Tori alone with McGuire because he "did bad things" to her; the neighbor further testified that she had never seen McGuire's wife abuse the child in any way. Furthermore, when being questioned by the police after Tori died, McGuire's wife stated that she observed bruises on the baby's body when bathing her. When asked by the police for an explanation, she replied, "I don't really know, you know, I am not the only one who is taking care of her." App. 131. The evidence described, along with other evidence in the record, convinces us that there was sufficient proof for the jury to conclude, if it so desired, that McGuire caused the prior rib and rectal injuries.

McGuire also contends that, even if the determination of the perpetrator was left to the jury, the instruction constituted a "propensity" instruction, allowing the jury to base its determination of guilt in part upon the conclusion that McGuire had committed the prior acts and therefore had a propensity to commit this type of crime. While the instruction was not as clear as it might have been, we find that there is not a "reasonable likelihood" that the jury would have concluded that this instruction, read in the context of other instructions, authorized the use of propensity evidence pure and simple. *Boyde v. California, supra*, 494 U.S. at 380. It seems far more likely that the jury understood the instruction, supra, at 481, to mean that if it found a "clear connection" between the prior injuries and the instant injuries, and if it found that McGuire had committed the prior injuries, then it could use that fact in determining that McGuire committed the crime charged. The use of the evidence of prior offenses permitted by this instruction was therefore parallel to the familiar use of evidence of prior acts for the purpose of showing intent, identity, motive, or plan. *See, e.g.*, Fed.Rule Evid. 404(b). Furthermore, the trial court guarded against possible misuse of the instruction by specifically advising the jury that the "[prior injury] evidence, if believed, was not received, and may not be considered by you[,] to prove that [McGuire] is a person of bad character or that he has a disposition to commit crimes." See n. 1, supra. Especially in light of this limiting provision, we reject McGuire's claim that the instruction should be viewed as a propensity instruction.[5]

We therefore hold that neither the introduction of the challenged evidence, nor the jury instruction as to its use, "so infused the trial with unfairness as to deny due process of law." *Lisenba v. California*, 314 U.S. 219, 228 (1941); *see also Donnelly v. DeChristoforo*, 416 U.S. at 643. The judgment of the Court of Appeals is therefore

Reversed.

Justice THOMAS took no part in the consideration or decision of this case.

Justice O'CONNOR, with whom Justice STEVENS joins, concurring in part and dissenting in part.

I agree with the Court that the evidence of battered child syndrome was relevant. The State had to prove that Mark McGuire intended to kill his daughter, and the evidence that Tori was a battered child was probative of causation and intent. I therefore join Part I of the Court's opinion.

I do not join Part II of the opinion because I think there is a reasonable likelihood that the jury misapplied the prior acts instruction. The trial court instructed the jury that evidence of Tori's prior injuries had been admitted to show that McGuire had committed offenses similar to that for which he was on trial, and that, if the jury found a "clear connection" between the

---

[5] Because we need not reach the issue, we express no opinion on whether a state law would violate the Due Process Clause if it permitted the use of "prior crimes" evidence to show propensity to commit a charged crime.

prior offenses and the charged offense, "it may be logically concluded that if the Defendant committed other offenses, he also committed the crime charged in this case." App. 41. In my view, the instruction encouraged the jury to assume that McGuire had inflicted the prior injuries and then directed the jury to conclude that the prior abuser was the murderer. Because the instruction may have relieved the State of its burden of proving the identity of Tori's murderer beyond a reasonable doubt, I would hold that the instruction was error and remand to the Court of Appeals for a determination of whether that error was harmless.

The fact that a 6-month-old child was repeatedly beaten in the course of her short life is so horrifying that a trial court should take special care to inform the jury as to the significance of that evidence. As the Court notes, the demonstration of battered child syndrome is relevant because it "'indicates that a child found with [serious, repeated injuries] has not suffered those injuries by accidental means,' " *ante*, at 480 (*quoting People v. Jackson*, 18 Cal.App.3d 504, 507; 95 Cal.Rptr. 919, 921 (1971)). I therefore agree that proof of Tori's battered child status, although "not linked by any direct evidence to McGuire," was properly admitted because "the evidence demonstrated that Tori's death was the result of an intentional act by someone, and not an accident." *Ante*, at 480. Precisely because the relevance of battered child syndrome is not tied to the identity of the abuser, however, I believe that a jury instruction clarifying the limited probative value of that evidence was required.

Instead of an instruction limiting the use of evidence of Tori's prior injuries, the trial judge gave an instruction limiting the use of evidence of McGuire's prior bad acts. In so doing, the trial judge himself appears to have assumed that the prior injuries could be attributed to McGuire. The judge told the jury that "[e]vidence has been introduced for the purpose of showing that the Defendant committed acts similar to those constituting a crime other than that for which he is on trial." *App.* 40. The State concedes that this category of evidence encompasses both the acts for which McGuire was positively identified as the actor (carrying the child by one arm and roughly pinching her cheeks) and the far more brutal acts for which no actor was identified (the fractured ribs and the rectal tearing). The grouping of these two distinct classes of evidence created a reasonable likelihood that the jury would believe that McGuire had been identified—at least in the eyes of the trial judge—as the prior abuser.

The trial court's error in implying that McGuire had been identified as the prior abuser was compounded by its further instruction that, if the jury found a "clear connection" between the prior offenses and the charged offense, "it may be logically concluded that if the Defendant committed other offenses, he also committed the crime charged in this case." The Court finds it "likely" that the jury understood the instruction to mean that "if it found a 'clear connection' between the prior injuries and the instant injuries, and if it found that McGuire had committed the prior injuries, then it could use that fact in determining that McGuire committed the crime charged." *Ante*, at 483. In my view, there is a reasonable likelihood that the jury did not understand this single sentence to establish a two-step process.

The jury was instructed to "consider" the evidence that McGuire had "committed acts similar" to the crime charged and to "determin[e]" whether there was a "clear connection" between these prior acts and the ones that resulted in Tori's death. App. 40, 41. The trial court did not instruct the jury that it must first "determine" whether McGuire had in fact inflicted the prior injuries. The part of the instruction relied upon by the Court—"it may be logically concluded that if the defendant committed other offenses, he also committed the crime charged in this case"—does not make clear that it is the jury's role to ascertain whether McGuire was the perpetrator of the prior abuse. Rather, coming as it does in the middle of what appears to be a conclusion of law, it is reasonably likely that the jury understood that such a determination had already been made and that its role was merely to determine if there was a "clear connection" between Tori's prior injuries and the injuries that killed her.

Although we "have defined the category of infractions that violate 'fundamental fairness' very narrowly," *Dowling v. United States*, 493 U.S. 342, 352 (1990), it is well established that the fundamental fairness guarantee of the Due Process Clause requires the prosecution to prove beyond a reasonable doubt every element of the offense. *In re Winship*, 397 U.S. 358, 364 (1970); *McMillan v. Pennsylvania*, 477 U.S. 79, 85 (1986). This constitutional principle "prohibits the State from using evidentiary presumptions in a jury charge that have the effect of relieving the State of its burden of persuasion beyond a reasonable doubt of every essential element of a crime." *Francis v. Franklin*, 471 U.S. 307, 313 (1985); *Sandstrom v. Montana*, 442 U.S. 510 (1979). Thus, we have held that mandatory presumptions violate the Due Process Clause if they relieve the State of the burden of persuasion on an element of the offense. *Patterson v. New York*, 432 U.S. 197, 215 (1977); *Sandstrom, supra*, 442 U.S. at 520-524. By contrast, a permissive inference is not a violation of due process because the State still has the burden of persuading the jury that the suggested conclusion should be inferred based on the predicate facts proved. *Ulster County Court v. Allen,* 442 U.S. 140, 157-163 (1979).

In this case, the instruction perhaps was intended to posit a permissive inference that whoever had inflicted Tori's prior injuries was likely to have inflicted the injuries that caused her death. But the trial court did not make clear that the State first had to prove the predicate facts from which the inference was to be drawn. Furthermore, the wording of the instruction is such that the jury may well have assumed that it had no choice but to "logically conclud[e]" that McGuire was the murderer once it found a "clear connection" between the prior injuries and the fatal ones.* Because I cannot say with any confidence that the instruction allowed a mere permissive inference drawing from proven facts, I think the instruction should be treated as a mandatory presumption that may have relieved the State of its burden of proving the identity of Tori's killer beyond a reasonable doubt.

Had the instruction been clearly worded, I would agree with the Court that there is sufficient circumstantial evidence in the record to support a finding that McGuire was the perpetrator of the prior injuries. After all, as the Court points out, "[t]he proof of battered child syndrome itself narrowed the group of possible perpetrators to McGuire and his wife, because they were the only two people regularly caring for Tori." *Ante*, at 483. In this case, however, it is important to remember that the other person regularly caring for Tori—Daisy McGuire—took the stand and testified, under a grant of immunity, that she was the one who inflicted the fatal injuries on the night of July 7, 1981.

McGuire's jury deliberated for three days before returning a verdict of guilty. Any evaluation of the jury instruction must be conducted against the background of Daisy McGuire's surprise testimony and the dilemma it so clearly posed for the jury. In my view, the jury instruction on similar acts was so "ambiguous," *ante*, at 482, that there was a reasonable likelihood that the jury was encouraged to make assumptions and conclusions about the identity of Tori's murderer that relieved the State of having to prove that element of the offense beyond a reasonable doubt. In cases where the Court has found that jury instructions included mandatory presumptions inconsistent with the guarantees of the Due Process Clause, the Court has remanded to determine whether the erroneous instruction was harmless,

---

* Although not dispositive, it is worth noting that California's model jury instructions on "evidence of other crimes" has since been revised to eliminate the phrase "so that it may be logically concluded." *See* 1 California Jury Instructions, Criminal 2.50 (5th ed. 1987).

which is the course that should be followed here. *See, e.g., Sandstrom, supra*, 442 U.S. at 526-527; *Rose v. Clark*, 478 U.S. 570, 584 (1986); *Carella v. California*, 491 U.S. 263, 266-267 (1989) (*per curiam*).

IX.
Conclusion

I have tried to give you a judge's-eye-view of the appellate process—what is likely to work and why; what hinders effective advocacy and why—so you can better represent your clients on appeal. I believe that if you follow my suggestions, you will increase your odds of winning on appeal. At the very least, however, I hope that this book encourages you to step back and examine what you've been doing and whether the things that you were taught by law school, mentors, or CLE appellate programs *really* make sense. Following that analysis, you should keep the techniques that you believe are helpful to effective, forceful advocacy, and jettison those that you believe are not helpful.

As I've mentioned, in giving you examples from the real world—in the *Micro Star* and *McGuire* cases—I have made suggestions as I would have framed the arguments, together with my reasons; I have attempted to do that without conforming those suggestions to the courts' ultimate decisions. Thus, you may see some of my suggested arguments echoed in the decisions that you read, and you may see other of my suggested arguments either ignored or rejected. In my nine years as a trial judge, from 1979 through 1988, I have been affirmed at times, and I have been reversed. During my twelve years as an appellate judge, decisions written by me have been both affirmed and reversed; my dissents have been both adopted and ignored. That is the nature of the process.

Throughout this book, I've written about the "odds" of winning; there is no "magic key," of course, that will guarantee victory each and every time you step before a jury or judge, or file an appellate brief. We live in an imperfect world—sometimes "justice" is not done. All we can hope for, in my view, is a process that maximizes the chances that "justice" will be done. In my view, our system only works if we have effective advocacy on both sides of a contested issue. It is in that spirit that I have written by *The "How-To-Win" Trial Manual* and this book. If in some case "justice" is done because a lawyer read either the trial manual or this book, and applied some of the techniques, this effort will have been successful.

INDEX

Cases:

Authorities cited by the parties and courts in the two cases we analyze: *Micro Star v. FormGen, Inc.* and *McGuire v. Estelle* are not indexed.